THE TRUTH ABOUT CHRISTIAN SCIENCE

The Founder and the Faith

By JAMES H. SNOWDEN

PHILADELPHIA
THE WESTMINSTER PRESS
1920

PREFACE

The author of this book is well aware that it falls among those "obnoxious books" which the founder of Christian Science forbade her followers to read in her endeavor by her censorship to protect them from any influence or light coming from outside the closed circle of her own books and other approved writings. It is not therefore written primarily for Christian Scientists, but if any of them should look into it, it is not thought they will find just ground of offense, however strong may be their dissent. It is difficult to be permanently offended with facts.

Every important statement in this book relating to the founder and faith of Christian Science is supported by quotations from her writings or is based upon trustworthy evidence. The most serious allegations pertaining to Mrs. Eddy are sustained by her own words found in her acknowledged writings, for in such matters she is always the most damaging witness against herself.

The author throughout this book has let Mrs. Eddy speak fairly for herself. Her teaching is entitled to a patient and even sympathetic hearing in its own behalf before any judgment is passed upon it. The author really had no particular prejudice against it when he began this investigation, and when asked by the publishers to write a book on it was even inclined to let Christian Science alone as a rather harmless vagary, and he formed his judgments of it as he proceeded with this study. It was close acquaintance with and insight into its real nature that led him to see that it is a graver error than he had supposed.

If anyone asks for the justification for another book on this subject, the author answers that he had doubts on this point himself until he began to look into its literature and then saw that there appears to be no book that covers the whole ground of the founder and the faith and brings its history up to the present time. This book not only endeavors to do this, but also as a distinctive feature seeks to see the elements of truth in Christian Science and recover them to their full use. It is a story that has often been told, but it will no doubt need to be told again and again and brought up to date and subjected to the criticism of new light.

J. H. S.

Pittsburgh, Pennsylvania.

TABLE OF CONTENTS

CONTENTS

WORKS CONSULTED

BATES, J. H., *Christian Science and Its Problems*, 1898.

BENSON, ROBERT HUGH, *A Book of Essays*, 1916.

BERKELEY, GEORGE, *The Principles of Human Knowledge*, Krauth's Edition.

BOWNE, BORDEN P., *The Immanence of God*, 1905.

BROWN, WILLIAM LEON, *Christian Science Falsely So Called*, 1911.

BUCKLEY, JAMES M., *Faith Healing, Christian Science and Kindred Phenomena*, 1892.

CABOT, RICHARD C., Article on "One Hundred Christian Science Cures," in *McClure's Magazine*, August, 1908.

CALKINS, MARY WHITON, *The Persistent Problems of Philosophy*, 1907.

CARPENTER, WILLIAM B., *Mental Physiology*, 1874.

CARROLL, H. K., *The Religious Forces of the United States*, 1912.

CARROLL, ROBERT S., *The Soul in Suffering*, 1919.

CLEMENS, SAMUEL L. (Mark Twain), *Christian Science*, 1907.

COAKELEY, THOMAS J., *Christian Science and the Catholic Church*, 1912.

COMBS, GEORGE HAMILTON, *Some Latter-Day Religions*, 1899.

COOKSEY, N. B., *Christian Science Under the Searchlight*, 1915.

COOMBS, J. V., *Religious Delusions*, 1904.

COPPAGE, L. J., *Christian Science in the Light of Reason*, 1914.

CORIAT, ISADOR H., *Religion and Medicine*, 1907.

CUTTEN, GEORGE BARTON, *The Psychological Phenomena of Christianity*, 1908.

DRESSER, HORATIO W., *Health and the Inner Life*, 1906; *A Physician of the Soul*, 1908; *The Philosophy of the Spirit*, 1908; *The History of the New Thought Movement*, 1919.

DRESSER, JULIUS A., *The True History of Mental Science*, 1887.

EDDY, MRS. MARY BAKER G., *Science and Health with Key to the Scriptures*, 1916; *Retrospection and Introspection*, 1891; *Unity of Good and Unreality of Evil*, 1915; *Pulpit and Press*, 1915; *Rudimental Divine Science*, 1915; *No and Yes*, 1915; *Christian Healing and the People's Idea of God*, 1912; *Christian Science versus Pantheism*, 1912; *Miscellaneous Writings*, 1883-1898; *The First Church of Christ Scientist and Miscellany*, 1914; *The Manual of the Mother Church*, 1919.

EDWARDS, MAURICE D., *Christian Science Reviewed*, 1906.

FARNSWORTH, EDWARD C., *The Sophistries of Christian Science*, 1909; *The Passing of Mary Baker Eddy*, 1911.

FISKE, A. A., *A Searchlight on Christian Science*, 1913.

FLOWER, B. O., *Christian Science as a Religious Belief and a Therapeutic Agent*, 1909.

FROTHINGHAM, OCTAVIOUS BROOKS, *Transcendentalism in New England*, 1897.

GRAY, JAMES M., *The Antidote of Christian Science*, 1907.

GREENBAUM, LEON, *Follow Christ*, 1916.

HALDEMAN, I. M., *Christian Science in the Light of Holy Scripture*, 1909.

HARRIS, WALTER S., *Christian Science and the Ordinary Man*, 1917.

HEGEMAN, J. WINTHROP, *Must Protestantism Adopt Christian Science?* 1914.

HUDSON, THOMAS JAY, *The Law of Mental Medicine*, 1903.

JAMES, WILLIAM W., *The Principles of Psychology*, 1893.

JOHNSON, THOMAS CARY, *Some Modern Isms*, 1919.

KRATZER, G. A., *Spiritual Man*, 1914.

KUHNS, OSCAR, *The Sense of the Infinite*, 1908.

LADD, GEORGE T., *Outlines of Physiological Psychology*, 1893.

LAMBERT L. A., *Christian Science Before the Bar of Reason*, 1908.

LARSON, CHRISTIAN D., *The Good Side of Christian Science*, 1916.

LEA, CHARLES HERMAN, *A Plea for the Thorough and Unbiassed Investigation of Christian Science*, 1915.

MCCOMB, SAMUEL, *Religion and Medicine*, 1907.

MACKAY, W. MACKINTOSH, *The Disease and Remedy of Sin*, 1919.

MARS, GERHARDT, *The Interpretation of Life: Relation of Modern Culture to Christian Science*, 1908.

MARSHALL, HENRY RUTGERS, *Mind and Conduct*, 1919.

MARSTEN, FRANCIS EDWARD, *The Mask of Christian Science*, 1909.

MILMINE, GEORGINE, *The Life of Mary Baker G. Eddy and the History of Christian Science*, 1909.

MOULTON T. G., *An Exposure of Christian Science*, 1906.

NEWTON, R. HEBER, *Christian Science*, 1899.

PAGET, STEPHEN, *The Faith and Works of Christian Science*, 1909.

PAULSEN, FRIEDRICH, *Introduction to Philosophy*, 1897.

PAYOT, JULES, *The Education of the Will*, 1909.

PEABODY, FREDERICK W., *The Religio-Medical Masquerade*, 1910.

PODMORE, FRANK, *Mesmerism and Christian Science*, 1903.

POWELL, LYMAN P., *Christian Science, the Faith and Its Founder*, 1907.

PURRINGTON, W. A., *Christian Science; An Exposition*, 1899.

RILEY, WOODBRIDGE, *American Thought from Puritanism to Pragmatism*, 1815.

RYDBERG, VIKTOR, *The Magic of the Middle Ages*, 1879.

SCHOFIELD, ALFRED T., *The Force of Mind; or, The Mental Factor in Medicine*, 1907.

SEARS, CLARA ENDICOTT, *Gleanings from Old Shaker Journals*, 1916.

SEWARD, THEODORE F., *How to Get Acquainted with God*, 1902.

SHELDON, HENRY C., *Christian Science So-Called*, 1913.

SLATER, JOHN ROTHWELL, and others, *Searchlight on Christian Science*, 1899.

STETSON, AUGUSTA E., *Give God the Glory*, 1911; *Vital Issues in Christian Science*, 1914.

STURGE, M. CARTA, *The Truth and Error of Christian Science*.

SWAIN, RICHARD L., *The Real Key to Christian Science*, 1917.

THOMPSON, W. HANNA, *Brain and Personality*, 1919.

TRINE, RALPH WALDO, *In Tune with the Infinite*, 1898; *The Alinement of Life*, 1913.

TROWARD, T., *The Edinburgh Lectures on Mental Science*, 1915.

WARFIELD, BENJAMIN B., *Counterfeit Miracles*, 1918.

WEAVER, EDWARD E., *Mind and Health with an Examination of Some Systems of Divine Healing*, 1913.

WHITE, ANDREW D., *History of the Warfare of Science with Theology*, 1897.

WHITNEY, MRS. A. D. T., *The Integrity of Christian Science*, 1900.

WILBUR, SIBYL, *The Life of Mary Baker Eddy*, 1907.

WILBY, THOMAS W., *What Is Christian Science?* 1915.

WOODBURY, JOSEPHINE C., *War in Heaven: Sixteen Years' Experience in Christian Science;* Article on "The Book and the Woman" in the *Arena*, May, 1899.

WORCESTER, ELWOOD, *Religion and Medicine*, 1907; *The Living Word*, 1908.

Arena, 1899.

Christian Science Journal, 1918, 1919.

Christian Science Sentinel, 1920.

McClure's Magazine, 1907, 1908.

Report of Clerical and Medical Committee on Spiritual Healing, 1914.

In the beginning God created the heavens and the earth.

—Genesis 1:1.

And Jehovah God formed man of the dust of the ground, and breathed into his nostrils the breath of life; and man became a living soul.

—Genesis 2:7.

I have never doubted that fire is hot and that ice is cold.

—Bishop Berkeley.

Dark is the world to thee: thyself art the reason why;
For is He not all but that which has power to feel "I am I."

—Tennyson.

A pseudoscience does not necessarily consist wholly of lies. It contains many truths and even valuable ones. The rottenest bank starts with a little specie. It puts out a thousand promises to pay on the strength of a single dollar, but the dollar is commonly a good one.

—Oliver Wendell Holmes.

One of the most important of all changes had taken place in the world—a change in the mode of thinking. The work of Descartes, Locke, and Sir Isaac Newton had become a common inheritance; the relation of physical effect with physical cause had become established even in ignorant and unthinking minds.

—Georgine Milmine

One of the most primitive and fundamental shapes which the relation of cause and effect takes in the savage mind, is the assumed connection between disease or death and some malevolent personal agency. . . The minds of civilized people have become familiar with the conception of natural law, and that conception has simply stifled the old superstition as clover chokes out weeds. . . . The disposition to believe was one of the oldest inheritances of the human mind, while the capacity for estimating evidence in the cases of physical causation is one of its very latest and most laborious acquisitions.

—John Fiske.

Hereby know ye the spirit of God: every spirit that confesseth that Jesus Christ is come in the flesh is of God: and every spirit that confesseth not Jesus is not of God.

—I John 4:2

THE TRUTH
ABOUT CHRISTIAN SCIENCE

CHAPTER I

INTRODUCTION

It is the purpose of the author of this book to ascertain and state, as accurately and impartially and fairly as he can, the facts as to the founder and the faith of Christian Science. While one cannot wholly escape from the limitations of his personal point of view and from the subjective coloring of his established convictions and unconscious preferences, yet objective truth should be his ideal, and this is the aim and effort of this study.

1. TRUTH AND ERROR IN RELIGION

Religion is our conscious relation to God. All human beings sustain vital unconscious relations to God, for in him we necessarily live and move and have our being, and we could no more escape from his presence and power than we could slip out of the grip of gravitation. But it is only as this relation emerges into the field of conscious life and becomes a matter of personal experience and choice and action that it becomes religion. This experience is one of the deepest and most universal and vital facts in our human world, as all history witnesses.

The truth in religion is open to us on the same terms as

truth in other fields: intuition, perception, judgment, evidence, reasoning, and experience. God is nigh us, even in our heart. Agnosticism, that peremptorily shuts its gate against any knowledge of God, is irresistibly battered down by the reasonings of our minds and the urgencies of our hearts, and we know God as surely as the child knows its father, or as the eye sees the sun.

The truth contained in religion is the most vital in the world, the foundation and framework of all our knowledge and life. "In the beginning God," is the sublime opening of the Bible, and it is the beginning of all our science and philosophy, religion and life. What we think about God is the bottom principle of all our thinking and shapes and colors our thoughts on every subject, as the center of a circle determines every point around its whole circumference. If we believe in no God, we have a world without a Cause, a universe without a system and center, a hopeless confusion and chaos, if not a wild dream of insanity as well as a colossal cruelty. Give us God, and the world falls into order and meaning and purpose around a central throne, and all things work together for good.

But everything depends on the kind of God we believe in. Any pantheistic God or impersonal principle or blind fate does not give us any light but only turns the light we have into a greater darkness. Our Christian faith believes in God our heavenly Father, and this fact is its Rock of ages and its glory. We are "infants crying in the night," and our cry is answered by our Father who folds us in his everlasting arm, close to his loving heart. When we have faith in God as our Father we can calm our perplexed minds and soothe our troubled hearts and be still and know that he is God. This simple faith solves our problems, makes plain our path, and gives us strength and courage to resist our temptations and bear our burdens and win the battle of life.

Yet the field of religion, which yields the most blessed fruits, also abounds in the most poisonous weeds. Its very light may turn to darkness, and then "how great is that darkness!" The best things are always subject to the worst perversion and abuse. The science and art that invent magic machines and multiply material goods and create all the wonders and splendors of our civilization, also produce the most diabolical devices of destruction and death that blast the very face of the earth and destroy millions of lives. All our education is only a sharp and cunning tool that bad men can use as powerfully as good men. The Devil can clothe himself in light seemingly as pure and beautiful as the holiness of any saint or the white robes of an angel, and often so artfully as to deceive the very elect.

It is not surprising, then, but inevitable that religion should be productive of error as well as of truth, of evil as well as of good. And this all history confirms. The records of religion present the aspect of a vast confusion and chaos and noise of conflicting beliefs and practices, "a dust of systems and of creeds." Religion divides into innumerable forms and sects that are all more or less at war with one another. Not only are there many antagonistic general religions, but each religion in itself splits into sects, and historic Christianity has not escaped this fate but has divided into upwards of two hundred denominations, each one of which has its own internal divisions.

In this field are intermingled all forms and varieties of

truth and error, wholesome grain and deadly weeds. There is no form of belief so false and fantastic that some religion or religionist has not held it as a doctrine, and no religious rite so inhuman and cruel and wicked that it has not been advocated and practiced as a sacred duty.

> In religion,
> What damned error but some sober brow
> Will bless it, and approve it with a text,
> Hiding the grossness with fair ornament.

Hatred and malice and murder and every kind of uncleanness have been consecrated on the altar of religion as truly as purity and love and service and sacrifice. No demon or Devil could be more vile and vicious in character and conduct than have been some gods that men have worshipped. On the other hand, it is not to be overlooked that such errors and misdeeds are not the general fact and fruit but are relatively rare in the history of religion, and that Christianity has an infinitely larger credit side to its account and has filled its pages with the best thoughts and noblest deeds and the whitest and most beautiful characters this world has ever known.

These errors and evils in religion are not all found in the past, but are still in the world and run rife in Christian lands and even disfigure professedly Christian forms of faith and worship. It is necessary to face the difficult task of discriminating the wheat from the tares, of trying the spirits whether they be of God, and of proving all things and holding fast only that which is good.

2. TRUTH AND ERROR IN CHRISTIAN SCIENCE

It is certain that there is truth in Christian Science. No pure error could ever last or even get a start in the world. Such an error would totally contradict itself so that no sane mind could entertain it. Every error not only impinges on and interlaces with truth around its whole boundary, but it also contains internal elements of fact. It is this truth in any erroneous system of belief and conduct that gives it some working value and enables it to live and last in the world. Tested by this principle, Christian Science has proved that it must contain large elements of important truth, for it has laid hold of many minds and spread rapidly among men. The adherents of this faith are generally people of intelligence and culture and some of them are of marked ability. It has also become institutionalized in a great mother church with thousands of members and with many branches and in a complex and powerful organization with its sacred book, its literature, magazines, and daily newspaper, and with an alert and efficient system of propaganda. It is less than fifty years old, and few religions have more to show in so short a time in practical results than has this modern cult.

Christian Science certainly meets some wide and deep need in our day. Its success indicates that it has either discovered some new truth, or else it has emphasized and utilized some old truth which other forms of religion have neglected and let fall into desuetude. However much error it may contain it has rendered a service by calling attention to this truth and forcing the Christian Church to do it justice in its own teaching and practice. It is the duty of Christians to see and accept and utilize this truth, and it is the purpose of this book to endeavor to do this in the study of it. The spirit of truth-seeking requires this and it is hoped it may be done in all fairness and frankness, both out of regard to justice to Christian Science and of duty to our Christian faith.

On the other hand, the reader will find and, even at the outset of study and without prejudicing fairness, can affirm, on the general ground of well-known admitted facts, that there is much error in Christian Science. The most superficial acquaintance with its doctrines and practices proves this. A system of belief that bodily casts overboard as utter delusions anatomy, physiology, biology, geology, astronomy, and all sciences, repudiates organized human knowledge and turns the whole natural world into a baseless illusion of the mind, must contain a huge error that is the mother of a whole brood of errors. It will be the business of this study to expose and refute these errors as it proceeds.

Few subjects have been so beset and beclouded with personal issues and controversial points as Christian Science, and it calls for a fair mind and clear vision to discriminate between the truth and error in this system; but the author will strive to see the facts in the light of objective truth and write in a spirit of candor and charity.

3. LITERATURE OF THE SUBJECT

The literature of Christian Science has become extensive, and a number of the more important books on the subject are named in the list of "Works Consulted" prefixed to this volume. It is the purpose of this section to name and characterize a few of the most important ones, especially of those on which this study is directly based.

First and foremost are the works of Mrs. Mary Baker Eddy. She has the right before all others to speak for herself and should be heard at every step and point.

Though at first she was a slow and untrained and even un-grammatical writer and had to learn after she had passed her fiftieth year the simplest rudiments of literary art, yet through patient and persistent practice she was able to turn out several books, but with what help will be told in later chapters. Her first and chief book is the well-known "Science and Health with Key to the Scriptures," which is the bible of Christian Science, the book that she claimed and that her followers claim was divinely inspired in the same sense that the Bible was inspired; the book that contains her authoritative official teaching and is officially enjoined to be used and is used along with the Bible in every Christian Science church and service the world over. Frequent reference to, and examination of, this book will be made in the course of this study. Of course every thorough student of this subject should read this book, and as a guarantee of good faith the writer declares that he patiently carried through the task of reading it from beginning to end: a wearisome labor that few people outside of the inner circle of the most devoted followers and practitioners of Christian Science have done or ever will do.

Another book by Mrs. Eddy is "Retrospection and Introspection," a brief and fragmentary autobiography which should be read and carefully compared with other sources of information as to her life. Several other books are listed among her writings, such as "Miscellaneous Writings, 1883-1896," and "The First Church of Christ Scientist and Miscellany," but these are mostly composed of selected articles, contributed to The Christian Science Journal and The Christian Science Sentinel and other journals, and of messages to her churches. A number of her sermons are also available, many of these being published separately. All of her books and writings are published by the official Christian Science Publishing Society in Boston, and the edition of "Science and Health," used in this study bears the date of 1916, except when otherwise indicated.

One of the most important books on this subject is "The Life of Mary Baker G. Eddy and the History of Christian Science," by Georgine Milmine. This book first appeared as a series of illustrated articles in McClure's Magazine in 1906-1907 and was then issued in book form. Christian Scientists hold this to be a prejudiced and hostile work, but in the judgment of the author it is a thoroughly scientific piece of historical investigation and composition. Miss Milmine made a comprehensive and searching inquiry into the facts of Mrs. Eddy's life and into the teaching and practice of Christian Science. She visited the scenes of Mrs. Eddy's career, followed her from town to town and through year after year, examined books and newspapers and court records, interviewed many persons who knew and had had personal relations with her, obtained affidavits on important matters, and secured photographs of many places and documents that enter into the story. Her book is based on the facts as thus obtained and is not only illustrated with many pictures from photographs of places and persons but is also fortified with facsimiles of some important documents. The book is written with an evident desire and effort to find and tell the truth, and it will ever stand as an authoritative history based on original investigation and backed up with names, dates, documents, and affidavits. The writer has made frequent use of and generous quotations from this book, of which due acknowledgments have been given.

Another book next in importance to Miss Milmine's is "Christian Science, the Faith and Its Founder," by Lyman P. Powell, Rector of St. John's Church, Northampton, Mass., and now president of Hobart College, Geneva, N. Y. Dr. Powell says in his preface that he has made free use of Miss Milmine's articles and adds: "I have taken the pains, however, in each instance to verify her statements by correspondence or by interviews with those concerned. For this purpose alone I have traveled more than twenty-five hundred miles and am glad to be able to testify to the singular accuracy of the articles and the thoroughness with which they have been prepared." This is a remarkable confirmation of the trustworthiness of Miss Milmine's book. Dr. Powell also contributes additional light of value on Christian Science as the result of his own investigations. The day for obtaining personal evidence from those that knew and had relations with Mrs. Eddy is about gone, and later writers will necessarily largely depend on these first-hand students and witnesses for the facts in the case.

Miss Milmine's articles in McClure's called forth an answer in the form of a series of articles that appeared in the journal, Human Life, and were then issued in a volume entitled "The Life of Mary Baker Eddy," (1907), by Sibyl Wilbur O'Brien, now Sibyl Wilbur. This book is published by The Christian Science Publishing Society, Boston, and is thus officially authorized. Mrs. Eddy herself published in the Christian Science Sentinel of March 12, 1910, the following authorization of the book, which is now printed in the book itself:

I have not had sufficient interest in the matter to read or to note from others' reading what the enemies of Christian Science are said to be circulating regarding my history, but my friends have read Sibyl Wilbur's book, "Life of Mary Baker Eddy," and request the privilege of buying, circulating, and recommending it to the public. I briefly declare that nothing has occurred in my life's experience which, if correctly narrated and understood, could injure me; and not a little is already reported of the good accomplished therein, the self-sacrifice, etc., that has distinguished all my working years. I thank Miss Wilbur and the Concord Publishing Company for their unselfish labors in placing this book before the public, and hereby say that they have my permission to publish and circulate this work.   Mary Baker Eddy.

It will be noted that Mrs. Eddy takes advantage of the occasion to write a recommendation of herself as well as of the book.

As to Miss Wilbur's book, it bears all the marks of an interested advocate's statement of facts in dispute and defense of a character under attack. It is partisan in the extreme, and everything is turned to Mrs. Eddy's glory. The many facts in her life that appear in an unfortunate and often painful light in Miss Milmine's book are by Miss Wilbur toned down and glossed over and clothed in a different aspect. Even the most desperate cases are made the best of, though the ugly truth cannot always be denied or explained away. The personal adulation of Mrs. Eddy, approaching divine worship, is nauseating. Even such a simple-minded soul and colorless limp personality as Asa Gilbert Eddy, Mrs. Eddy's third husband, at whose "calm, sweet eyes" the presiding judge in a celebrated trial "must have wondered," is ridiculously adulated. In contrast with Miss Milmine's book, which is abundantly supplied with quotations from and references to authorities and documents, Miss Wilbur's book is almost bare of such quotations and references. It ob-

viously lacks objective authority and gives the impression
that it is largely a subjective production. It is based
in no small measure on conversations with and explanations and private disclosures which must have come from
Mrs. Eddy herself. Such statements occur as "Mrs.
Eddy has told the author," and "Mrs. Eddy has recently
pointed out to the author." There are many of these
confidential revelations, so that one is led to believe that
the book is largely the result of the intimate communings
of the author with Mrs. Eddy and that it is little more
than what Mrs. Eddy wants the world to believe about
herself. The book, however, is a valuable document in
the case and confirms more than it explains away.

Having in hand the books of Mrs. Eddy, Miss Milmine,
Dr. Powell, and Miss Wilbur the student can get at the
essential facts as to the founder and the faith of this cult.

Many other books throw important corroborative light
and critical illumination on it, among which may be
named the following: "The Interpretation of Life," New
York, (1908), by Gerhardt C. Mars, a New York "lecturer," purports to show "the relation of Modern Culture
to Christian Science." It displays considerable learning
and acumen and strongly supports Mrs. Eddy's claims,
granting her "preternatural insight," but distinguishing
"two phases in Mrs. Eddy's life—as indeed in all our
lives—which are to be borne in mind, viz.: her human
personality, with its mortal limitations, and her spiritual
individuality which is ever seeking to express itself through
the human form," a distinction apparently after the
manner of the infallibility of the pope, who is infallible
only when speaking in his official and not in his private
capacity.

A dispassionate exposition of the system is found in Thomas W. Wilby's "What Is Christian Science?" On the other hand, "A Plea for the Thorough and Unbiassed Investigation of Christian Science," by Charles Herman Lea, an English writer, is anything but "unbiassed" in its intensely dogmatic and heated defense of this faith. If italics and black letter type were logic, Mr. Lea would be very convincing.

"The Religio-Medical Masquerade, a Complete Exposure of Christian Science," (1910), is by Frederick W. Peabody, a Boston lawyer who was counsel in several cases brought against Mrs. Eddy and has had intimate relations with many of the people involved in this story. He tells us in the introduction to his book that "the facts herein set forth are, almost without exception, based, either upon Mrs. Eddy's own published utterances, her private correspondence, the sworn testimony of witnesses, or the admissions under oath of her most influential friends and followers." Mr. Peabody's book, written in a trenchant style, reveals much inside information and is a damaging document in the case he presents against Christian Science.

"The Faith and Works of Christian Science," (1909), is an examination of the system, especially in it claims of healing, by Stephen Paget, M. D., an eminent London medical authority. Mark Twain's "Christian Science," (1907), is the humorist's terribly sarcastic but really serious exposure of the cult, illuminating and sharp as a flash of lightning. It by no means lacks logic, for so keen a logician as Dr. Francis L. Patton, of Princeton, when he was asked what book he read in refutation of Christian Science, answered with a characteristic snap of his mouth, "Mark Twain!" "Mesmerism and Christian Science," (1909), by Frank Podmore, an English psychologist and member of the Society for Psychical Research, is written with a psychologist's insight and in a judicial spirit. A small but important book is "The True History of Mental Science," by Julius A. Dresser, (1887), who was a patient of Dr. Quimby and then a teacher of his system and had inside and intimate knowledge of the facts that lie at the very origin and root of Christian Science.

The title of this book occurred to and was adopted by the writer in May, 1919, and he had almost completed the manuscript when he discovered that a book with the same title (except the subtitle) had appeared in 1916, the author being George M. Searle, of the Paulist Fathers and formerly Professor of Mathematics in the Catholic University, Washington, D. C. Father Searle's book is confined to a critical examination of "Science and Health," and is a keen piece of work.

CHAPTER II

THE SUBSOIL OF CHRISTIAN SCIENCE

Every system of thought and movement in society has deep roots and distant connections, and we must understand these in order to comprehend it. Christian Science has such roots.

1. PHILOSOPHICAL IDEALISM

Philosophical idealism is as old as Plato and has come down into our day in a deepening gulf stream of thought. It found classical expression in Berkeley's "Principles of Human Knowledge," a book of singular lucidity which readers untrained in philosophy can understand. Briefly, this system holds that mind or spirit is the ultimate and sole reality and that matter is a mode of its activity. The doctrine usually maintains that God is the infinite and eternal Spirit, who has posited or created finite spirits, and that the material world is a mode of the divine will and life. As finite spirits we are environed in God, in whom "we live and move and have our being," and our experience of the world is caused by the activity of God which we in some degree share with him. Idealism, then, does not at all deny the reality of matter or resolve it into a subjective illusion or delusion, but only discovers and demonstrates, as it believes, the true nature of matter as a mode of the divine life.

14

Dr. Powell says of P. P. Quimby, the mind healer of Portland, Me., from whom Mrs. Eddy, as we shall see, derived her ideas: "He read much. The Bible was ever in his hand, and sometimes Berkeley." Quimby taught that "error is matter." The uneducated Portland clock maker thus had obtained a perverted notion of Berkeley's idealism, and this trickled down into Mrs. Eddy's mind. She mentions Berkeley but only to disown him and it is not likely that she ever read him, but in some way she got an inkling of this philosopher's theory in the form that matter, instead of being a phenomenal experience of objective spiritual reality, is a pure subjective delusion to be "denied" and cast out of the mind; and this initial mistake lies at the root of her system and is the beginning of all her trouble. The basis of Christian Science is a misunderstood and spurious form of idealism. Philosophical idealism in all its forms repudiates Christian Science as an illegitimate and deformed child and will acknowledge no responsibility for it.

2. NEW ENGLAND TRANSCENDENTALISM

Mrs. Eddy grew up in New England at a time when a peculiar type of transcendentalism was running its course and blighting the roots of historic Christian faith. Reaction against the extreme Calvinism of Jonathan Edwards and his successors had swung to Unitarianism and then had escaped from the gravitation of Christianity into free thought. Channing and Parker, Frothingham and Freeman Clarke were leaders in the movement that gave the world "the pale negations of Boston Unitarianism." Emerson went beyond them and became lost in the pantheistic Oversoul. He was a seer of wonderful insight and taught truth of imperishable value, yet he emitted a cold, white light that corruscated brilliantly in the brain but gave no warmth to the heart and little religious satisfaction to the soul. The literary genius of Longfellow and Lowell and Holmes produced some high-grade poetry, but yielded very thin religion. Transcendentalism reached its limit in A. Bronson Alcott whose "orphic sayings" and subjective exhalations were bits of pale clouds that have long since evaporated into nothingness.

New England transcendentalism thus did some notable literary work and emitted some splendid fireworks, but it burned New England over with a kind of slow-consuming fire of religious indifference and skepticism that left the ground ready for a new crop of reactionary movements. Such a crop is sure to spring up. Deprive people of religious bread and they will take to stones rather than do without any spiritual food. When the human soul is swept and left empty, it is in a dangerous condition, and if nothing else comes in, devils will. As faith in the mythological gods died out in the ancient Greek and Roman world, it swarmed with all manner of wild, fantastic cults. Dead orthodoxy becomes the rank hothouse and seedbed of heresy. As rational faith withers, fads flourish. The human heart is "incurably religious" and will have its god and its cult, and if robbed of one thing it will take to another, though it be a god as false and foolish as a hideous idol of wood or stone.

New England in the middle decades of the last century was just the soil in which Christian Science could strike root and flourish, and it took advantage of its opportunity.

3. FAITH HEALING AND SPIRITUALISM

New England was prolific in these strange cults. At East Canterbury, New Hampshire, within five miles of Tilton, Mary Baker's childhood home, was the main community of the Shakers, a sect that had been founded by Ann Lee. Their peculiar doctrines and still more peculiar practices were the cause of much popular excitement and of considerable indignation in the region round about, and the impressionable young girl who afterwards became Mrs. Eddy must have heard and seen much of these strange doings. While Shakerism and Christian Science are not closely connected, yet they have many points of affinity and contact. The Shakers always prayed to "Our Father and Mother which art in heaven," while Mrs. Eddy's "spiritually interpreted" version of The Lord's Prayer begins, "Our Father-Mother God." The Shakers proclaimed Ann Lee to be the woman of the Apocalypse, and Mrs. Eddy made the same suggestion with reference to herself. The Shakers called Ann Lee "Mother," and Mrs. Eddy arrogated this name to herself and forbade her followers to bestow it upon others, although afterwards she withdrew the privilege of applying it to herself and denied that she had ever authorized such use. The Shakers claimed that Ann Lee was inspired, and Mrs. Eddy made the same claim. Ann Lee declared that she had the gift of healing, and this was Mrs. Eddy's chief stock in trade. The Shakers called their organization "The Church of Christ," and Mrs. Eddy adopted this name with the addition of "Scientist." The Shakers forbade audible prayer, and Mrs. Eddy disapproved of it and has none of it, except The Lord's Prayer with her "interpretation" of it, in her services.

Ann Lee enjoined celibacy, and Mrs. Eddy, though practicing marriage liberally herself, discouraged it in others.[1]

Andrew Jackson Davis, born in Orange County, N. Y., in 1826, was a clairvoyant and magnetic healer and later a spiritualist, who attained notoriety as a traveling lecturer, and published several volumes setting forth his doctrines and methods of healing. He used in a peculiar sense such terms as "truth," "error," and especially "principle," in very much the same way as they were adopted as characteristic terms in Mrs. Eddy's teaching. "Truth," he says, "is positive principle; error is a negative principle." "Power, wisdom, goodness, justice, mercy, truth, are the gradual developments of an eternal and internal principle, constituting the divine, original essence." He taught that Christ employed animal magnetism in making cures, and that to dispel disease the divine principle has provided certain remedial agents.[2] Dr. Warren F. Evans, in a work entitled "Mental Medicine" and published three years before the first edition of Mrs. Eddy's book "Christian Science," said: "Disease being in its root a wrong belief, change that belief and we cure the disease. By faith we are thus made whole."[3] He will appear later in this study.

Another remarkable man was Thomas Lake Harris, born in 1823, who established a community at Brocton, N. Y., fell into trances, and spoke rhapsodically by inspiration, discouraged marriage as a "terrible" thing, and had strange hypnotic power over his followers, even

---

[1] See Clara Endicott Sears, *Gleanings from Old Quaker Journals*, and Milmine, *History*, pp. 494, 495.
[2] Milmine *History*, pp. 489, 493.
[3] Ibid, p. 483.

captivating and enslaving Lady Oliphant and her well-known son Laurence Oliphant.[1]

Joseph Smith, born in 1805 at Sharon, Vt., of illiterate and neuropathic parents, and who became dissatisfied with the clash of creeds at Palmyra, N. Y., whither his parents had removed in 1815, began to have "visions" and the "Book of Mormon" was produced which was the start of Mormonism, another religious vagary with roots running back into New England. Mormonism and Christian Science have many points of affinity. Both sprang from the same region at about the same time out of the same social and religious conditions; both had founders of neurotic, physical constitution and hysterical temperament, who had very meager education and claimed to receive divine revelations; both have an alleged inspired book or bible, and both of these books, it is charged, were plagiarized by their authors from other writings; both claim to be a later revelation and higher form of Christianity; both hold peculiar views on the marriage relation; and both in their practices have come into conflict with the civil law.

In the meanwhile mesmerism was spreading like wildfire over New England. Charles Poyen, a French disciple of Mesmer, traveled through the region lecturing and performing feats of mesmeric influence in the same towns in which Mary Baker then lived. In 1837 he published "Animal Magnetism," in which he called his system "Truth," "the Power of Mind over Matter," a "demonstration," a "discovery given of God" and a "science."[2]

[1] Podmore, *Mesmerism and Christian Science.* Ch. XIII.
[2] Milmine, *History*, p. 23.

The teaching and work of P. P. Quimby, the faith healer of Portland, Me., will be considered later.

The excitement over the alleged spirit rappings of the Fox sisters at Rochester, N. Y., broke out in 1853 and spread through New York and New England. Alleged "mediums" multiplied and "communications" from departed spirits became a common belief and practice. Judge Edmonds, of the Supreme Court of New York, and Dr. Dexter, an eminent physician of New York City, investigated the subject and published a work that became an authority and gave wide currency and respectability to belief in the system.

"Thus in the '30's," to quote Miss Milmine, "the first wave of mental science, animal magnetism, and clairvoyance swept over New England. The atmosphere was charged with the occult, the movement ranging all the way from phrenology and mind-reading to German transcendentalism. Quimby's interest was directly stimulated by the visit of Charles Poyen, the well-known French mesmerist, who came to lecture in Belfast (Me.). The inquiring clock maker became absorbed in Poyen's theories, formed his acquaintance, and followed him from town to town. . . Then, as now, the public mind associated occult sciences with the cure of physical disease. Clairvoyants, magnetisers, and mind readers treated all imaginable ills. . . Hundreds of men, women, and children, 'whose cases the doctors had given up as hopeless,' fervently testified to their power. Consumptives, according to popular report, began to get well, the blind saw, and the halt walked."[1]

This state of things in New England was the soil out of

[1] *History*, pp. 45, 46.

which Christian Science grew, the environment in which
Mary Baker was reared, the atmosphere she breathed,
the mental and religious influences that unconsciously
molded and colored her highly nervous, neurotic, impressionable nature. Christian Science had its roots
in this soil; both the founder and the faith are the proper
fruits of such seeds.

CHAPTER III

LIFE OF MRS. MARY BAKER G. EDDY

The following is a rapid outline of the life of the remarkable woman who was the founder of Christian Science and the veritable incarnation of the whole system. It takes a large volume to trace all the windings and disentangle all the knots in her strangely checkered career, and only the more important points can be touched on here.

1. EARLY YEARS

Mary A. Morse Baker, the youngest of the six children of Mark and Abigail Ambrose Baker, was born July 16, 1821, in Bow township, near Concord, New Hampshire. The parents were members of the Congregational Church, and the father was a man of narrow mind and dogmatic temper who pushed his opinions on other people and had a conscience that gave great trouble to his neighbors. The mother was of a quiet disposition and faithfully attended to her home cares and church duties. The family were in meager circumstances, and hard work on a lonely farm in the days when there were no railroads and few newspapers was the daily routine of their life.

Mary early attracted attention as a beautiful and bright child, but even in infancy she was subject to attacks of a hysterical nature. The irascibility of her father came out in her in intensified temper and weakened self-control. The family soon learned that they must yield to her whims, and all rules were in abeyance when she had one of her "fits." The Sabbath was an especially dangerous day with her, and even her domineering father had then to relax some of his rules, "for she invariably had one of her bad attacks, and the day ended in excitement and anxiety." "Mrs. Baker, the mother, often told her friends that Mary, of all her children, was the most difficult to care for, and they were all at their wits' end to keep her quiet and amuse her."[1] She attended the district school for a short time, but on account of her peculiar disposition she was allowed to stop and went no more until she had reached her fifteenth year.

In her autobiography, "Retrospection and Introspection," Mrs. Eddy relates, as her chief remembrance of the Bow farm days, the following incident:

For some twelve months, when I was about eight years old, I repeatedly heard a voice, calling me distinctly by name, three times, in an ascending scale. I thought this was my mother's voice, and sometimes went to her, beseeching her to tell me what she wanted. Her answer was always: "Nothing, child! What do you mean?" Then I would say: "Mother, who did call me? I heard somebody call 'Mary' three times!" This continued until I grew discouraged, and my mother was perplexed and anxious.

The similarity to the call of the child Samuel, I Sam., ch. 3, is obvious, and Mrs. Eddy completes the parallel as follows:

My mother read to me the Scriptural narrative of little Samuel, and bade me, when the voice called again, to reply as he did, "Speak, Lord; for thy servant heareth." The voice came; but I did not answer. Afterward I wept, and prayed that God would forgive me, resolving to do, next time, as my mother had bidden me. When the call came again I did answer, in the words of Samuel, but never again to the material senses was that mysterious call repeated.[2]

[1] These and other quotations without references are from Miss Milmine's *History*.

[2] *Retrospection and Introspection*, pp. 8, 9.

Mark Baker lived on the Bow farm from 1785 to 1836) and then removed to Tilton (then Sanborton Bridge) eighteen miles north of Concord, where he lived until his death in 1865. Here Mary again went to the district school, and as she was backward in her studies she was placed in a class with younger children. Miss Milmine interviewed a number of her classmates and quotes one of them as follows: "I remember Mary Baker very well," said one of her classmates living (1907) in Tilton. "She began to come to district school in the early summer of 1836. I recollect her very distinctly because she sat just in front of me, and because she was such a big girl to be in our class. I was only nine, but I helped her with her arithmetic when she needed help. We studied Smith's Grammar and ciphered by ourselves in Adam's New Arithmetic, and when she left school in three or four weeks we had both reached long division. She left on account of sickness."

Turning to "Retrospection and Introspection," we read Mrs. Eddy's own account of these days. She says that she was kept out of school because her father was taught to believe that her brain was too large for her body; that her brother Albert, then a student in college, taught her Greek, Latin, and Hebrew; that her favorite childhood studies were natural philosophy, logic, and moral science; that at ten years of age she was as familiar with Lindley Murray's Grammar as with the Westminster Catechism; and that she graduated from Dyer H. Sanborn's Academy at Tilton. Her schoolmates when interviewed by Miss Milmine could not reconcile these statements with their own knowledge. They do not believe her brother taught her Greek, Latin, and Hebrew, for he entered college when Mary was nine and left home when she was thirteen years old. Dyer H. Sanborn did not conduct an "academy" and there were no "graduations" from it; and they insist that Mary left school when she had only reached long division. Mrs. Eddy further says in her autobiography, "After my discovery of Christian Science, most of the knowledge I had gleaned from schoolbooks vanished like a dream"! As she never gave any indication of ever having possessed any knowledge of "Hebrew, Greek, and Latin," "natural philosophy, logic, and moral science," it is evident that her belief or claim that she once had such learning was a dream also. "Learning was so illumined," she continues, "that grammar was eclipsed." There is plenty of evidence of this in her own unassisted writings. "Etymology was divine history, voicing the idea of God in man's origin and signification." Her "spiritual sense, which is also their original meaning" of words as given in her "Glossary" in "Science and Health," is always purely fanciful and often screamingly ridiculous. "Syntax was spiritual order and unity." Her syntax may have been "spiritual," but it certainly was not grammatical. "Prosody, the song of angels, and no earthly inglorious theme." If angels sang in her prose, they refused to do so in her "poetry."[1]

One other incident in these earliest years may be mentioned. She tells us that "at the age of twelve years I was admitted to the Congregational (Trinitarian) Church." She had a horror of the doctrine of predestination and denied it before the deacons of the church. "Distinctly do I recall what followed. I stoutly main-

[1] *Retrospection and Introspection*, p. 10.

tained that I was willing to trust God, and take my chance of spiritual safety with my brothers and sisters—not one of whom had then made any profession of religion. . . This was so earnestly said, that even the oldest church-members wept. After the meeting was over they came and kissed me. To the astonishment of many, the good clergyman's heart was melted, and he received me into their communion, and my protest along with me." Her recollection is "distinctly" vivid as to details, but on the one concrete fact wherein it can be tested, she is wrong. Instead of being twelve she was seventeen years of age at this time. The official record of the Tilton Congregational Church contains this entry: "1838. July 26, Received into this church, Stephen Grant, Esq., John Gilly and his wife Hannah, Mrs. Susan French, wife of William French, Miss Mary A. M. Baker, by profession, the two former receiving the ordinance of baptism. Greenaugh McQuestion, Scribe."[1] Why was this incident put at the age of twelve years? The visit of Jesus to the Temple at the same age may have suggested another parallel.

Through these early years the hysterical, cataleptic nature of Mary Baker continued to give anxiety to the Baker household and to be a subject of general talk in the neighborhood. On this point Miss Milmine writes ·

At home Mary was still allowed to have her own way as completely as in her baby days. Indeed, by this time she, as well as the family, had come to consider this privilege a natural right, and she grew constantly more insistent in her demands upon her parents and brothers and sisters, who had found by long experience that the only way to live at all with Mary was to give in to all her whims. . . . Mary's hysteria was, of course, her most effective argument

[1] Milmine, *History*, p. 20.

in securing her way.   Like the sword of Damocles, it hung perilously over the household, which constantly surrendered and conceded and made shift with Mary to avert the inevitable climax. . . These attacks, which continued until very late in life, have been described to the writer by many eyewitnesses, some of whom have watched by her bedside and treated her in Christian Science for her affliction.   Mary fell headlong to the floor, writhing and screaming in apparent agony.   Again she dropped as lifeless, and lay limp and motionless, until restored.   At other times she became rigid like a cataleptic, and continued for a time in a state of suspended animation. . .   Nothing had the power of exciting Mark Baker like one of Mary's "fits," as they were called.   His neighbors in Tilton remember him as he went to fetch Dr. Ladd, how he lashed his horse down the hill, standing upright in his wagon and shouting in his tremendous voice, "Mary is dying." . . .   A neighbor, passing the house one morning, stopped at Mark's gate and inquired why Mary, who was at that moment rushing wildly up and down the second-story piazza, was so excited; to which Mark replied bitterly: "The Bible says Mary Magdalen had seven devils, but our Mary has got ten." [1]

It was in these days that Charles Poyen, the French mesmerist, appeared as a lecturer in the neighborhood of Tilton, and while it is not known that Mary Baker heard him personally, she must have heard about him and his theories and practice, because of the fact that "Animal Magnetism" came to occupy a large place in her own teaching and life. The influences of Shakerism and transcendentalism and other peculiar cults that were then rife in New England were also in the air and must have reached and left their impress on her sensitive and absorbent nature. She grew up in a kind of hotbed of "isms," and her life was the proper outgrowth of such a nature in such an environment.

2. EARLY MARRIAGES

In December, 1843, at the age of twenty-two Mary Baker was married to George Washington Glover, who

[1] *History*, pp. 19, 20.

is described as "a big, kind-hearted, young fellow," whose parents were neighbors of the Bakers at Bow. "Wash" Glover was a bricklayer and, attracted by higher wages, had gone South. On one of his visits back home he married Mary Baker and took her as his bride to Wilmington, N. C. Within six months, in June, 1844, the young husband died of yellow fever and left his widow without money among strangers. The Freemasons, to whose order George Glover belonged, provided the means for the funeral and for the return of the widow to her parents' home at Tilton.

In September of the same year Mrs. Glover gave birth to a son, her only child, whom she named George Washington after his father. The relation of the mother to this son is one of the peculiar things in Mrs. Eddy's career. Her sisters and brothers were now married and gone from home, and her parents were growing old. Mrs. Glover "took it for granted that she was to receive not only sympathy of her relatives but their support and constant service, and that they should assume the care of her child." She frequently left it with her aged parents or with her married sister, or with a neighbor woman, while she went off visiting. The child annoyed her irritable nature, and her father said, "Mary acts like an old ewe that won't own its lamb. She won't have the boy near her."

When the boy was seven years old the mother gave him to Mahala Sanborn, who had served as a nurse in the family, and, when this worthy woman was married to Russell Cheney and was about to move from Tilton, she begged her to take the boy with her. The Cheneys lived for a time at Groton, N. H., where Mrs. Glover

would see her son occasionally, but in 1857 they removed to
Enterprise, Minn.   In 1861 George W. Glover enlisted
in the Union Army and made an excellent record as a
soldier, and afterwards settled in Lead, S. D., where
he was appointed United States marshall.   Mrs. Eddy
never saw her son after his removal to the West at the
age of thirteen until 1878, when he was thirty-four years
of age and was married and had two children.

Mrs. Eddy's own account of her relations with her son
is given in "Retrospection and Introspection" as follows:

A few months before my father's second marriage, . . my little
son, about four years of age, was sent away from me, and put under
the care of our family nurse, who had married, and resided in the
northern part of New Hampshire.   I had no training for self-
support, and my home I regarded as very precious.   The night
before my child was taken from me, I knelt by his side throughout
the dark hours, hoping for a vision of relief from this trial. . .   My
dominant thought in marrying again was to get back my child,
but after our marriage his stepfather was not willing he should
have a home with me.   A plot was consummated for keeping us
apart.   The family to whose care he was committed, very soon
removed to what was then regarded as the Far West.   After his
removal a letter was read to my little son informing him that his
mother was dead and buried.   Without my knowledge he was
appointed a guardian, and I was then informed that my son was
lost.   Every means within my power was employed to find him,
but without success.   We never met again until he had reached the
age of thirty-four, had a wife and two children, and by a strange
providence had learned that his mother still lived, and came to see
me in Massachusetts.[1]

However, when her son did want to come to visit her
he received small encouragement.   In fact, she wrote
him a letter in which she positively forbade him to come,
and said, "If you come after getting this letter I shall
feel you have no regard for my interest or feelings, which

[1] Pp. 20, 21.

I hope not to be obliged to feel." This was in 1907. In 1902 Mrs. Eddy built her son a handsome house and otherwise provided for him. In 1907, for some reason she tried to get from her son all the letters she had ever written him, saying: "My dear Son: The enemy to Christian Science is by the wickedest powers of hypnotism trying to do me all the harm possible by acting on the minds of people to make them lie about me and my family." She then asked him to "send by express all the letters of mine that I have written you. This will be a great comfort to your mother if you do it. Send all—all of them." This letter with its peculiar request appears to have been occasioned by the fact that her son was about to bring action against ten leading Christian Scientists on the ground that they were controlling her property and that she through age and failing faculties was incompetent to manage it. Mrs. Eddy met this by placing her property in the hands of trustees, and several months later the suit was withdrawn. With this incident is closed our account of the relations of Mrs. Eddy with her son.

In these early years of her life spiritualism swept in a wave over the region, and Mrs. Glover developed her susceptibility as a medium. Seances were held at Mark Baker's house and there was considerable excitement over the strange phenomena. One elderly woman recalls a night spent with Mrs. Glover when her rest was frequently disturbed by mysterious "rappings" and by Mrs. Glover's announcements of the "appearance" of different spirits as they came and went. A few years later she received "messages" from her deceased brother Albert. Mrs. Eddy in "Science and Health," second edition,

(1878), denied that she ever was a medium, but said, "We have explained to the class calling themselves Spiritualists how their signs and wonders were wrought, and have illustrated them by doing them."[1] At this time also Mrs. Glover began to do some writing and "there was a tradition that she wrote a love story for 'Godey's Lady's Book,' and this gave her some local fame as an 'authoress.'"

In 1853 after having been a widow for nine years and at the age of thirty-two Mrs. Glover was married to Daniel Patterson, a peripatetic dentist who made occasional visits to Tilton. Mrs. Glover was so ill on the day of the wedding that Dr. Patterson had to carry her downstairs for the ceremony and then back again. He is described as a handsome man with a full black beard, who wore a frock coat and a silk hat and was popular with his patrons. Nevertheless he earned only a meager and precarious income, and their married life was a struggle with hard circumstances. They first settled in Franklin, a village near Tilton.

The Pattersons moved from place to place, leaving behind them a trail of stories about Mrs. Patterson's invalidism and hysteria and "fits" and quarrels with her neighbors.[2] During the Civil War Dr. Patterson went South seeking employment as an army surgeon and, straying into enemy lines, was captured and held as a prisoner, and Mrs. Patterson again went back to her relatives. On his release and return the Pattersons settled in Lynn, Mass., where the doctor opened an office in 1864. Two years later Dr. Patterson left his wife, and they never

1 Milmine, *History*, pp. 30, 66.
2 Ibid, *History*, p. 38.

lived together again. Mrs. Eddy, in a published statement in the Boston Post, of March 7, 1883, said that her "husband had eloped with a married woman," but her neighbors never heard of such an elopement, and Dr. Patterson told her family that he could not endure her any longer. Dr. Patterson paid his wife an annuity of $200 for several years, but in 1873 she obtained a divorce from him, and he dropped out of her life, dying in 1896.

It was while living with Dr. Patterson that Mrs. Patterson heard of Dr. P. P. Quimby, the mind healer of Portland, Me., and went to him and received help from him for her illness and also derived from him her ideas, but this affair in her life is so important that it will be reserved for a separate chapter, and this outline will be continued as a framework for the events more directly connected with her main work.

3. WANDER YEARS

Mrs. Patterson first visited Quimby in 1862 and again in 1864, and then after her separation from her husband she wandered around staying with various families until she settled in Lynn in 1870. The story of these years is one of a constant succession of quarrels in these homes. Although only a visitor occasionally paying a nominal rent, yet she was extremely exacting in her demands, doing no work and requiring everyone to serve her. "Untrained in any kind of paid work, she fell back upon the favor of her friends or chance acquaintances, living precariously upon their bounty, and obliged to go from house to house, as one family after another wearied of her." During these years she was practicing healing

herself, calling it "Moral Science" and attributing it
to Quimby. Her first announcement appeared in the
Banner of Light, a Spiritualist organ, on July 4, 1868,
and read in part: "Any Person desiring to learn how to
heal the sick can receive of the undersigned instructions
that will enable them to commence healing on a principle
of science with a success far beyond any of the present
modes. . . Address, Mrs. Mary B. Glover, Amesbury,
Mass." In all her teaching she represented her system as
being that of P. P. Quimby, as will be brought out later on.

When her husband left her at Lynn, Mrs. Patterson
went to room at the Russells, but she soon had to leave
because Russell's "wife, who had greatly admired her
when she first came, soon declared she could not endure
Mrs. Patterson's remaining there." She then went to
Mrs. Clark, and then to the home of Mrs. Armenius
Newhall, but soon afterward .left the house, at Mrs.
Newhall's request. Mrs. James Wheeler, of Swampscott,
"then offered her shelter," where, according to an affidavit
of Mrs. Julia Walcott, a sister of Mrs. Patterson's former
landlord and an intimate friend of Mrs. Wheeler, "Mrs.
Patterson was the means of creating discord in the Wheeler
family." From the Wheelers she went to live with Mrs.
Mary Ellis, and next we find her with Hiram Craft at
East Stoughton, where, according to an affidavit of Ira
Holmes, a brother of Mrs. Craft, "she caused trouble in
the household, and urged Mr. Craft to get a bill of divorce
from his wife, Mary Craft." She then went to the home
of Captain Webster, in Amesbury, Mass. A long affidavit
by Mary Bartlett, a granddaughter of Captain Webster,
gives an account of her trouble-making in this home,
which at last grew so exasperating that Captain Webster's

son put Mrs. Patterson out of the house and locked the door against her.

The friendless woman was then taken into the home of Miss Sarah Bageley, a dressmaker and Spiritualist of Amesbury, Mrs. Patterson teaching her the Quimby method of healing. By this time it was understood that Mrs. Glover, who had now again adopted this name, was writing a book, and she was working at manuscripts which eventually resulted in "Science and Health." From Amesbury she drifted to Stoughton, Mass., to the home of Mrs. Sally Wentworth, another Spiritualist, where she had the usual quarrel and on leaving was charged with having tried to set the house on fire.[1]

While with the Wentworths Mrs. Glover was writing manuscripts, and she wrote out instructions for Mrs. Wentworth, to direct her in healing the sick. Horace T. Wentworth, a son, had these instructions in Mrs. Glover's own handwriting in his possession when Miss Milmine wrote her "History" and she gives two pages from the original manuscript, literally reproducing the spelling and punctuation. We here insert them as they contain the germ of Mrs. Eddy's system and also show her unassisted English style:

An argument for the sick having what is termed fever chills and heat with sleepless nights, and called spinal inflammation.

The patient has been doctoring the sick one patient is an opium eater, with catarrh, great fear of the air, etc. Another had inflammation of the joints or rheumatism, and liver complaint another scrofula and rheumatism, and another dyspepsia, all of them having the most intense fear.

First the fever is to be argued down. What is heat and chills we answer nothing but an effect produced upon the body by images

[1] Affidavits giving the details of this affair made by a son and a niece of Mrs. Wentworth are given in Milmine, *History*, p. 125.

of disease before the spiritual senses wherefore you must say of heat and chill you are not hot you are not cold you are only the effect of fright there is no such thing as heat and cold if there were you would not grow hot when angry or abashed or frightened and the temperature around not changed in the least.

Inflammation is not inflammation or redness and soreness of any part this is your belief only and this belief is the red dragon the King of beasts which means this belief of inflammation is the leading lie out of which you get your fright that causes chills and heat. Now look it down cause your patient to look at this truth with you call upon their spiritual senses to look with your view which sees no such image and thus waken them out of their dream that is causing them so much suffering.[1]

These years were strewn with a constant succession of personal quarrels and estrangements. After the death of Mark Baker, Mrs. Eddy's father, in 1865, her own sister, Mrs. Tilton, closed her door against her. On this point Miss Milmine writes:

When Mrs. Tilton, who had taken care of Mrs. Patterson from childhood and supported her in her widowhood, finally turned against her sister, she was as hard as she had been generous before. "I loved Mary best of all my sisters and brothers," she said to her friends, "but it is all gone now." The bitterness of her feeling lasted to the day of her death. She instructed her family not to allow Mary to see her after death nor to attend her funeral, and her wishes were carried out.[2]

When the Christian Science Church in Concord, N. H., was dedicated on July 16, 1904, a North Groton correspondent, under the head, "Time Makes Changes," wrote in the "Plymouth Record":

With the dedication of the Christian Science Church at Concord, the gift of Mary Baker Glover Patterson Eddy, the thoughts of many of the older residents have turned back to the time when Mrs. Eddy, as the wife of Daniel Patterson, lived in this place.

[1] Milmine, *History*, pp. 130, 131.
[2] Ibid, p. 108.

These people remember the woman at that time as one who carried herself above her fellows. With no stretch of the imagination they remember her ungovernable temper and hysterical ways, and particularly well do they remember the night ride of one of the citizens who went for her husband to calm her in one of her unreasonable moods. The Mrs. Eddy of to-day is not the Mrs. Patterson of then, for this is a sort of Mr. Hyde and Dr. Jekyll case, and the woman is now credited with many charitable and kindly acts.[1]

From the Wentworths in Stoughton Mrs. Glover returned to her friend, Miss Bageley in Amesbury, where two years before she had met with Richard Kennedy, then a youth of eighteen, and had discerned in him a promising student and had given him lessons in the Quimby art of healing. She now proposed to him a partnership in which she would teach and he would practice this art. Up to this time she had little success herself in healing, and in fact she was chary of trying her hand at the business down to the end of her life. This arrangement was entered into, and this agreement marked a turning point in Mrs. Eddy's life and brought these troubled wander years to an end.

4. AT WORK IN LYNN

In June, 1870, a sign appeared in the yard in front of a house in Lynn, bearing the announcement, "Dr. Kennedy." Several rooms on the second floor had been sublet from a young woman who conducted a school on the first floor. Kennedy used the front room as an office, and Mrs. Glover occupied the other rooms as her living quarters and as a schoolroom for her pupils, her card bearing the announcement, "Mrs. Mary Glover, Teacher of Moral Science." Soon patients began to

[1] Milmine, *History*, pp. 35, 36.

appear in Dr. Kennedy's office and students in Mrs. Glover's classes, and for the first time in her life Mary Baker Glover began to be eased of the burden of poverty and to experience the joys of prosperity. Her students were required to copy a Quimby manuscript which she called "The Science of Man," and they obligated themselves to pay one hundred dollars in advance for the course of lessons and ten per cent of their annual income from their practice.

For twelve years Mrs. Eddy continued her work in Lynn, until she removed to Boston in 1882. These were trying years in many ways and brought out the masterful qualities of her strange personality. She was nearly fifty years of age, with no means or influential friends and with very meager education, and was burdened and often tortured with ill health, when she found herself and started out on her course that was destined to grow into a great career and world-wide fame. During these years she developed her system of healing and wrote her book "Science and Health," the first edition of which she was able to get published in 1875. Her classes grew, her charges increased from one hundred to three hundred dollars for a course of twelve lessons and then the course was reduced to seven lessons for the same price, and gold began to flow in copious streams into her coffers; within eighteen months she had $6000 to her credit in the bank. She began to extend her private teaching to public speaking and at length developed her system of healing into a religion and founded a church. At last she assumed the office of minister and blossomed out as the "Rev. Mary Baker Eddy," only stopping short of appending a "D. D." to her name. She was already dreaming of a great religion and world fame, and one day she said to Kennedy, "Richard, you will live to hear the church bells ring out my birthday." Her dream came true.

At this time Miss Milmine gives us a vivid glimpse into her classroom:

Whatever disagreement Mrs. Glover had with individual students, their number constantly increased, and for every deserter there were several new adherents. Her following grew not only in numbers but in zeal; her influence over her students and their veneration of her were subjects of comment and astonishment in Lynn. Of some of them it could be truly said that they lived only for and through Mrs. Glover. They continued to attend in some manner to their old occupations, but they became like strangers to their own families, and their personalities seemed to have undergone an eclipse. Like their teacher, they could talk of only one thing and had but one vital interest. One disciple let two of his three children die under metaphysical treatment without a murmur. Another married the woman whom Mrs. Glover designated. . . The closer students, who constituted Mrs. Glover's cabinet and bodyguard, executed her commissions, transacted her business, and were always at her call. To-day some of these who have long been accounted as enemies by Mrs. Eddy, and whom she has anathematized in print and discredited on the witness stand, still declare that what they got from her was beyond equivalent in gold or silver. They speak of a certain spiritual or emotional exaltation which she was able to impart in her classroom; a feeling so strong that it was like the birth of a new understanding and seemed to open to them a new heaven and a new earth. . . They lived by a new set of values; the color seemed to fade out of the physical world about them; men and women became shadow-like, and their humanity grew pale. The reality of pain and pleasure, sin and grief, love and death, once denied, the only positive thing in their lives was their belief—and that was almost wholly negation.

5. ENTER: ASA GILBERT EDDY, THIRD HUSBAND

Among those who came within the sphere of her attraction was Daniel H. Spofford, a worker in a shoe factory, who became her student in 1875 and was soon "Dr.

[1] *History*, pp. 155, 156.

Spofford, Scientific Physician," and had a flourishing practice. Spofford brought Asa Gilbert Eddy to Mrs. Glover as a student, and presently he gave her the name that she took and made famous as the founder of a new religion. Eddy was a weaver and was described by people who knew him in Lynn "as a quiet, dull, little man, docile and yielding up to a certain point, but capable of dogged obstinancy. He was short of stature, slow in his movements, and always taciturn." He was a bachelor who did his own washing and his sister-in-law said "he could do up a shirt as well as any woman." This simple-minded plastic soul at once yielded to Mrs. Glover's magnetic personality and was presently her favorite so obviously as to excite comment and jealousy among the other students. On Sunday evening, December 31, 1876, Eddy brought to Spofford a note which read as follows: "Dear Student: For reasons best known to myself I have changed my views in respect to marrying and ask you to hand this note to the Unitarian clergyman and please wait for an answer. Your teacher, M. B. G." "Hand or deliver reply to Dr. Eddy."

Spofford was astonished out of measure and said: "You've been very quiet about all this, Gilbert." "Indeed, Dr. Spofford," said Eddy, "I didn't know a thing about it myself until last night." On looking at the marriage license Spofford noticed that the ages of both the bride and groom were put down at forty years. As he knew that Eddy himself was only forty but that Mrs. Glover was then fifty-six, "he remarked upon the inaccuracy, but Mr. Eddy explained that the statement of age was a mere formality and that a few years more or less was of no consequence." It will be remembered that Mrs.

Eddy also misstated her age at which she was received into the Congregational Church, and this was another instance in which "a few years more or less was of no consequence." "Dr." Eddy was a very useful addition to Mrs. Eddy's establishment. "He would solicit students for his wife or take up the collection at the Sunday service when she preached the sermon." "He did what he was told," and after his marriage he had plenty of it to do.

6. LAWSUITS AT LYNN

These years at Lynn were also marked by interminable quarrels and lawsuits. Her relations with Richard Kennedy lasted only two years, and she then regarded him as one of her bitterest enemies and poured upon him the vials of her wrath, charging him with exercising "Malicious Animal Magnetism" against her and branding him in the third edition of "Science and Health" as "the Nero of to-day." Next, Daniel H. Spofford, who had become the publisher of her book, fell under her displeasure and was expelled from the Christian Scientists' Association, receiving the following notice: "Dr. D. H. Spofford of Newburyport has been expelled from the Association of Christian Scientists for immorality and as unworthy to be a member." The word "immorality" as used by Mrs. Eddy did not at all mean the sin that usually goes under that name, but only personal disagreement with her. This is only one of the instances in which she uses words in a sense wholly peculiar to herself. Years afterwards she accused a prominent woman in the mother church in Boston of being "an adulteress," and when the frantic woman begged to know the ground of such a charge, she replied, "You have adulterated the Truth; what are you, then, but an adulteress?" It would take a long catalogue of names to mention all the students that met a like fate. Already she was exercising the powers of an absolute despot and her simple and sudden word would dismiss anybody from her school or church and blacken the name of the victim with some grave but utterly unfounded charge.

Lawsuits flew thick and fast. The air was surcharged with litigation. She brought suit against George Tuttle and Charles Stanley, two of her students, for unpaid tuition. The case was tried before Judge George F. Choate, and in rendering a decision for the defendant Judge Choate said:

> Upon a careful examination I do not find any instructions given by her nor any explanations of her "science" or "method of healing" which appear intelligible to ordinary comprehension, or which could in any way be of value in fitting defendant as a competent and successful practitioner of any intelligible art or method of healing the sick, and I am of the opinion that the consideration for the agreement has wholly failed, and I so find.

This court decision is interesting as being the first legal evaluation of Christian Science.

In 1877 George W. Barry, one of her students, brought suit against Mrs. Eddy for service rendered in attending to her business and obtained judgment against her. In 1878 she sued Richard Kennedy for two years' instruction and lost. The same year she sued Daniel Spofford to recover royalty on his practice and lost. She lost every case brought for the recovery of tuition.[1]

[1] Peabody, *Masquerade*, p. 123.

7. MALICIOUS ANIMAL MAGNETISM

The case of Daniel Spofford, which was brought to trial at Salem, Mass., in May, 1878, introduces the subject of Malicious Animal Magnetism, which came to be known in the Eddy household as "M. A. M.," and also as "Malicious Mesmerism." Every religion must have a devil, and "M. A. M." was Mrs Eddy's Satan. By this name she meant the power of one mind, called by her "mortal mind," to influence and injure and even poison and drive insane and kill another mind. This notion became her obsession and infatuation that plagued her day and night, the mortal fear that tortured her and gave her no security and rest. It early became implanted in her mind, and in the first edition (1875) of "Science and Health" we read:

In coming years the person or mind that hates his neighbor will have no need to traverse his fields, to destroy his flocks and herds, and spoil his vines; or to enter his house to demoralize his household; for the evil mind will do this through mesmerism; and not *in propria personae* be seen committing the deed. Unless this terrible hour be met and restrained by science, mesmerism, that scourge of man, will leave nothing sacred when mind begins to act under direction of conscious power.[1]

In the thirteenth edition of the same book she says:

The evidence of the power that the mind exercises over the body has accumulated in weight and clearness until it culminates, at this period, in scientific statement and proof. Our courts recognize the evidence that goes to prove the committal of crime; then, if it be clear that the so-called mind of one mortal has killed another, is not this mind proved a murderer, and shall not the man be sentenced whose mind, with malice aforethought, kills?

[1] *Science and Health,* 1875, p. 123.

This demon proved all its powers of ubiquitous presence and evil influence and malignant destructiveness in her own household. It bedeviled her printers, froze her water pipes, and made the boiler leak. It got into her household furniture and kitchen utensils, her coal and blankets and feather pillows and silver spoons and caused them to disappear as if by some magician's wand. She accused nearly all her servants of stealing and charged their perversity to "M. A. M." She would send servants to outlying towns to mail letters and dispatch telegrams so that they would not pass through Boston where the mail clerks and telegraph operators were supposed to be "mesmerized" and could poison the messages with their evil power. A long succession of tenants and housekeepers went wrong under the same evil influence. Any personal annoyance or irritation that she experienced was instantly charged to this devil. Friend after friend fell under this accusation and was forthwith excommunicated. No language could be bitter enough, no punishment could be dire enough to express her sense of the horror of this evil thing.[1]

The first one to fall under this condemnation in its fell fury was Richard Kennedy, and the following passage from the chapter on "Demonology" in "Science and

[1] This obsession as to the evil presence and power of the Devil was rampant in the Middle Ages and was one of the terrors of those dark days. "The highest authorities of the Church constantly nourished that awe of the Devil and his tools which filled the mind, and they could do it without scruple, being themselves seized by the same terror. Thus Pope John XXII promulgated, A.D. 1303, two letters in which he complains that he himself not less than countless numbers of his sheep, was in danger of his life by the acts of sorcerers who could send devils into mirrors and rings, and make away with men by their words alone." Viktor Rydberg, *The Magic of the Middle Ages*, p. 162.

Health," edition of 1881, was aimed at him and illustrates her style and spirit:

> The Nero of to-day, regaling himself through a mental method with the tortures of individuals, is repeating history, and will fall upon his own sword, and it shall pierce him through. Let him remember this when, in the dark recesses of thought, he is robbing, committing adultery, and killing; when he is attempting to turn friend away from friend, ruthlessly stabbing the quivering heart; when he is clipping the thread of life, and giving to the grave youth and its rainbow hues; when he is turning back the reviving sufferer to her bed of pain, clouding her first morning after years of night; and the Nemesis of that hour shall point to the tyrant's fate, who falls at length upon the sword of justice.

And now we come to the case of Daniel Spofford. After her quarrel with him her hatred for him grew until it could no longer contain itself. "Accordingly," as Miss Milmine tells the story, "Mrs. Eddy got out a postscript to 'Science and Health.' The second edition, which Mr. Spofford had labored to prepare, was hastily revised and converted into a running attack upon him, hurried to press, labeled Volume II., and sent panting after 'Science and Health,' which was not labeled Volume I., and which had already been in the world three years. This odd little brown book, with the ark and troubled waves on the cover, is made up of a few chapters snatched from the 1875 edition, interlarded with vigorous rhetoric such as the following apostrophe to Spofford:"

> Behold! thou criminal mental marauder, that would blot out the sunshine of earth, that would sever friends, destroy virtue, put out truth, and murder in secret the innocent befouling thy track with the trophies of thy guilt—I say, "Behold the cloud no bigger than a man's hand," already rising in the horizon of truth, to pour down upon thy guilty head the hailstones of doom.

This "doom" came down upon "the guilty head" of Spofford in the form of a bill filed before the Supreme Judicial Court at Salem in the spring of 1878, charging him with practicing witchcraft upon one of Mrs. Eddy's former students, Lucretia L. S. Brown. Miss Brown was a maiden woman of fifty years of age, who was an invalid and had been healed by Christian Science and suffered a relapse. Mrs. Eddy persuaded her that Dr. Spofford was practicing "Malicious Animal Magnetism" upon her and that was the cause of her relapse; and she selected twelve of her students and trained them to serve as witnesses, saying to one of them, who protested at the railway station as they were about to take the train for Salem that she did not know anything about the case, "You will be told what to say."

The case came to trial before a crowded court room, for it attracted great attention in the newspapers. Mr. Spofford did not appear, but his attorney filed a demurrer, which Judge Gray sustained, "declaring with a smile that it was not within the power of the court to control Mr. Spofford's mind."

Miss Milmine concludes her detailed account of this celebrated case with these striking comments:

So, after a lapse of nearly two centuries, another charge of witchcraft was made before the court in Salem village. But it was an anachronism merely and elicited such ridicule that it was hard to realize that, because of charges quite as fanciful, one hundred and twenty-six persons were once lodged in Salem jail, nineteen persons were hanged, and an entire community was plunged into anguish and horror.

During the long years that the grass had been growing and withering above the graves of Martha Corey and Rebecca Nurse and their wretched companions, one of the most important of all possible changes had taken place in the world—a change in the mode of thinking. The works of Descartes, Locke, and Sir Isaac Newton had become a common inheritance; the relation of physical effect with physical cause had become established even in ignorant and unthinking minds, and a schoolboy of 1878 would have rejected as absurd the evidence upon which Judge Hawthorne condemned a woman like Mary Easty to death.[1]

A fitting climax and conclusion of Mr. Spofford's relations with the Eddy people in Lynn came in a celebrated case which was brought in the Municipal Court in December following the trial at Salem. To this case Miss Milmine devotes an entire chapter (ch. XIII) of her "History," giving part of the court records and of the testimony. Mr. Peabody gives an account of it from a lawyer's point of view (in ch. XI of his book), strongly hinting that Mrs. Eddy was back of the "conspiracy," but Dr. Powell in his book (page 80) condenses it into a brief summary which is sufficient for our purpose and the writer here transcribes it:

The last strange chapter in as strange a story as ever yet was told of Mrs. Eddy's strange career was the indictment the following December of Asa Gilbert Eddy, Mrs. Eddy's husband, and Edward J. Arens, one of her students, by the grand jury on the charge of conspiracy to murder Daniel H. Spofford. The evidence was dubious and inconsequential. No inference can to-day be drawn from it except that there was probably hysteria on one side and panic on the other. The case was *nolle prossed*, and never came to trial. Mr. Eddy paid the costs, and Mr. Spofford still lives (1907) and at the age of sixty-five enjoys the confidence of those who know him well.

[1] *History*, pp. 218–244. On Malicious Animal Magnetism, see also Powell, *Christian Science*, ch. VI, and Peabody, *The Religio-Medical Masquerade*, ch. XII. For an account of the belief in and the torture of witches, "which must forever be considered as among the most fearful calamities in human history," see A. D. White's *History of the Warfare of Science with Theology*, vol. I, pp. 350–363, II: 135–167.

Miss Wilbur also devotes to this case a chapter (ch. XVI) of her "Life of Mary Baker Eddy," which virtually gives Mrs. Eddy's version of the affair, stating that the "monstrous charge was thus dismissed without a trial," and deploring that "the men accused were made to appear too insignificant in the world's affairs to warrant a full and clear exoneration." It seems to be a perplexing point in the case that Dr. Eddy was willing to pay the costs when it was dismissed.

In closing this account of Mrs. Eddy's work at Lynn it will be sufficient to note that she organized the Christian Science Church in 1879 and her Metaphysical College in 1881. But the numerous quarrels and lawsuits and dissensions of the Christian Scientists made them unpopular in that city, "and to this day the Christian Science Church there has never prospered. . . They were constantly quarreling and bickering among themselves, accusing each other of fraud, dishonesty, witchcraft, bad temper, greed of money, hypocrisy, and finally of a conspiracy to murder. Unquestionably Mrs. Eddy, as the accepted messenger of God, was more severely criticized for her part in these altercations than if she had appeared before the courts merely as a citizen of Lynn, and this criticism had much to do with the cloud of suspicion and distrust which hung over the Church when, in the early part of the winter of 1882, Mrs. Eddy left Lynn forever behind her and went to Boston."[1]

8. LIFE IN BOSTON

Boston! the "hub of the universe," the "literary Athens of America," redolent of memories of Emerson and Lowell

---

[1] Milmine, *History*, p. 279.

and Holmes; the seat of Harvard University; the luminary that has emitted the cold, white light of Unitarianism and liberal thought; distinguished from colonial days by eminent scholars and divines and statesmen and literary geniuses; Boston with all its literary and social exclusiveness and superiority and pride; that this city set on a hill should become the home and throne of Christian Science is surely the paradox and irony of history. How are the mighty fallen! If the light that is in Boston turn to darkness, how great is that darkness!

The home and throne of Christian Science is what Boston became when Mary Baker Eddy, at the age of sixty-one years, set foot in its precincts and located her establishment on Columbus Avenue, afterwards transferring it to the fashionable Commonwealth Avenue. On Columbus Avenue she set up her "Massachusetts Metaphysical College," of which she herself was the entire faculty and in which she charged three hundred dollars for a course of seven lessons. Half a dozen of her students made their home with her, and the business of teaching on her part and of practicing on their part began in this city.

In June of the same year the death of Dr. Eddy occurred, for death, which according to Mrs. Eddy and her "Science" is only a "false belief" and "delusion" and "myth" and "nothing," has never spared the followers of Mrs. Eddy, not even her own husbands. Mrs. Eddy had an autopsy performed by a regular physician, who pronounced the cause of death to be organic disease of the heart. "Dr. Rufus K. Noyes of Boston," says Mr. Peabody, "who performed the autopsy, tells me that, having removed the diseased organ from Mr. Eddy's

breast, he exhibited it upon a platter to the sorrowing
widow, who craved the ocular demonstration, and pointed
out to her curious and eager inspection the precise cause
of death in its diseased condition. And it was after,
and notwithstanding, her close scrutiny of the physical
heart that had so robustly throbbed with love for her,
that, much to Dr. Noyes' amusement, Mrs. Eddy gave
out the statement, to the extent of a column or more in
the newspapers, that arsenical poison mentally administered by absent treatment had in fact torn her loved
one a third time, and finally, from her clinging grasp."[1]

The following are several extracts from this interview
which appeared in the Boston Post, June 5, 1882, the
"Dr. Eastman" mentioned in it being one of Mrs. Eddy's
students and not a graduate of any regular medical school:

My husband's death was caused by malicious mesmerism. Dr.
C. J. Eastman, who attended the case after it had taken an alarming
turn, declares the symptoms to be the same as those of arsenical
poisoning. On the other hand, Dr. Rufus K. Noyes, late of the
City Hospital, who held an autopsy over the body to-day, affirms
that the corpse is free from all material poisons, although Dr. Eastman still holds to his original belief. I know it was poison that
killed him, not material poison, but mesmeric poison. My husband
was in uniform health, and but seldom complained of any kind of
ailment. During his brief illness, just preceding his death, his
continual cry was, "Only relieve me of this continual suggestion,
through the mind, of poison, and I will recover." It is well known
that by constantly dwelling upon any subject in thought finally
comes the poison of belief through the whole system. . Oh, isn't
it terrible, that this fiend of malpractice is in the land! The only
remedy that is effective in meeting this terrible power possessed by
the evil-minded is to counteract it by the same method that I use in
counteracting poison. They require the same remedy. Circumstances debarred me from taking hold of my husband's case. He
declared himself perfectly capable of carrying himself through, and
I was so entirely absorbed in business that I permitted him to try,

[1] *Masquerade*, p. 44.

and when I awakened to the danger it was too late. . . We all know that disease of any kind cannot reach the body except through the mind, and that if the mind is cured the disease is soon relieved. Only a few days ago I disposed of a tumor in twenty-four hours that the doctors had said must be removed by the knife. I changed the course of the mind to counteract the effect of the disease. This proves the myth of matter.[1]

It was really unfortunate for the poor husband that a wife with such power was "so entirely absorbed in business" that "circumstances debarred [her] from taking hold of [his] case."

Soon after Mr. Eddy's death Mrs. Eddy called into her service Calvin A. Frye, who ever after played a large and intimate part in her life until her death. He was a striking exception among her many students and followers in that she did not quarrel with him and dismiss him peremptorily under a charge of "Malicious Mesmerism" or "Malpractice." He was a machinist employed at Lawrence, Mass., when at the age of twenty-seven he was summoned to come to Mrs. Eddy, from whom he had formerly received instruction. Writing in 1908, Miss Milmine gives the following summary account of him:

For twenty-seven years Mr. Frye has occupied an anomalous position in Mrs. Eddy's household. He has been her house steward, bookkeeper, and secretary. When he attends her upon her cere- monial drives in Concord, he wears the livery of a footman. In a letter to her son, George Glover, written April 27, 1898, Mrs. Eddy describes Mr. Frye as her "man-of-all-work." Since Mrs. Eddy's retirement [1889] to Concord eighteen years ago, Calvin Frye has lived in an isolation almost as complete as her own, the object of surmises and insinuations. He has no personal friends outside of the walls of Pleasant View, and the oft-repeated assertion that in twenty-seven years he has not been beyond Mrs. Eddy's call for twenty-four hours is perhaps literally true. Although her treatment

[1] Milmine, *History*, pp. 286, 287.

of him has often been contemptuous in the extreme, his fidelity has been invaluable to Mrs. Eddy; but the actual donning of livery by a middle-aged man of some education and of sturdy, independent New England ancestry, is a difficult thing to understand.   Whether he feels the grave charges which have recently been brought against him, or the ridicule of which he has long been the object, it is not likely that anyone will ever learn from Mr. Frye.[1]

Mr. Peabody offers like testimony as to the strange relations of this man and woman.   "He is," he says, "her major-domo, master of ceremonies in her pretentious establishment, and director of her large retinue of assistant secretaries, literary experts, personal healers, mental protectors, and domestic servants.   These positions Mr. Frye has adorned, as a resident member of Mrs. Eddy's family, occupying an adjoining room, for upwards of thirty years."   For years he held the legal title of all her property down to the very jewels she wore, and this condition continued until Mr. Peabody, who was associate counsel in a legal case in connection with Mrs. Eddy's property, called attention to it and Mr. Frye reconveyed it to Mrs. Eddy.   In view "of all these circumstances, taken with the confident opinion of one long a member of her household," Mr. Peabody, speaking with an inside knowledge of the facts, expresses his judgment of the relations of these two people, which anyone interested in knowing it can find recorded in his book.[2]

The seven years that Mrs. Eddy spent in Boston at the head of her complex and growing establishment, consisting of her household, Metaphysical College and church, were marked by the usual personal quarrels, church dissensions, lawsuits, and mesmeric monomania.   The devil

[1] *History*, pp. 293, 294.
[2] *Masquerade*, pp. 45, 46.

of "M. A. M." was very busy in Boston and let no day
pass without some visible mark of his presence and displeasure. One who spent several years in her Boston
household declares it was "a madhouse." Miss Milmine
gives the following glimpse into it:

> The atmosphere of Mrs. Eddy's house derived its peculiar char-
> acter from her belief in malicious mesmerism, which exerted a
> sinister influence over everyone under her roof. Her students could
> never get away from it. Morning, noon, and night the thing had
> to be reckoned with, and the very domestic arrangements were
> ordered to elude or to combat the demoniacal power. If Mrs. Eddy
> had kept in her house a dangerous maniac or some horrible physical
> monstrosity which was always breaking from confinement and
> stealing around her chambers and hallways, it could scarcely have
> cast a more depressing anxiety over her household. Those of her
> students who believed in mesmerism were always on their guard
> with each other, filled with suspicion and distrust. If a member
> of that household denied the doctrine, or even showed a lack of
> interest in it, he was at once pronounced a mesmerist and requested
> to leave. Mr. Eddy's death had given malicious animal magnetism
> a new vogue. Mrs. Eddy was now always discovering in herself
> and her students symptoms of arsenical poisons or of other baneful
> drugs. Her nocturnal illnesses, which she had for years attributed
> to malicious mesmerism, were now more frequent and violent than
> ever.[1]

In 1888, Mrs. Eddy at the age of sixty-eight adopted as
her legal son Ebenezer Johnson Foster, a man of forty-
one, who then became known as Ebenezer J. Foster Eddy.
He was a homeopathic physician and Mrs. Eddy was
glad to have a medically trained man in her service so
that on occasion she could use him for her own purposes.
Dr. Foster Eddy served her well for a time and became
publisher of her books, but in time he was charged with
being short in his accounts and with having conducted
himself improperly with a married woman, and Mrs.

[1] *History*, p. 301.

Eddy then sent him to Philadelphia to build up a church. When it was found that discreditable stories had followed him to that city Mrs. Eddy wrote to him: "Dear Doctor, I have silenced every word of the slander started in Boston about that woman by saying that I had not the least idea of any wrong conduct between you and her, for I know you are chaste. . . This silly stuff is dead. Always kindly yours, Mary Baker Eddy." Dr. Foster Eddy left Philadelphia, but he was already under suspicion with Mrs. Eddy, and soon after when he sought to see her, she "cut short the interview and went upstairs while he was speaking," and he drops out of this history.

Mrs. Eddy was having almost constant trouble with her publishers and editors whom she appointed and dismissed at her own arbitrary pleasure. In one letter she reprimanded W. G. Nixon, her publisher, for not affixing her name whenever he mentioned "Science and Health" in the Christian Science Journal, and in another letter reproof fell on his unlucky head for having omitted the title "Reverend" before her name. Mr. Nixon thought that the Journal should not be conducted simply as the personal organ of Mrs. Eddy and ventured to suggest to her that it would be more dignified to keep her name a little more in the background, but this drew from her the following note:

Those who are trying to frighten you over my name at suitable intervals and who are crying personality are the very ones that persist in their purpose to keep my personality before the public through abusing it and to harness it to all the faults of other personalities and make it responsible for them. But neither of these efforts disposes of personality nor handle it on the rule our Master taught nor deal with mortal personality scientifically.

On Sept. 30, 1889, Mrs. Eddy wrote to Mr. Nixon,

saying: "God our God has just told me who to recommend to you for the Editor of C. S. Jour. but you are not to name me in this transaction. It is Rev. Charles Macomber Smith, D. D., 164 Summer St., Somerville, Mass. . . . Get him sure." But before Mr. Nixon could act on this letter she wrote him again, saying, "I regret having named the one I did for Editor. It is a mistake, he is not fit. It was not God evidently that suggested that thought but the person who suggests many things mentally but I have before been able to discriminate I wrote too soon after it came to my thought." It thus appears that she was not always able to discriminate between God's revelation and the suggestion of her mesmeric devil "M. A. M." In these disputes Mrs. Eddy always had one argument that was unanswerable. Looking her opponent directly in the eye she would slowly say, "God has directed me in this matter. Have you anything further to say?"

In the spring of 1889 Mrs. Eddy suddenly left Boston, driven out as she said by malicious mesmerism. This evil presence had filled and poisoned the whole city. Her mail, her clothes, her house were saturated with it. The very atmosphere had become so impregnated with it that she said it choked her. The only relief for her was "flight," escape anywhere to get away from Boston. The city of culture that had once attracted her now repelled her and sent her flying from it as for her very life.

9. RETIREMENT AND CLOSING YEARS

From Boston Mrs. Eddy went to Concord, N. H., where she lived in a beautiful home with surrounding grounds known as Pleasant View, from which she could look out over the hills among which lies the farm where she spent her childhood. In this retirement she lived nineteen years, but though withdrawn from public life she yet kept her hand on her church and all her affairs and even tightened her autocratic grip. Only four times during these years did she visit Boston. She ceased to teach and preach as long before she had ceased to give treatment to the sick; and she published a notice that no one must seek to consult her or write to her. Her followers would go out from Boston on pilgrimages to Pleasant View, where for a number of years she appeared to them on the occasion of the June communion. But she withdrew into ever closer seclusion and even published a prohibition forbidding her followers to linger on the road so as to see her as she went by in her carriage. Her life grew increasingly isolated and lonely, and writing to her son George Washington Glover in 1898 she said: "Now what of my circumstances? I name first my home, which of all places on earth is the one in which to find peace and enjoyment. But my home is simply a house and a beautiful landscape. There is not one in it that I love as I love everybody. I have no congeniality with my help inside of my house; there are no companions and scarcely fit to be my help."

She was so closely guarded that her son came to believe that his letters were not reaching her and that Calvin Frye answered some of them. When he sent a letter to her by express he was notified that Mrs Eddy could not receive it except through her secretary Frye. Mr. Glover then brought action against ten leading Christian Scientists, as we have already related, when Mrs Eddy transferred her property to a trusteeship, and then the action was withdrawn.

On Sunday, January 26, 1908, Mrs. Eddy was taken on board a special train at Concord and removed to Newton, Mass., where a fine mansion had been bought and prepared for her. This removal was effected with great secrecy and precaution and was an utter surprise to her followers and the public. The reason for this final change of residence is given by Miss Milmine as follows:

It is very probable that Mrs. Eddy left Concord for the same reason that she left Boston years ago; because she felt that malicious animal magnetism was becoming too strong for her there. The action brought by her son in Concord the previous summer she attributed entirely to the work of mesmerists who were supposed to control her son's mind. Mrs. Eddy always believed that this strange miasma of evil had a curious tendency to become localized; that certain streets, mailboxes, telegraph offices, vehicles, could be totally suborned by these invisible currents of hatred and ill-will that had their source in the minds of her enemies and continually encircled her. She believed that in this way an entire neighborhood could be made inimical to her, and it is quite possible that, after the recent litigation in Concord, she felt that the place had become saturated with mesmerism and that she would never again find peace there.[1]

Mrs. Eddy was now eighty-seven years of age, and her highly nervous organization that had withstood the strain and storms of so many years was visibly approaching the end.   Yet she still showed wonderful vitality and grip on her affairs and at times the old fire would flash up in the dying embers. Her death occurred on December 3, 1910. A physician was called in near the end, and her attendants said that for several days she had been "in error."   She was buried at Newton, where a costly monument has been

[1] *History*, p. 459.

reared over her grave. But her real monument is the strange system of belief and practice she built up and the strange book she wrote and the church that acknowledges her as its founder. Whatever view may be taken of her character and teaching and work, it must be admitted that she was one of the most remarkable women of her day.

CHAPTER IV

WHERE DID MRS. EDDY GET HER SYSTEM OF HEALING?

This is a vital question in the story of Mrs. Eddy's life and the history of Christian Science. If the system is based on a false claim of originality and has purloined its ideas from another healer, it falls into the class of stolen goods. It is true that the essential truth and worth of the ideas of a system may be independent of their origin and authorship, but a religion founded by a false prophet cannot retain the respect of the world, and will not endure.

1. MRS. EDDY'S CLAIMS

Mrs. Eddy makes very positive claims as to her own discovery of Christian Science, but as usual she is at this point her own most confusing and contradictory witness against herself. At different times she fixes on different dates for this discovery; and while the development of an idea may pass through degrees of growth, yet her definite dates do not carry this implication, especially as she says in one of her letters, "I discovered the art in a moment's time." In a letter to the Boston Post of March 7, 1883, she says: "We made our first experiments in mental healing about 1853, when we were convinced that mind had a science, which, if understood, would heal all disease." But in the first edition of "Science and Health," 1875, she says: "We made our first discovery that science mentally

58

applied would heal the sick, in 1864, and since then have tested it on ourselves and hundreds of others and never found it fail to prove the statement herein made for it."

In later editions of "Science and Health," she fixes on 1866 as the date of the discovery, and this is the date given in a more elaborate account in her autobiography "Retrospection and Introspection" (1892), which is as follows:

It was in Massachusetts, February, 1866, and after the death of the magnetic doctor, Mr. P. P. Quimby, whom spiritualists would associate therewith, but who was in no wise connected with this event, that I discovered the science of Divine Metaphysical healing, which I afterward named Christian Science. The discovery came to pass in this way. During twenty years prior to my discovery I had been trying to trace all physical effects to a mental cause; and in the latter part of 1866 I gained the scientific certainty that all causation was Mind, and every effect a mental phenomenon. My immediate recovery from the effects of an injury caused by an accident, an injury neither medicine nor surgery could reach, was the falling apple that led me to the discovery how to be well myself and how to make others so. Even to the homeopathic physician who attended me, and rejoiced in my recovery, I could not then explain the modus of my relief. I could only assure him that the Divine Spirit had wrought the miracle, a miracle which later I found to be in perfect Scientific accord with divine law.[1]

She refers to this recovery in the first edition of "Science and Health" and also in a letter written to Mr. W. W. Wright, in which she says: "I have demonstrated upon myself in an injury occasioned by a fall, that it did for me what surgeons could not do. Dr. Cushing of this city pronounced my injury incurable and that I could not survive three days because of it, when on the third day I rose from my bed and to the utter confusion of all I

[1] *Retrospection and Introspection*, p. 24.

commenced my usual avocations and notwithstanding misplacements, I regained the natural position and functions of the body."

But two weeks after this miraculous recovery, which she says occurred on the third day after her accident, Mrs. Eddy wrote to Julius A. Dresser, a former student of Quimby, as follows:

Two weeks ago I fell on the sidewalk, and struck my back on the ice, and was taken up for dead, came to consciousness amid a storm of vapors from cologne, chloroform, ether, camphor, etc., but to find myself the helpless cripple I was before I saw Dr. Quimby. The physician attending said I had taken the last step I ever should, but in two days I got out of my bed alone and will walk; but yet I confess I am frightened, and out of that nervous heat my friends are forming, spite of me, the terrible spinal affection from which I have suffered so long and hopelessly. . . Now can't you help me? I believe you can. I write with this feeling: I think that I could help another in my condition if they had not placed their intelligence in matter. This I have not done, and yet I am slowly failing. Won't you write to me if you will undertake for me if I can get you?

And Dr. Cushing, the physician in the case, in 1907 made a long affidavit, based on notes of the case written at the time, giving an account of it in which he said:

I did not at any time declare, or believe, that there was no hope for Mrs. Patterson's recovery, or that she was in a critical condition, and did not at any time say, or believe, that she had but three or any other limited number of days to live. Mrs. Patterson did not suggest, or say, or pretend, or in any way whatever intimate, that on the third, or any other day, of her said illness, she had miraculously recovered or been healed, or that, discovering or perceiving the truth of the power employed by Christ to heal the sick, she had, by it, been restored to health. As I have stated, on the third and subsequent days of her said illness, resulting from her said fall on the ice, I attended Mrs. Patterson and gave her medicine; and on the 10th day of the following August, I was again called to see her, this time at the home of a Mrs. Clark, on Summer Street, in said city of Lynn.

As Dr. Cushing attended Mrs. Eddy on the third day after her fall, when she says she experienced an "immediate recovery" which astonished her physician, an alleged fact which he utterly denies, and also attended her for at least two days subsequent to this third day, and as she herself wrote two weeks later to Julius A. Dresser that she was "slowly failing" and made a frantic appeal to him to help her, her claim to have discovered Christian Science in 1866 in connection with a miraculous recovery from a fall is discredited and disproved by her physician and especially by her own subsequent testimony.

2. PHINEAS PARKHURST QUIMBY

Phineas Parkhurst Quimby, as has been seen, was an uneducated clock maker of Portland, Me., who practiced mental healing. He was born in Lebanon, N. H., in 1802 and died at Belfast, Me., in 1866. He was a man of Christian faith and fine character and sterling worth, whose simple goodness and kindliness won the instinctive confidence of all who came into contact with him, and this faith in himself which he inspired was, no doubt, the chief secret of his healing power. While uneducated, he was yet not an ignorant man, but was a constant reader of the Bible and even read some philosophical books. About 1838 he became interested in the power of the mind as exhibited in mesmerism, clairvoyance, and Scriptural healing by laying on of hands. Charles Poyen, the French mesmerist who has been mentioned before, was then traveling around and lecturing in New England, and Mr. Quimby heard him and was influenced by him. He practiced his method of healing for a time, but soon abandoned it and began to heal diseases by the silent treatment, declaring "Truth" to be the healer. Though he said that "error is matter," yet he did not mean to deny the reality of matter and was little interested in metaphysics. "His explanations were concrete, and he saw no reason for denying natural facts."[1] He ceased to practice mesmerism or hypnotism because he discovered that "any person or drug which could put the patient in this attitude of mental receptivity and give his own mind a chance to work upon the disease, would accomplish the same result." He then gave up manipulating his patients and declared the cure was purely mental. Finally he lost all faith in the science of medicine and thought that doctors were hypocrites. "Instead of gaining confidence in the doctors, I was forced to the conclusion that their science was false. .ˑ . . My theory exposes the hypocrisy of those who undertake to cure in this way."[2] Mr. Quimby was a simple-minded man who found no difficulty in thinking that all his own opinions were infallible knowledge and that all other men's opinions were false.

In one of his circulars he described his method as follows:

My practice is unlike all medical practice. . . I give no medicines and make no outward applications, but simply sit by the patient, tell him what he thinks is his disease, and my explanation is the cure. . . If I succeed in correcting his errors, I change the fluids of his system, and establish the truth or health. The truth is the cure. This mode of treatment applies to all cases.[3]

[1] Horatio W. Dresser, *History of the New Thought Movement*, p. 120.

[2] Julius A. Dresser, *True History of Mental Healing*, p. 17.

[3] For extensive quotations from Mr. Quimby's manuscripts see the *True History of Mental Healing*, by Julius A. Dresser who was a

Mr. Quimby divided man into two parts or elements, "the spiritual power in man," and "the natural man," or "animal matter or life." He uses the word "matter" for the lower nature of the senses and also appears to mean by it very much the same as we mean by the "subconsciousness," but he never employs it in Mrs. Eddy's sense of "nothingness," and of a delusion of "mortal mind," a term he does not use. "My theory," he says, "is founded on the fact that mind is matter; and, if you will admit this for the sake of listening to my ideas, I will give you my theory. . . All knowledge that is of man is based on opinions. This I call this world of [spiritual] matter. It embraces all that comes within the so-called senses. Man's happiness and misery are in his belief; but the wisdom of science is of God, and not of man. Now to separate these two kingdoms is what I am trying to do. . . Disease is the invention of man, and has no identity in Wisdom." Disease is thus a wrong belief rooted down in the subconscious life of man, and it is cured by Truth or Wisdom which is the power of God working in the soul.[1] This is Quimby's root idea which Mrs. Eddy appropriated, only she added to it the idea of the nonreality of matter, which he never held, as well as many other absurd notions.

patient of Mr. Quimby and then a teacher of his methods, and who says, "All these writings I have read, being in the confidence of George A. Quimby, the son, who holds them." His book, based on personal intimate knowledge of the facts, gives convincing testimony as to the way in which Mrs. Eddy appropriated Mr. Quimby's principle and methods.

[1] For an exposition of Mr. Quimby's theory, see H. W. Dresser's *History of the New Thought Movement*, ch. II and III.

3. REV. WARREN F. EVANS, FIRST EXPOSITOR OF QUIMBY

Dr. Quimby soon began to attract not only patients but also students and followers who took up his system and began to teach and practice it for themselves. Among these was the Rev. Warren F. Evans, a Swedenborgian minister of Claremont, N. H., who came to Dr. Quimby in poor health in 1863 and was healed. He was acquainted with philosophical idealism and was able to grasp Dr. Quimby's ideas and work them out for himself. As a result of his study and experience he became the first expositor of Dr. Quimby's theory, which he set forth in six volumes, the first three of which, with their titles and dates of publication, were the following: "The Mental Cure," 1869; "Mental Medicine," 1872; and "Soul and Body," 1875. It will be noted that these three books appeared before the first edition of Mrs. Eddy's "Science and Health." A quotation from the second of these volumes, "Mental Medicine," will indicate Mr. Evans' general teaching:

Disease being in its root a wrong belief, change that belief and we cure the disease. By faith we are thus made whole. There is a law here the world will sometime understand and use in the cure of the diseases that afflict mankind. The late Dr. Quimby, one of the successful healers of this or any age, embraced this view of the nature of disease, and by a long succession of most remarkable cures proved the truth of the theory and the efficiency of that mode of treatment. Had he lived in a remote age or country, the wonderful facts which occurred in his practice would have been deemed either mythical or miraculous. He seemed to reproduce the wonders of the Gospel history.[1]

It will be seen that Mr. Evans not only reproduces Dr. Quimby's fundamental teaching but also expressly

---

[1] For account of Rev. W. F. Evans and his teaching, see Dresser's *History of the New Thought Movement*, ch. IV.

attributes it to him, in which respect he stands in wide
contrast with Mrs. Eddy. It is an important fact in
this history that Mrs. Eddy had some knowledge of Dr.
Evans' books, for "as a direct rebuke to those who had
become interested in the writings of Dr. Evans, she issued
instructions to the members of the Christian Scientists'
Association that they should read no other works upon
mental healing than those written by herself, and she
printed in the Journal a set of rules to the effect that all
teachers of Christian Science should require that their
students read no literature upon the subject of mind
cure but her own."[2]

4. MRS. EDDY'S RELATIONS WITH DR. QUIMBY

Mrs. Eddy, then Mrs. Patterson, was wandering
around with her peripatetic dental husband and was
trying various means of cure for her ill health, when she
heard of Dr. Quimby and went to him in Portland in
1862. She was so weak on her arrival that she had to
be helped up into the waiting room and so poor that he
personally obtained for her a room at a reduced rate.
After a stay of three weeks her spinal trouble left her and
she thought she was cured. But she obtained more than
healing from Dr. Quimby: she obtained from him something that she had hitherto lacked, an idea and a mission,
a purpose that would unify her discordant life and call
out her latent personality and power. She haunted Dr.
Quimby's office, "asking questions, reading manuscripts,
and observing his treatment of patients." The kindly
old man took an interest in her and said, "She's a devilish
bright woman."

2 Milmine, *History*, p. 349.

Soon after her recovery she wrote a long letter to the Portland Courier, of the date of November 7, 1862, in which she pays a laudatory tribute to Dr. Quimby and explains his mode of healing. In these early letters of Mrs. Eddy's, she is discovered in the act of writing her unassisted and unedited English, and from the opening paragraph of this letter this specimen is given:

When the startled alchemist discovered, as he supposed, an universal solvent, or the philosopher's stone, and the more daring Archimedes invented a lever wherewithal to pry up the universe, I cannot say that in either the principle obtained in nature or in art, or that it worked well, having never tried it. But, when by a falling apple, an immutable law was discovered, we gave it the crown of science, which is incontrovertible and capable of demonstration; hence that was wisdom and truth. When from the evidence of the senses, my reason takes cognizance of truth, although it may appear in quite a miraculous view, I must acknowledge that as science which is truth uninvestigated.

In reading the following extract from her letter bearing on Dr. Quimby's method of healing, let the fact be kept in mind that afterward she affirmed that he was a mesmerist and used animal magnetism in his work:

Is it by animal magnetism that he heals the sick? Let us examine. I have employed electro-magnetism and animal magnetism, and for a brief interval have felt relief, from the equilibrium which I fancied was restored to an exhausted system or by diffusion of concentrated action. But in no instance did I get rid of a return of all my ailments, because I had not been helped out of the error in which opinions involved us. My operator believed in disease, independent of the mind; hence I could not be wiser than my master. But now I can see dimly at first, and only as trees walking, the great principle which underlies Dr. Quimby's faith and works; and just in proportion to my right perception of truth is my recovery. This truth which he opposes to the error of giving intelligence to matter and placing pain where it never placed itself, if received understandingly, changes the currents of the system to their normal action; and the mechanism of the body goes on undisturbed. That this is a science capable of demonstration, becomes clear to the minds of those patients who reason upon the process of their cure. The truth which he establishes in the patient cures him (although he may be wholly unconscious thereof); and the body, which is full of light, is no longer in disease. At present I am too much in error to elucidate the truth, and can touch only the keynote for the master hand to wake to harmony. May it be in essays, instead of notes! say I. After all, this is very spiritual doctrine; but the eternal years of God are with it, and it must stand firm as the rock of ages. And to many a poor sufferer may it be found, as by me, "the shadow of a great rock in a weary land."[1]

This letter brought ridicule upon both Dr. Quimby and herself, and a correspondent of the Portland Advertiser exclaimed, "P. P. Quimby compared to Jesus Christ?" Again Mrs. Eddy wrote to the Courier:

Noticing the paragraph in the Advertiser, commenting upon some sentences of mine clipped from the Courier, relative to the science of P. P. Quimby, concluding, "What next?" we would reply in due deference to the courtesy with which they define their position. P. P. Quimby stands upon the plane of wisdom with his truth. Christ healed the sick, but not by jugglery or with drugs. As the former speaks as never man before spake, and heals as never man healed since Christ, is he not identified with truth? And is not this the Christ which is in him? We know that in wisdom is life, "and the life was the light of man." P. P. Quimby rolls away the stone from the sepulcher of error, and health is the resurrection.[2]

Mrs. Patterson returned from Portland to Sanbornton Bridge apparently in restored health, and "Quimby became the great possession of her life." She talked of him incessantly and wrote him many letters, containing such statements as: "I am to all who see me a living wonder, and a living monument of your power. . . My explanation of your curative principle surprises people,

[1] Milmine, *History*, pp. 58, 59.
[2] Ibid, p. 60.

especially those whose minds are all matter." A few
days later she writes asking him for "absent treatment,"
and to "please come to me and remove this pain."

In 1864 Mrs. Patterson again spent two or three months
in Portland. Dr. Quimby now gave her much of his time,
and Mrs. Sarah Crosby, a patient of Dr. Quimby with
whom Mrs. Patterson became intimate, says of her, "She
would work with Dr. Quimby all afternoon, and then she
would come home and sit up late at night writing down
what she had learned during the day." Again she left
Portland and wrote more letters to Dr. Quimby full of
gratitude and praise. "Who is wise but you? . . . Doctor,
I have a strong feeling of late that I might be perfect
after the command of science."

Mr. Quimby died on January 16, 1866, of an abdominal
tumor, and many mourned the good man's death. None
more than Mrs. Patterson, who wrote to Julius Dresser
a letter inclosing some lines of poetry on the death of
Dr. Quimby, the letter beginning: "I enclose some lines
of mine in memory of our much-loved friend, which
perhaps you will not think overwrought in meaning:
others must of course." The concluding lines of the poem
are: "Rest should reward him who hath made us whole,
seeking, though tremblers, where his footsteps trod."

What was Mrs. Patterson doing in the years 1864-1870?
These were the "wander years" during which she went
from home to home, creating more or less trouble in almost
every one of them. She was teaching the Quimby
"science" of healing, using for this purpose a manuscript
which she said had been written by "Dr. P. P. Quimby"
and having her students copy it, while she guarded it
most jealously. There is an unbroken chain of witnesses

and affidavits and other evidences to prove this important fact beyond a doubt.

She spent two years, 1868-1870, at the home of Mrs. Sally Wentworth in Stoughton, Mass. Here she used the Quimby manuscript in instructing Mrs. Wentworth, who made a copy of it. Mrs. Wentworth's son, Horace T. Wentworth, had his mother's copy in 1907, and in a long affidavit, made in that year, he minutely describes it and states:

I became acquainted with Mrs. Mary Baker G. Eddy, now of Concord, N. H., and known as the Discoverer and Founder of Christian Science, in the year 1868, when she was the wife of one Daniel Patterson, with whom she was now living, and was known by the name of a former husband, one George W. Glover, and called herself Mrs. Mary M. Glover. . . Said Mrs. Glover, upon coming to my mother's house, lent my mother her manuscript copy of what she, Mrs. Glover, said were writings of said Quimby, and permitted my mother to make a full manuscript copy thereof, and said manuscript copy of the writings of said Quimby, in my mother's handwriting, and with corrections and interlineations in the handwriting of Mrs. Glover, is now, and has been since my mother's death, in my possession. On the outside, said copy is entitled "Extracts from Doctor P. P. Quimby's Writings," and at the head of the first page, on the inside, said copy is further entitled "The Science of Man, or the Principle Which Controls All Phenomena." There is a preface of two pages with Mrs. Mary M. Glover's name signed at the end. The extracts are in the form of fifteen questions and answers and are labeled, "Questions by patients, Answers by Dr. Quimby." Annexed hereto, marked "Exhibit A," is a full and complete copy of my mother's said copy of Mrs. Glover's said copy of Dr. Quimby's writings. Annexed hereto, marked "Exhibit B" is a photograph of the first page of Mrs. Wentworth's manuscript plainly showing the additions made in a handwriting not my mother's. All of the said first page shown in Exhibit B is in my mother's handwriting except the words "Wisdom Love &" added to the beginning of the fifteenth line, the word "of" and the symbol "&" added to the sixteenth line and the words "is in it" added to the seventeenth line, none of which additions is in my mother's handwriting.

Mr. Wentworth in his affidavit proceeds to say that,

while he is not familiar with Mrs. Glover's writing, "having compared these corrections with unquestionable writing of said Mrs. Glover's, found with my mother's papers, and seen them to be strikingly similar, I am confidently of the opinion that they are the writing of the only person interested in the correction of said Mrs. Glover's preface to said Dr. Quimby's writings, to wit, said Mrs. Mary M. Glover—Mrs. Mary Baker G. Eddy— herself."

Miss Milmine gives a facsimile of the first page of this manuscript with its corrections in a different handwriting as described in Mr. Wentworth's affidavit.[1]

Affidavits similar to that of Horace T. Wentworth were made by Charles O. Wentworth, his brother, Mrs. Arthur L. Holmes, his sister, and Mrs. Catherine I. Clapp, his cousin, these being all the members of the Wentworth family living at the time. Mrs. Clapp, when asked if she had ever heard Mrs. Glover say that she learned her system from Dr. Quimby, said: "Yes, and I am not likely to forget it. It is fixed in my memory by a very reprehensible proceeding of my own. You see, Mrs. Glover used to say this to everybody who came in. She wasn't content with mentioning it once or twice that she had learned it from Dr. Quimby, she repeated it so often that we girls got dreadfully tired of hearing it." The "reprehensible proceeding of her own" was that she used to mock Mrs. Glover who "would fold her hands softly in her lap, smile gently, nod her head slowly at almost every word, and say in a sweet voice, 'I learned this from Dr. Quimby and he made me promise to teach it to at least two persons before I die.'" There was one particular

[1] *History*, p. 128.

passage in Mrs. Glover's instructions which Mrs. Clapp, then a young girl, "used to scoff at and make fun of to her intimates." It ran as follows:

> The daily ablutions of an infant are no more natural or necessary than would be the process of taking a fish out of water every day and covering it with dirt to make it thrive more vigorously thereafter in its native element.

Years afterward, Mrs. Clapp picked up a copy of "Science and Health," and opened it at this identical passage which had so excited her girlish derision.[1] Much other testimony and evidence are available to prove that this manuscript that Mrs. Glover used in her teaching during the years 1864-1870 was a manuscript or a copy of a manuscript of P. P. Quimby's and embodied his system of healing.

Finally we have the explicit proof given by Miss Milmine as follows:

> George A. Quimby of Belfast, Me., has lent the writer one of his father's manuscripts, entitled, "Questions and Answers." This is in the handwriting of Mr. Quimby's mother, the wife of Phineas P. Quimby, and is dated, in Mrs. Quimby's handwriting, February, 1862—nine months before Mrs. Eddy's first visit to Portland. For twenty closely written pages, Quimby's manuscript, "Questions and Answers," is word for word the same as Mrs. Glover's manuscript, "The Science of Man."[2]

The proof has reached demonstration that Mrs. Eddy had Quimby's manuscript and derived her teaching from

---

[1] Peabody, *Masquerade*, pp. 87, 89. Mr. Peabody locates this precious passage on page 41 of the 1898 edition of *Science and Health*, but it is now found on page 413 of that changeable book.

[2] *History*, pp. 128, 129.

him and attributed it to him. The contents of this
manuscript will be reserved until the next chapter.

It remains only to add that as late as 1871, after Mrs.
Eddy had settled in Lynn, she acknowledged that she
derived her "art" from Dr. Quimby. In a letter written
on March 7, 1871, to Mr. W. W. Wright, of Lynn, who
had asked her, "Has this theory ever been advertised or
practiced before you introduced it, or by any other individual?" she replied:

Never advertised, and practiced by only one individual who
healed me, Dr. Quimby of Portland, Me., an old gentleman who had
made it a research for twenty-five years, starting from the standpoint of magnetism thence going forward and leaving that behind.
I discovered the art in a moment's time, and he acknowledged it to
me; he died shortly after and since then, eight years I have been
founding and demonstrating the science. . . please preserve this,
and if you become my student call me to account for the truth of
what I have written. Respectfully, M. M. B. Glover.

Let it be noted that in this letter Mrs. Eddy acknowledges that Dr. Quimby started "from the standpoint
of magnetism thence going forward and leaving that
behind."

5. MRS. EDDY'S DENIAL OF DEPENDENCE ON QUIMBY

In the face of all this evidence and of her own written
and published acknowledgments of indebtedness to him,
will it be believed that Mrs. Eddy, after she launched
out on her public career as a mental healer and founder
of a religion, positively and repeatedly denied that she
had derived her ideas from P. P. Quimby, but affirmed that
he had derived his ideas from her? He had not taught
her, but she had taught him! Yet this is what she did
and, as usual, over her own signature.

When Mrs. Eddy turned against Dr. Quimby, she began by representing that he was a mesmerist and magnetic healer, although she herself had said that Dr. Quimby had started by this method but had gone forward, "leaving that behind." Julius A. Dresser, a student and follower of Quimby, resented this misrepresentation of Quimby and wrote a letter to this effect in the Boston Post of February 24, 1883. Mrs. Eddy replied in a letter to the same paper of March 7, 1883, in which she made this barefaced statement:

We never were a student of Dr. Quimby's. . . Dr. Quimby never had students, to our knowledge. He was a Humanitarian, but a very unlearned man. He never published a work in his life; was not a lecturer or teacher. He was somewhat of a remarkable healer, and at the time we knew him he was known as a mesmerist. We were one of his patients. He manipulated his patients, but possibly back of his practice he may have had a theory in advance of his method. . . We knew him about twenty years ago, and aimed to help him. We saw he was looking in our direction, and asked him to write his thoughts out. He did so, and then we would take that copy to correct, and sometimes so transform it that he would say it was our composition, which it virtually was; but we always gave him back the copy and sometimes wrote his name on the back of it.[1]

In "Science and Health," edition of 1884, Mrs. Eddy says of Quimby:

The old gentleman to whom we have referred had some very advanced views on healing, but he was not avowedly religious neither scholarly. We interchanged thoughts on the subject of healing the sick. I restored some patients of his he failed to heal, and left in his possession some manuscripts of mine containing corrections of his desultory pennings which I am imformed, at his decease, passed into the hands of a patient of his, now residing in Scotland. He died in 1865 and left no published works. The only manuscript that we ever had of his, longer than to correct it, was one of perhaps a dozen pages, most of which we composed.

[1] Milmine, *History*, p. 96.

It is true that Mr. Quimby "left no published works" but he was not "illiterate," as Mrs. Eddy in another statement declared, and he left manuscripts of "over eight hundred pages, covering one hundred and twenty subjects, written previous to March, 1862, more than six months before Mrs. Eddy went to Dr. Quimby." In her controversy with Mr. Julius A. Dresser, Mrs. Eddy published the following remarkable challenge:

Mr. George A. Quimby, son of the late Phineas P. Quimby, over his own signature and before witnesses, stated in 1883, that he had in his possession at that time all the manuscripts that had been written by his father. And I hereby declare that to expose the falsehood of parties publicly intimating that I have appropriated matter belonging to the aforesaid Quimby, I will pay the cost of printing and publishing the first edition of those manuscripts with the author's name. Provided, that I am allowed to examine said manuscripts, and do find that they were his own compositions, and not mine, that were left with him many years ago, or that they have not since his death, in 1865, been stolen from my published works. Also that I am given the right to bring out this one edition under the copyright of the owner of said manuscripts, and all the money accruing from the sale of said book shall be paid to said owner. Some of the purported writings, quoted by Mr. D—— were my own words as near as I can recollect them.

It is needless to say that such an offer was not accepted. Mrs. Eddy would quickly have found that these alleged manuscripts of Mr. Quimby were not "his own compositions," but were her own, or had "been stolen" from her own "published works."[1]

[1] The question is often asked, Why are not these Quimby manuscripts published so that the world may see their contents for itself? On this point Horatio W. Dresser, Ph. D., the son of Julius A. Dresser, in his "History of the New Thought Movement," p. 338, says: "For reasons best known to himself, Mr. George A. Quimby steadily refused to publish the manuscripts during the life-time of Mrs. Eddy. By previous arrangement with Mr. Quimby our family copies were returned to him in 1893, and we were not permitted to quote any of

When Mrs. Eddy was confronted by Julius A. Dresser, in a letter in the Boston Post, the same letter to which reference has already been made, making public some of the articles and letters which she had written acknowledging her indebtedness to Dr. Quimby, she in her letter to the same paper, March 7, 1883, made this remarkable statement:

Did I write those articles purporting to be mine? I might have written them twenty or thirty years ago, for I was under the mesmeric treatment of Dr. Quimby from 1862 until his death in 1865. He was illiterate and I knew nothing then of the Science of Mind-healing, and I was as ignorant of mesmerism as Eve before she was taught by the serpent. Mind Science was unknown to me; and my head was so turned by animal magnetism and will-power, under his treatment, that I might have written something as hopelessly incorrect as the articles now published in the Dresser pamphlet. I was not healed until after the death of Dr. Quimby; and then healing came as the result of my discovery in 1866, of the Science of Mind-healing, since named Christian Science.

When in 1887 Mrs. Eddy asked Rev. James Henry Wiggin, her literary adviser and reviser, to answer the charge brought against her on the basis of her public acknowledgments of her indebtedness to Quimby, he asked her if she had written the letters to the Portland newspapers, the poem on Quimby's death and other effusions.

the articles in full either in 'The Philosophy of P. P. Quimby,' 1895, or in 'Health and the Inner Life,' 1896. Mr. Quimby died without making any provision for the disposition of the manuscripts. It remains for the historian to edit and publish these writings at some future time. The historian has been personally acquainted with all the patients and followers of P. P. Quimby who have had the use of the manuscripts. Miss Milmine was allowed to reproduce part of a page of one of them for her life of Mrs. Eddy published in McClure's Magazine." In a personal letter from Dr. Dresser he tells the author that he himself is the "historian" referred to. The Dressers, father and son, who had personal access to and knowledge of the Quimby manuscripts, had no doubt of Mrs. Eddy's indebtedness to them for her ideas.

When she admitted that she had, he said to her, "Then there is nothing to say."

In a personal letter to a friend, Mr. Wiggin said:

> What Mrs. Eddy has, as documents clearly prove, she got from P. P. Quimby, of Portland, Me., whom she eulogized after death as the great leader and her special teacher. . . . She has tried to answer this charge of the adoption of Quimby's ideas, and called me in to her counsel about it; but her only answer (in print!) was that if she said such things twenty years ago, she must have been under the influence of Animal Magnetism.[1]

So ended and so stands the case of the relation of Mrs. Eddy to P. P. Quimby. That she should have derived her system, at least in idea and germ, from him was nothing to her discredit and nothing unusual in the history of ideas, which are rarely or never discovered as an absolute originality but are always derived from or suggested by or related to the work of other thinkers. Such derivation is always proper and honorable, provided, of course, it is acknowledged and not denied. Mrs. Eddy at first did make this acknowledgment in the fullest and frankest measure, but afterwards when she became established in her public career as a healer and founder of a religion she came to think that any acknowledgment of indebtedness to Mr. Quimby was a reduction on her own standing and especially that it was fatal to her claim of receiving her discovery by divine revelation; a claim which she presently made; and therefore she disowned Quimby, denied her own words, set up a claim to false originality and backed it up with a deliberate untruth. And of this indebtedness and this denial she is convicted out of her own mouth.

[1] Milmine. *History,* pp. 102, 103.

CHAPTER V

"SCIENCE AND HEALTH": THE MAKING OF THE BOOK

It is now time to consider "Science and Health," the book which claims to be the inspired bible of Christian Science. There will be given, first, some account of the making of this remarkable work, and then a summary of its contents.

1. CONTENTS OF THE QUIMBY MANUSCRIPT

It is in order at this point to give an outline of the contents and teaching of the manuscript which Mrs. Eddy used in her instruction in 1864–1870 and which it has been proved she derived from P. P. Quimby and during these years constantly acknowledged as his. This manuscript, which was lent to Miss Milmine by George A. Quimby, Dr. Quimby's son, consisted of twenty closely written pages and was entitled "Questions and Answers." Mrs. Eddy headed the copy she used at the top with "Extracts from Doctor P. P. Quimby's Writings," and underneath this with "The Science of Man." Quotations from this manuscript are given by Miss Milmine,[1] Dr. Powell,[2] and Mr. Peabody,[3] in their respective books. The arrangement of these quotations with parallel quotations from Mrs. Eddy's "Science and Health," here given, is taken from Mr. Peabody, with the exception of several quotations, which are from Dr. Powell.

[1] *History*, pp. 129, 130.
[2] *Christian Science*, pp. 48, 49.
[3] *Masquerade*, pp. 92–94.

From Quimby's
"Science and Man."

Christian Science.[1]

Science of Health.
Matter has no intelligence.
If I understand how disease originates in the mind and fully believe it, why cannot I cure myself?

Never get in a passion, but in patience possess ye your soul, and at length you weary out the discord and produce harmony by your Truth destroying error. Then it is you get the case. Now if you are not afraid and argue down, then you can heal the sick.
Error is sickness. Truth is health.
In this science the names are given; thus God is Wisdom. This Wisdom, not an individuality but a principle, embraces every idea form, of which the idea, man, is the highest, hence the image of God, or the Principle.

Understanding is God.

Truth is God.
Wisdom, Love, and Truth are principle.

From Mrs. Eddy's
"Science and Health."

Christian Science.

Science and Health.
Matter cannot produce mind.
Disease being a belief, a latent delusion of mortal mind, the sensation would not appear if this error was met and destroyed by Truth.
When we come to have more faith in the Truth of Being than we have in error, more faith in spirit than in matter, then no material conditions can prevent us from healing the sick and destroying error through Truth.

Sickness is part of the error which Truth casts out.
God is the principle of man; and the principle of man remaining perfect, its idea or reflection—man—remains perfect. Man was and is God's idea. Man is the idea of divine principle. What is God? Jehovah is not a person, God is principle.
Understanding is a quality of God.
Truth is God.
Adhere to its divine Principle, and follow its behests, abiding steadily in Wisdom, Love, and Truth.

[1] Miss Milmine gives a facsimile of a part of another manuscript by Dr. Quimby in his own handwriting containing the words "Christian Science." As this manuscript bears the date 1863, this is incontestable proof that Mrs. Eddy did not originate this name, as she says she did. See *McClure's Magazine*, vol. XXVIII, p. 511, for this facsimile. The use of the word "science," however, in this peculiar sense goes back of Quimby. It was so used by Charles Poyen. See p. 19.

Error is matter.
To give intelligence to matter is an error which is sickness.

Matter has no intelligence of its own, and to believe intelligence is in matter is the error which produces pain and inharmony of all sorts.
For matter is an error, there being no substance, which is Truth in a thing which changes and is only that which belief makes it.

Matter is mortal error.
The fundamental error of mortal man is the belief that matter is intelligent.
Laws of matter are nothing more or less than a belief of intelligence and life in matter, which is the procuring cause of all disease.
There is no life, truth, intelligence, or substance in matter.

The identity of teaching extending to the very words in these two writings is obvious and undeniable. The key words of Mrs. Eddy's book, "science," "truth," "principle," "mind," "error," "matter," "belief," which she uses in a peculiar sense as a kind of jargon or lingo, are all derived from Quimby who used them in the same peculiar sense. Such expressions as "Truth is God," "God is Principle," "Matter is Error," "There is no intelligence in matter," which Mrs. Eddy repeats thousands of times with wearisome and infinite repetition in her book, are all taken bodily from Quimby. He built his instructions and practice around these same ideas and phrases and wrote them indelibly into his manuscripts, where they stand to this day published in facsimile and can be seen and read of all men. The merest superficial acquaintance with Mrs. Eddy's "Science and Health" shows that her book is built up around the same ideas and words and phrases. She repeats the same ideas, practices the same healing art, speaks the same language. Mrs. Eddy was right and was simply telling the truth when she kept telling her students during 1864–1870, "I learned this from Dr. Quimby."

Thus the roots of Mrs. Eddy's teaching and book run back into P. P. Quimby and through him and others down into the subsoil of New England transcendentalism and other "isms" that grew so rank in that region. Of course she elaborated these germinal ideas or at least repeated them and spun them out into her system and book. It cannot be claimed that she had no originality and was a mere echo of other voices. She had a mind and especially a will and purpose of her own, and she wrought these out into her book and her church. But the substance and core of her teaching were not her own, but came from the humble and benevolent clock maker at whose feet she obediently sat and then rose up at first to praise him extravagantly and follow him loyally, and then to deny and disown him and even to claim that he had taken from her what she had purloined from him.

In the face of these proven facts she had the effrontery to assert in the original first preface to "Science and Health," "Not one of our printed works was ever copied or abstracted from the published or from the unpublished writings of anyone;" and she had the further boldness to insert in her autobiography a chapter on "Plagiarism" in which she denounces this thing and declares that it "does violence to the ethics of Christian Science"!

2. THE EDITIONS OF "SCIENCE AND HEALTH"

During the years from 1864 to 1870 in all the households where she stopped Mrs. Eddy was writing, writing, and referring to her manuscripts as her "Bible." As early as 1866 when she was at Lynn she said she "was writing a Bible, and was almost through Genesis." At Mrs. Wentworth's at Stoughton, where she spent two years, 1868–1870, she "pointed affectionately to a pile of notepaper tied up with a string, which lay on her desk, and told Mrs. Clapp (Mrs. Wentworth's niece) that it was her Bible, and that she had completed the book of Genesis."[1]

For at least eight years she had been at work on her manuscript before she sought a publisher. It was while she was with Mrs. Wentworth that she took the book to a Boston printer, and when he demanded payment in advance for publishing it she tried to borrow the money from her, but the money was not forthcoming. "Had Mrs. Glover," says Miss Milmine, "then been successful in her search for a publisher, Christian Science in its present form would never have existed; for at that time she had not dreamed of calling her system anything but Quimby's Science."[2]

The book first saw the light in 1875, when she was at work in Lynn, and two of her students, Miss Elizabeth Newhall and George Barry, furnished the money, $1500, to secure its publication, the expense of Mrs. Eddy's many changes in the plates increasing the cost to $2200. In spite of her intense faith in her book, she was chary about venturing her own money on it and saw that others ran the risk of any loss while she would reap any gain. The book contained 456 pages and sold at $2.50. The first edition consisted of 1000 copies, but when the book fell flat on the market the price was reduced to $1.00. Copies were sent for review to the New England newspapers, and to some notable institutions and people, such as the University of Heidelberg and Thomas Carlyle.

[1] Milmine, *History*, pp. 131, 132.
[2] Ibid, p. 176.

But it received little notice other than flippant references to its vagaries, and the "ill-made, cheap-looking affair" seemed to drop into the waters of oblivion. One woman, however, still had indomitable faith in its future, and her faith in due time was justified.

By 1877 Mrs. Eddy was busily at work on a second edition of her book, when it was hurried to the press on account of her quarrel with her publisher, Daniel Spofford, and it has already been noted how she turned into a bitter personal attack upon him this edition which consisted of an "odd little brown book," labeled Volume II, although the first edition has not been labeled Volume I.[1]

The third edition, which appeared in 1881, was also turned into a personal polemic and attack on Richard Kennedy. A new chapter appeared in this edition, entitled "Demonology," which poured out all the vials of her wrath against her former student and partner. From this a characteristic quotation has been given.[2]

Prosperity was now smiling upon Mrs. Eddy, and new editions of "Science and Health" came thick and fast. The "Key to the Scriptures" was added to the book in 1884. The book has now passed through about five hundred editions. They were announced as new editions up to near this point, but of late years this is no longer done and only the year of publication is given. Of course these "editions" are mostly simply additional printings and are not properly editions, but in a surprising number of them the book underwent revision and sometimes radical change. For a number of years the book was in a state of flux and its contents floated around within the covers in the most astonishing way. Not

[1] Page 44.
[2] Page 44.

only were there constant additions and subtractions, but the order of the chapters was frequently changed. On this point Dr. Powell writes:

No matter what editions you may chance to be comparing, there is an unexpected instability of arrangement in a book which the author claims is of the nature of "final revelation." Mrs. Eddy is not content to let the sequence remain permanent.   Of four editions dated, respectively, 1881, 1888, 1898, and 1906, the chapter which comes first in the first and second of the four editions comes fifth in the third and sixth and fourth.   The second chapter in the first and second editions is third and eighth respectively in the third and fourth.   The third chapter in the first edition appears as the fifth in the second, the second in the third, and the seventh in the fourth. Chapter IV in the first edition is Chapter XII in the second and XIV in the third and fourth editions.   Chapter V in the first is IX in the second, XII in the third and fourth.   And the variation lasts throughout.[1]

While the chapters were thus being shuffled around into new arrangements, changes were being introduced in their paragraphs, and some of these are significant. For example, in the 1903 edition on page 274 there is this declaration: "Until it is learned that generation rests on no sexual basis, let marriage continue."   But in the 1909 edition this declaration is found on page 64 and has been changed to read as follows: "Until it is learned that God is the Father of all, marriage will continue." In both cases it is implied that generation does not rest on a sexual basis, but until this fact is conceded the first version permits marriage to Christian Scientists and the second version simply declares that marriage will continue: the first version grants a permission which the second version does not allow; but either way it reads the statement is a subtle blow at the foundation of marriage and brands it as a temporary delusion, which, should give way to "a more spiritual adherence."

[1] *Christian Science*, pp. 18, 19.

The sale of the book, of course, has been enormous and it has proved probably the richest literary gold mine of a century; and as every Christian Scientist is supposed and sometimes commanded to purchase the latest issue, the point of these many "editions" is easily seen.

3. WHO WROTE THE BOOK?

Mark Twain refuses to believe that Mrs. Eddy unaided wrote "Science and Health." He devotes many pages to a higher critical examination of her ideas and style in her early and acknowledged writings to show that the same hand could not have written the generally smooth and intelligent English of her main book. To believe this he says "is more than difficult, it is impossible." He continues:

Largely speaking, I have read acres of what purported to be Mrs Eddy's writings, in the past two months. I cannot know, but I am convinced, that the circumstantial evidence shows that her actual share in the work of composing and phrasing these things was so slight as to be inconsequential. Where she puts her literary foot down, her trail across her paid polisher's page is as plain as the elephant's in a Sunday-school procession. Her verbal output, when left undoctored by her clerks, is quite unmistakable. It always exhibits the strongly distinctive features observable in the virgin passages from her pen already quoted by me:

> Desert vacancy, as regards thought.
> Self-complacency.
> Sentimentality.
> Affectations of scholarly learning.
> Lust after eloquent and flowery expression.
> Repetition of pet poetic picturesquenesses.
> Confused and wandering statement.
> Metaphor gone insane.
> Meaningless words, used because they are pretty, or showy or unusual.
> Sorrowful attempts at the epigrammatic.
> Destitution of originality.[1]

[1] *Christian Science*, pp. 130, 131.

He concludes that "it is not believable that the hand that wrote those clumsy and affected sentences wrote the smooth English of "Science and Health." Mark Twain was right in his higher critical instinct and guess[1] that Mrs. Eddy must have had "a paid polisher" and "clerks" to put her own lucubrations in shape, but it is the general opinion that he does more than justice to the English of "Science and Health." That is bad enough in the later editions of the book, but in the early editions it is Mrs. Eddy's own thought and style beyond a doubt.

The author has not been able to obtain or even to see a copy of the first edition of "Science and Health," although he has applied for it to the Christian Science publishers and headquarters,[2] but Miss Milmine gives an extended quotation from it that bears the marks of its being in Mrs. Eddy's own unaided style, a fine specimen[3] of which has already been given.

A portion of Miss Milmine's extract is the following:

The belief that fasting or feasting enables man to grow better, morally or physically, is one of the fruits of "the tree of knowledge" against which Wisdom warned man, and of which we had partaken in sad experience; believing for many years we lived only by the strictest adherence to dietetics and physiology. During this time we also learned a dyspeptic is very far from the image and likeness of God, from having "dominion over the fish of the sea, the fowls of the air, or beasts of the field;" therefore that God never made one; while the Graham system, hygiene, physiology, materia medica, etc., did, and contrary to his commands. Then it was that we promised God to spend our coming years for the sick and suffering; to unmask this error of belief that matter rules man. Our cure for dyspepsia

[1] Mark Twain wrote his book in 1902 and 1903 and therefore was not acquainted with the later disclosures as to the part played by the Rev. James Henry Wiggin as Mrs. Eddy's literary reviser.

[2] "The first edition of *Science and Health* has been so far as possible suppressed."   H. W. Dresser, *The New Thought Movement*, p. 111.

[3] Page 34.

was, to learn the science of being, and "eat what was set before us, asking no question for conscience' sake; yea to consult matter less and God more."[1]

Miss Milmine also describes the first edition of "Science and Health" as follows:

Even after eight years of struggle with her copy, the book, as printed in 1875, is hardly more than a tangle of words and theories, faulty in grammar and construction, and singularly vague and contradictory in its statements. Although the book is divided into chapters, each having a title of its own, there is no corresponding classification of the subject, and it is only by piecing together the declarations found in the various chapters that one may make out something of the theories which Mrs. Glover had been trying for so long to express.[2]

The conclusion is that Mrs. Eddy did write "Science and Health" as it appeared in its first and early editions.

4. ENTER: REVEREND JAMES HENRY WIGGIN, LITERARY REVISER

At this point there enters upon the scene Rev. James Henry Wiggin who plays an important part in this story. He is the "paid polisher" whose hand Mark Twain discerned in Mrs. Eddy's book by an improvement in her style, as Leverrier detected the presence of an unknown planet by its influence on another planet.

Mr. Wiggin was a Unitarian minister, a graduate of the Meadville (Pa.) Theological Seminary in the class of 1861, who had retired from the active ministry in 1875, although for years he continued occasionally to occupy a pulpit. He was a large man physically, who had a rich sense of humor and enjoyed life. He was a lover of music, an inveterate theatergoer, and had Shakspere on

[1] *History*, p. 81.
[2] Ibid, p. 178.

the end of his tongue so that he could furnish an apt
quotation from the poet to adorn any subject or occasion.
Edward Everett Hale and other distinguished literary
men were among his associates. He was a man of wide
reading and fine culture and was specially fitted for the
peculiar task to which he was called.

One day in August, 1885, Calvin Frye called on Mr.
Wiggin and introduced himself as the secretary of a lady
who had written a book and wished to engage him to
revise it. A few days later Mrs. Eddy herself appeared
and completed the engagement. Mr. Wiggin went to
work for her and continued to serve as her literary adviser
and reviser for four years. Mrs. Eddy placed in his
hands the bulky manuscript of a new edition of "Science
and Health" which she had prepared, and Mr. Wiggin
took it with him on his vacation for leisurely examination.
Such examination soon showed him that the revision the
book needed was practically a rewriting of it. "The
faulty spelling and punctuation could have been corrected
readily enough, as well as the incorrect historical references and the misuse of words; but the whole work was
so involved, formless, and contradictory that Mr. Wiggin
put the manuscript away and thought no more about it
until he returned to Boston."

Upon his return from his vacation he intimated to
Mrs. Eddy his views about the book and his proposal as
to what should be done with it, and to his surprise she
willingly consented. During the autumn he worked upon
the task of virtually rewriting the book, she keeping a
close watch upon him to see that he did not change her
teaching and that he continued to use her technical words
in her peculiar sense. Miss Milmine gives several para-

graphs as they appeared in the 1884 edition and the corresponding paragraphs as they appeared in the 1886 edition as revised by Mr. Wiggin, and the reader will at once see the improvement in almost every sentence. The following paragraph is from the 1884 edition:

What is man? Brains, heart, blood, or the entire human structure? If he is one or all of the component parts of the body, when you amputate a limb, you have taken away a portion of man, and the surgeon destroys manhood, and worms are annihilators of man. But losing a limb, or injuring structure, is sometimes the quickener of manliness; and the unfortunate cripple presents more nobility than the statuesque outline, whereby we find "a man's a man, for a' that."

The same passage in the 1886 edition as revised by Mr. Wiggin reads:

What is man? Brains, heart, blood, the material structure? If he is but a material body, when you amputate a limb. you must take away a portion of the man; the surgeon can destroy manhood, and the worms annihilate it. But the loss of a limb or injury to a tissue, is sometimes the quickener of manliness, and the unfortunate cripple may present more of it than the statuesque athlete, teaching us, by his very deprivations, that "a man's a man, for a' that."

Sometimes, however, his revision went deeper than mere diction and cut into the form and substance of her teaching, as in the following instance. The paragraph is from Mrs. Eddy's own 1884 edition:

The glorious spiritual signification of the life and not death of our Master—for he never died—was laying down all of earth to instruct his enemies the way to heaven, showing in the most sublime and unequivocal sense how heaven is obtained. The blood of Jesus was not as much offered on the cross as before those closing scenes of his earth mission. The spiritual meaning of blood is offering sacrifice, and the efficacy of his life offering was greater than that of his blood spilled upon the cross. It was the consecration of his

whole being upon the altar of Love, a deathless offering to Spirit.
O, highest sense of human affections and higher spiritual conceptions
of our Infinite Father and Mother, show us what is Love!

The following is the same passage as rendered by Mr.
Wiggin in the 1886 edition:

The material blood of Jesus was no more efficacious to cleanse
from sin, when it was shed upon the "accursed tree," than when it
was flowing in his veins as he went daily about his Father's business.
His spiritual flesh and blood were his Life; and they truly eat his
flesh and drink his blood, who partake of that Life. The spiritual
meaning of blood is sacrifice. The efficacy of Jesus' spirit-offering
was infinitely greater than can be expressed by our mortal sense of
human life. His mission was fulfilled. It reunited God and man by
his career. His offering was Love's deathless sacrifice; for in Jesus'
experience the human element was gloriously expanded and absorbed
into the divine.[1]

Mr. Wiggin had a still deeper hand in the reconstruction
of Mrs. Eddy's book. He actually supplied and was the
author of one of the chapters that appeared in the 1886
edition. He drew up for her the outline of a sermon
upon the "city that lieth foursquare," which she preached
in her pulpit on January 24, 1886, "with great success,
though the Journal, in reporting the occasion, says that
Rev. Mrs. Eddy laboured under some disadvantage, as
she had left her manuscript at home." Mr. Wiggin was
present in the audience and went up at the close of the
service to speak to her as she stood in the midst of her
admirers. When she saw him "her eyes began to twinkle,
and, putting her hand to her lips, she shot him a stage
whisper: 'How did it go?'" Miss Milmine completes
the story of the new chapter as follows:

[1] Milmine, *History*, pp. 329, 330.

When Mr. Wiggin persuaded her to omit the libelous portion of
the chapter on mesmerism from the 1886 edition of "Science and
Health" after the plates for the edition had been made, Mrs. Eddy,
at Mr. Wiggin's suggestion, cut this sermon to the required length
and, by inserting it was able to send the book to press without
renumbering the remaining pages.   The chapter was called "Wayside Hints (Supplementary)," and Mrs. Eddy put her seal upon it
by inserting under the subject of "squareness" a tribute to her
deceased husband: "We need good square men everywhere.   Such a
man was my late husband, Dr. Asa G. Eddy."[1]

The reader of "Science and Health" as it stands to-day,
however, will think that Mrs. Eddy's "paid polisher"
still left much work that might have been done in im-
proving that much-tinkered book.   It is still characterized
by affectation and obscurity and ineptitude and infinite
repetition and especially by Mrs. Eddy's lingo or jargon
of words which she uses in her own peculiar sense, though
this lingo was also derived from Quimby and others of
her literary forbears.   She sometimes uses words with as
ludicrous misapprehension of their real meaning as does
Mrs. Partington.   For instance, she thinks the name of
the Assyrian god Sin is the same word as our word "sin,"[2]
thinks "mysticism" means the same as "mystery,"[3]
frequently confuses "pantheism" with "materiality,"[4]
confuses "adulteration" with "adultery," and makes
many such mistakes that escaped the pen of her paid
polisher.   Some of her etymologies and definitions in
her "Glossary" in "Science and Health" are fearfully
and wonderfully made.   "Abel" means "Watchfulness,"
"Canaan" means "A sensuous belief," "Dan" means
"Animal magnetism," and "Gad" means "Science."   We

[1] *History*, p. 335.
[2] *Science and Health*, p. 103.
[3] Ibid, p. 80.
[4] Ibid, p. 522.

had always thought very highly of Moses but in this "Glossary" we learn to our disappointment that "Moses" means "A corporeal mortal." This entrance in the Glossary is specially puzzling: "IN. A term obsolete in Science if used with reference to Spirit, Deity." Hebrew etymology exercises little restraint upon Mrs. Eddy, although at times she airily refers to the Hebrew as if she knew all about it, forgetting that her knowledge of "Greek, Latin, and Hebrew," which her brother taught her when she was only nine years of age, "after" her "discovery of Christian Science" "vanished like a dream."

A sense of humor would have saved Mrs. Eddy from all this, but she did not have a drop of it in her whole system. She takes all her pompous affectations of learning and shallow ignorance and ridiculous blunders and confused thinking and doggerel poetry and solemn incomprehensibilities in dead earnest.[1] They are all equally inspired and infallible to her. How did Mr. Wiggin, with all his sense of humor, restrain himself from loud laughter as his censor's pen passed these things? Doubtless he did go as far as he could or was permitted to go in cutting such things out, and as it was not his book he had to let its author have her way at many points which he would have quickly polished away.

Doctor Powell, who is himself a good literary writer and critic, passes this judgment on this book:

> The difficulty is not merely with the style, which though often marred by absurdity, turgidity, and faulty diction, possesses a certain lofty distinctiveness, a certain sonorous authoritativeness,

[1] Robert Hugh Benson, an English Roman Catholic prelate, says: "I am certain that Christian Science rises almost entirely from a lack of the sense of humor." *A Book of Essays*, p. 18.

which a book that claims to be a revelation ought to have to command the interest of the undiscriminating. The difficulty is also with the arrangement of the work. There is a woeful want of sequence both in thought and word. The reader can begin anywhere and stop anywhere without serious loss or gain. Mrs. Eddy in one section states that certain of her sentences read backward mean as much as when read forward, and many not of her persuasion will readily agree with her. . . Mrs. Eddy has undoubtedly improved greatly in her power to express herself on paper, since her literary helper twenty years ago testified she was constantly confusing such words as physics and physiology, gnostic and agnostic, and putting him to his wits' end to save her "from making herself ridiculous and flatly contradicting herself." But there is still some justification for Mark Twain's sweeping judgment that Mrs. Eddy "so lacks in the matter of literary precision that she can seldom put a thought into words that express it lucidly to the reader and leave no doubts in his mind as to whether he has rightly understood or not.[1]

This account of the relations of Mr. Wiggin with Mrs. Eddy is closed with a brief reference to the sad fate that finally overtook this good man. Like nearly all the students and associates and helpers of Mrs. Eddy, with the exception of Calvin A. Frye, he at length fell from her grace into deep condemnation. The devil of "M. A. M." at last got him. Signs of the coming end began when she charged him with a "most shocking flippancy in notations" upon her proofs. He seems to have indulged in some humorous marginal scribblings, and she could not stand any humor or wit in him, as she could not appreciate it in anybody else. In a letter to her publisher in which she complains about the "flippancy" she says of him: "When he returned the first proofs a belief (but don't name this to anyone) prevented my examining them as I should otherwise have done, and, to prevent delay, the proof was sent to the printer." The "belief" referred to was simply an attack of illness which prevented Mrs.

[1] *Christian Science,* pp. 17–20.

Eddy from examining Mr. Wiggin's proofs. He not only "changed his own marginal references" but also "took back the word 'cannot' throughout the entire proofs, which he had before insisted upon using thereby causing another delay." Evidently her "paid polisher" was getting too independent and flippant toward her book, and this was a very grave offense in her sight. Three months later (November, 1890) she again complained about his proofs and says: "This is M. A. M. [Malicious Animal Magnetism] and it governs Wiggin as it has done once before to prevent the publishing of my work. . . I will take the proof-reading out of Wiggin's hands." This sealed his doom and he drops out of this history.

In a letter to a college friend, from which a brief quotation has been made, dated December 14, 1889, and published by Miss Milmine in her "History," Mr. Wiggin gives his private view of Christian Science and of Mrs. Eddy, which Miss Milmine says is "an interesting criticism of Christian Science" and "probably the most trenchant and suggestive sketch of Mrs. Eddy that will ever be written." He was then about through with Mrs. Eddy and speaks confidentially but freely and unsparingly, yet not unkindly. The reader will be interested in the following extracts:

Christian Science, on its theological side, is an ignorant revival of one form of ancient gnosticism, that Jesus is to be distinguished from the Christ, and that his earthly appearance was phantasmal, not real and fleshly. On its moral side, it involves what must follow from the doctrine that reality is a dream, and that if a thing is right in thought, why right it is, and sin is nonexistent, because God can behold no evil. Not that Christian Science believers generally see this, or practice evil, but the virus is within.

Religiously, Christian Science is a revolt from orthodoxy, but unphilosophically conducted, endeavoring to ride two horses. Physically it leads people to trust all to nature, the great healer, and so does some good. Great virtue in imagination! . . . Where there is disease which time will not reach, Christian Science is useless.

As for the High Priestess of it, . . . She is—well I could tell you, but not write. An awfully (I use the word advisedly) smart woman, acute, shrewd, but not well read, nor in any way learned. What she has, as documents clearly show, she got from P. P. Quimby of Portland, Maine, whom she eulogized after death as the great leader and her special teacher. . . She tried to answer the charge of the adoption of Quimby's ideas, and called me in to counsel her about it; but her only answer in (print!) was that if she said such things twenty years ago, she must have been under the influence of "animal magnetism," which is her devil. No church can get along without a devil, you know. Much more I could say if you were here.

One of Mrs. Eddy's followers went so far as to say that if she saw Mrs. Eddy commit a crime she should believe her own sight at fault, not Mrs. Eddy's conduct. An intelligent man told me in reference to lies he knew about, that the wrong was in us. "Was not Jesus accused of wrongdoing, yet guiltless?"

Only experience can teach these fanatics, i. e., the real believers, not the charlatans who go into it for money. . . As for the book, if you have any edition since December, 1885, it had my supervision. Though now she is getting out an entirely new edition, with which I had nothing to do and occasionally she has made changes whereof I did not know. The chapter B—— told you of is rather fanciful, though, to use Mrs. Eddy's language in her last note, her "friends think it a gem." It is the one called "Wayside Hints," and was added after the work was not only in type, but cast, because she wished to take out some twenty pages of diatribe on her dissenters. I do not think it will greatly edify you, the chapter. As for clearness, many Christian Science people thought her early editions much better, because they sounded more like Mrs. Eddy. The truth is, she does not care to have her paragraphs clear, and delights in so expressing herself that her words may have various readings and meanings. Really, that is one of the tricks of her trade. You know how sibyls have always been thus oracular, to "keep the word of promise to the ear, and break it to the hope." . . . No, Swedenborg, and all other such writers, are sealed books to her. She cannot understand such utterances, and never could, but dollars and cents she understands thoroughly.[1]

5. MRS. EDDY'S CLAIMS TO DIVINE INSPIRATION

The bottom of the alleged basis and origin of this book has not yet been reached. A divinely accredited and

[1] *History*, pp. 337–339.

well-equipped religion must have an inspired revelation or Bible, and Mrs. Eddy did not overlook this point. She nowhere acknowledged her indebtedness to Mr. Quimby and Mr. Wiggin for their part in the production of "Science and Health," but she was voluble in her claims that God helped her to write it, or rather that he wrote it so that it was, as she called it, "God's book." She began to hint at this claim as early as 1877 when, in a letter to a student, she said: "I know the crucifixion of the one who presents Truth in its higher aspect will be this time through a bigger error, through mortal mind instead of its lower strata or matter, showing that the idea given of God this time is higher, clearer, and more permanent than before."[1]

In her autobiography we may read:

The divine hand led me into a new world of light and Life, a fresh universe—old to God, but new to his "little one."

And a little further on we read:

Even the Scriptures gave no direct interpretation of the scientific basis for demonstrating the spiritual Principle of healing, until our heavenly Father saw fit, through the "Key to the Scriptures," in "Science and Health," to unlock this "mystery of religion."[2]

This puts "Science and Health" with "Key to the Scriptures" above the Bible as a later and more perfect revelation, "higher, clearer, and more permanent," as she herself says. One may read in this book such statements as "when God impelled me," and "God has since shown me."

[1] Milmine, *History,* p. 73.
[2] *Retrospection and Introspection,* pp. 27 and 37.

Turning to "Science and Health" we read:

In the year 1866, I discovered the Science of Metaphysical Healing, and named it Christian Science. God had been graciously fitting me, during many years, for the reception of a final revelation of the absolute Principle of Scientific Mind-healing. No human pen or tongue taught me the science contained in this book. . . and neither tongue nor pen can overthrow it.[1]

The advent of this understanding is what is meant by the descent of the Holy Ghost—that influx of divine Science which so illuminated the Pentecostal Day and is now repeating ancient history. . . . In the words of St. John: "He shall give you another Comforter, that he may abide with you *forever*." This Comforter I understand to be divine Science.[2]

Writing in 1901 she said:

I should blush to write of "Science and Health," with "Key to the Scriptures" as I have, were it of human origin and I, apart from God, its author, but as I am only a scribe echoing the harmonies of Heaven in divine metaphysics, I cannot be supermodest of the Christian Science textbook.[3]

In every Christian Science church every sermon by the rules of the church is preceded by the following declaration:

The canonical writings, together with the word of our textbook ("Science and Health"), corroborating and explaining the Bible texts in their spiritual import and application to all ages, past, present and future, constitute a sermon undivorced from truth, uncontaminated and unfettered by human hypotheses, and authorized by Christ.

In "Miscellaneous Writings" she says:

The works I have written on Christian Science contain absolute Truth, and my necessity was to tell it; therefore I did this even as a surgeon who wounds to heal.   I was a scribe under orders; and who can refrain from transcribing what God indites, and ought not that one take the cup, drink all of it, and give thanks?[4]

[1] *Science and Health*, 1898 edition, pp. 550 ff.
[2] Ibid, 1916 edition, pp. 43 and 55.
[3] Peabody, *Masquerade*, p. 57.
[4] Page 3.

Once more, to conclude these claims of inspiration which might be further multiplied, in her organ, the Christian Science Journal, of January, 1901, Mrs. Eddy says:

It was not myself . . . which dictated "Science and Health" with "Key to the Scriptures." It was the divine power of Truth and Love, infinitely above me.[1]

She thus boldly and unblushingly claims that her book is not "of human origin," but was "dictated" by "divine Truth and Love," and revelation by "dictation" is the extremest form of plenary verbal inspiration.

But this is not the limit. Something far more painful is yet to come. Mrs. Eddy's followers are daring enough, and she herself does not hesitate, to exalt her to equality with Christ and crown her with deity. In "Science and Health," 1898 edition, she says:

The impersonation of the Spiritual idea had a brief history in the earthly life of our Master; but of his kingdom there shall be no end; for Christ, God's idea, will eventually rule all nations and peoples—imperatively, absolutely, finally—with Divine Science. This immaculate idea, represented first by man and last by woman, will baptize with fire.[2]

In her autobiography she writes:

No person can take the individual place of the Virgin Mary. No person can compass or fulfill the individual mission of Jesus of Nazareth. No person can take the place of the author of "Science and Health," the discoverer and founder of Christian Science.[3]

In the Christian Science Journal for April, 1889,

[1] Mark Twain, *Christian Science*, p. 144.
[2] Page 550.
[3] *Introspection and Retrospection*, p. 95.

which was then owned and published by Mrs. Eddy, an
article appeared which made an elaborate argument to
prove that she was the equal of Jesus. "Now a word,"
said the writer, "about the horror many good people
have of our making the author of 'Science and Health'
equal with Jesus."[1]

In 1894 Mrs. Eddy wrote and published a "poem"
illustrated with a picture in which Jesus is represented
as seated on a stone holding the right hand of a woman,
who in her left hand holds a scroll bearing the inscription
"Christian Science," thus identifying the woman with
Mrs. Eddy herself. About the head of each figure there
is a halo, and on the opposite page, illustrated by the
picture, are the lines, "As in blessed Palestine's hour,
so in our age 'tis the same hand unfolds his Power and
writes the page." Mrs. Eddy not only wrote the "poem,"
but also claimed a share in making the illustrations,
"which," Mr. Peabody says, "her man Hanna called
'exquisite bits of art,' but which are, doubtless, the
vulgarest products of the art of bookmaking of many
years."[2] This performance called forth such an outcry
of protest and indignation, even from some of her followers,
that she withdrew the little book (which was sold for $3.00)
from circulation, with the remark, "Scientists sometimes
take things too seriously."

Mrs. Eddy early began to identify herself with the
"woman" in the book of Revelation. She quotes ch.
12:1 and then says: "The Revelator saw also the spiritual
ideal as a woman clothed in light, a bride coming down
from heaven, wedded to the Lamb of Love. . . The

1 Peabody, *Masquerade*, p. 51.
2 *Masquerade*, pp. 51, 52.

woman in the Apocalypse symbolizes generic man, the spiritual idea of God; she illustrates the coincidence of God and man as the divine Principle and divine idea."[1]

In time she began to think of herself as the incarnation of the motherhood of God, and the idea that she should be worshiped as the correlative and coequal of the Father was not unwelcome to her mind. This seems to be the purport and point of her audacity in rendering the opening of The Lord's Prayer as "Our Father-Mother God." In the nineties "Mother Mary" became a common designation of her by her followers. Everybody spoke of her as "Mother." She sometimes signed herself "Mother Mary." The President of the National Christian Science Association on one occasion said, "There is but one Moses, one Jesus; and there is but one Mary."[2]

This idea culminated in one of the by-laws of her church, written by herself, which reads as follows:

The Title of Mother. In the year 1895 loyal Christian Scientists had given the author of their textbook, the Founder of Christian Science, the individual and endearing term of Mother. Therefore, if a student of Christian Science shall apply this title, either to herself or to others, except as the term for kinship according to the flesh, it shall be regarded by the Church as an indication of disrespect for their pastor emeritus, and unfitness to be a member of the mother church.[3]

Thus was this woman deified by her followers and herself, exalted to equality with and, indeed, to superiority to, Christ and finally raised to equality with God himself, and possibly she meant to join her name with his in the adoration of our Father-Mother God!

[1] *Science and Health*, pp. 560, 561.
[2] Powell, *Christian Science*, pp. 150, 151.
[3] In later editions of the *Church Manual*, Christian Scientists are instructed to substitute "Leader" for "Mother."

There is, however, an interesting sequel to this matter of Mrs. Eddy's use of the name "mother." After the appearance of Mark Twain's sarcastic book in which he punctures with his sharp pen many of the pretensions of Mrs. Eddy she issued a statement in the press in which she said:

In view of the circulation of certain criticisms from the pen of Mark Twain, I submit the following statement: It is a fact, well understood, that I begged the students who first gave me the endearing apellative "Mother" not to name me thus. But, without my consent, that word spread like wildfire. I still must think the name is not applicable to me. I stand in relation to this century as a Christian discoverer, founder, and leader. I regard self-deification as blasphemous; I may be more loved, but I am less lauded, pampered, provided for, and cheered than others before me —and wherefore? Because Christian Science is not yet popular, and I refuse adulation. . . I believe in but one incarnation, one Mother Mary, and I know I am not that one, and never claimed to be.

Mark Twain did not fail to see and seize his opportunity, and he replies to her in a scintillating chapter in his book, the opening sentences of which are: "I feel almost sure that Mrs. Eddy's inspiration works are getting out of repair. I think so because they made some errors in a statement which she uttered through the press on the 17th of January." The following is an extract:

She still thinks the name of our Mother not applicable to her; and she is also able to remember that it distressed her when it was conferred upon her, and that she begged to have it suppressed. Her memory is at fault here. If she will take her by-laws, and refer to Section 1 of Article XXII, written with her own hand—she will find that she has reserved that title to herself, and is so pleased with it that she threatens with excommunication any sister Scientist who shall call herself by it.

He also reproduces a telegram she sent on May 27,

25273

1890, to the National Christian Science Association then in session in New York in reply to one from the secretary of the association, who was "instructed to send to our Mother greetings and words of affection from her assembled children." Her response was: "All hail! He hath filled the hungry with good things and the sick hath he not sent empty away.—Mother Mary."

"Thus it stands proven," continues Mark Twain, "and established that she is that Mary and isn't, and thought she was and knows she wasn't. That much is clear. She is also 'The Mother,' by the election of 1895, and did not want the title, and thinks it is not applicable to her, and will excommunicate anyone that tries to take it away from her. So that is clear." Mark Twain was also distressed because Mrs. Eddy perverted the Scripture text she used in her telegram (which reads, in Luke 1:53, "and the rich hath he sent empty away") and marveled that this perversion "in that massed convention of trained Christians created no astonishment, since it caused no remark, and the business of the convention went tranquilly on, thereafter, as if nothing had happened."[1]

It stands indelibly written in her own writings, however, that she did make all these claims to divine inspiration and equality with Jesus, if not with God, and did adopt and use the name "Mother Mary," and forbade others to use it under pain of excommunication, and her subsequent denial of these claims is only one more instance of her inveracity, proved out of her own mouth.

[1] Mark Twain, *Christian Science*, pp. 331–342.

CHAPTER VI

"SCIENCE AND HEALTH": THE CONTENTS OF THE BOOK

It is difficult to give a condensed summary of the contents of "Science and Health" because of the lack of order and system in its arrangement and in its ideas. The chapters themselves have several times been shifted around in a different order, and they might be shuffled again without any loss of logic. The very titles of the chapters sometimes have little aptness as designations of their contents. The order of the paragraphs in the chapters also follows no inherent plan and progress and frequently baffles the reader to find and follow any thread of connection. There are only a few fundamental ideas in the book, and these are endlessly iterated and reiterated until one's sense of interest and attention is dulled into drowsiness: reading the book is like listening to a player on a violin who keeps sawing on one string and making few variations on that. One really has to maintain a firm grip on his attention to keep from falling into a stupor while perusing these monotonous pages. The style is trying enough because of its peculiar lingo and its frequent obscurity, although there are passages of clear English and here and there a purple patch of fine writing, some of these patches, however, being affected and stilted to a degree. Of course, also, there is much truth in the book, even fundamental truth and wholesome teaching, wheat in its chaff, grains of gold in its sand, and this will be brought out later. The present purpose, however, is to seize the principal points in each chapter and illustrate them with brief quotations. There is danger, it is true, in making such quotations of tearing them out of their context so as to pervert their meaning, but the author will guard against this tendency and will endeavor only to let Mrs. Eddy express her ideas in her own way.

1. PRAYER

The book starts abruptly in the middle of things with seventeen pages of rambling remarks and paragraphs on prayer, with little apparent continuity and progression. The point most frequently mentioned and strongly emphasized is that prayer is a subjective state which is not helped but hindered by audible expression and that its value is purely its reflex and subjective influence. "Audible prayer is impressive; it gives momentary solemnity and elevation to thought. But does it produce any lasting benefit? Looking deeply into these things, we find that 'a zeal not according to knowledge' gives occasion for reaction unfavorable to spiritual growth, sober resolve, and wholesome perception of God's requirements." The reader is therefore told that "lips must be silent and materialism silent," and that "we must close the lips and silence the materialistic senses." In accordance with this teaching only silent prayer is engaged in at Christian Science services, with the exception of the repetition of The Lord's Prayer together with Mrs. Eddy's interpretation of it.

It is expressly declared that "God is not influenced by man," and that "prayer cannot change the Science of being, but it tends to bring us into harmony with it."

The usual obsession as to the nonreality of matter and sin runs through the chapter. In praying "we must deny sin and plead God's allness," and yet sin is also constantly spoken of as a reality.

The chapter concludes with Mrs. Eddy's interpretation which she says she understands "to be the spiritual sense of The Lord's Prayer." It is here given as it stands in the 1916 edition of the book, but an entirely different version of her interpretation appeared in earlier editions of the same book.

Our Father which art in heaven,
　Our Father-Mother God, all-harmonious,
Hallowed be thy name.
　Adorable One.
Thy kingdom come.
　Thy kingdom come: Thou art ever-present.
Thy will be done in earth, as it is in heaven.
　Enable us to know, as in heaven, so on earth,—God is omnip-
　　otent, supreme.
Give us this day our daily bread.
　Give us grace for to-day; feed the famished affections.
And forgive us our debts, as we forgive our debtors.
　And Love is reflected in love;
And lead us not into temptation, but deliver us from evil;
　And God leadeth us not into temptation, but delivereth us
　　from sin, disease, and death.
For thine is the kingdom, and the power, and the glory,
　for ever.
　For God is infinite, all-power, all Life, Truth, Love, over all,
　　and All.

2. ATONEMENT AND EUCHARIST

This chapter extends to thirty-eight pages, but very little of it relates either to the atonement or the Eucharist. In reading these pages one soon gets the impression that one chapter runs without change of subject into another and that all are cut from the same cloth. The reader is

told at once that "the atonement of Christ reconciles man
to God, not God to man; for the divine Principle of Christ
is God, and how can God propitiate himself?" The
chapter never gets beyond the subjective influence of the
atonement, or the moral influence theory of it.   "The
atonement is a hard problem in theology, but its scientific
explanation is, that suffering is an error of sinful sense
which Truth destroys, and eventually both sin and
suffering will fall at the feet of everlasting love." The
atonement is indeed "a hard problem in theology," but
no light is imparted in the statement that "suffering is an
error of sinful sense," when the reality of both "suffering"
and "sinful sense" is denied and these are declared to be
"nothing." "Divine Science reveals the necessity of
sufficient suffering, either before or after death, to quench
the love of sin.   To remit the penalty due for sin, would
be for Truth to pardon error." It is puzzling to know
how there can be a "necessity of sufficient suffering"
when "suffering" is "nothing"; and the reader may be
satisfied with the orthodoxy of the statement that "to
remit the penalty due for sin, would be for Truth to
pardon error" until one remembers that both "penalty"
and "sin" are "dreams" of "mortal mind."   Mrs. Eddy
has the courage of her convictions when she declares that
"the universal belief in death is of no advantage," and
that "death will be found at length to be a mortal dream,
which comes in darkness and disappears with the light."
As soon as we quit believing in death, death itself will
cease.

The Eucharist which Christian Scientists observe is not
the Lord's Supper which Jesus instituted with his disciples
on the evening before his crucifixion, but is the "morning

meal" at which he was present with his disciples on the shore of the Sea of Galilee after his resurrection. The disciples, it will be recalled, had spent a night of fruitless toil in fishing on the lake when Jesus appeared on the shore and called to them to cast the net on the right side of the boat, and then they drew the net up swollen full. Here is Mrs. Eddy's account and interpretation of this incident:

> Convinced of the fruitlessness of their toil in the dark and wakened by their Master's voice, they changed their methods, turned away from material things, and cast their net on the right side. Discerning Christ, Truth, anew on the shore of time, they were enabled to rise somewhat from mortal sensuousness, or the burial of mind in matter, into newness of life as Spirit. This spiritual meeting with our Lord in the dawn of the new light is the morning meal which Christian Scientists commemorate.

This is a characteristic instance of the way in which Mrs. Eddy handles Scripture. She frequently quotes it, but often there is no remotest connection between her "science" and her Scripture "proof." Out of any text she extracts the most fanciful or fantastic meaning that suits her purpose, or rather she blandly attributes such a meaning to a text. The simple act of casting the net on the right side of the boat is made to mean that the disciples "turned away from material things" and "were enabled to rise somewhat from mortal sensuousness, or the burial of mind in matter, into newness of life as Spirit." According to this method of exegesis, anything can mean anything and all is indeed a "dream," it may be of "mortal mind," but certainly not of a rational mind.

The chapter concludes with another characteristic

misuse and perversion of Scripture, as follows: "In the words of Saint John: 'He shall give you another Comforter, that he may abide with you forever.' This Comforter I understand to be divine Science"!

3. MARRIAGE

This chapter contains fourteen pages, much of it having no connection with its subject, but frequently slipping into the obsession that "we must not attribute more and more intelligence to matter, but less and less, if we would be wise and healthy." This notion that everybody, except Christian Scientists, does "attribute intelligence to matter" runs all through these pages and receives endless repetition, whereas of course nobody, except an occasional crass materialist, does anything of the kind. This is only another instance of Mrs. Eddy's ignorance of what she is talking about.

Many good sentiments are expressed in this chapter as to the relation of husband and wife. "Kindred tastes, natures, and aspirations are necessary to the formation of a happy and permanent companionship." Divorce is discouraged, and "mutual compromises will often maintain a compact which otherwise might become unbearable." "Both sexes should be loving, pure, tender, and strong." "The entire education of children should be such as to form habits of obedience to the moral and spiritual law, with which the child can meet and master the belief in so-called physical laws, a belief which breeds disease." But again she is slipping into her obsession, which she can hardly avoid for a single paragraph. Children are to be deliberately taught that there is no such thing as "physical laws," and this falsehood is to be crammed into them in their earliest education.[1]

Mrs. Eddy's peculiar view as to the marriage relation appears in the very first paragraph of this chapter and runs as a subtle undertone all through it. She begins by quoting what Jesus said to John the Baptist in relation to his own baptism: "Suffer it now: for thus it becometh us to fulfil all righteousness." Her inference (and, as usual, a false one) from this passage is: "Jesus' concessions (in certain cases) to material methods were for the advancement of spiritual good." The point of this inference is that marriage is only a temporary arrangement to be regarded only as long as we believe in "mortal mind" and is to be cast aside as soon as we rise above this delusion. "The human mind will at length demand a higher affection," and "there will ensue a fermentation over this as over many other reforms." These views run through the chapter, and they are specifically set forth in the following paragraphs:

Marriage is the legal and moral provision for generation among human kind. Until the spiritual creation is discerned intact, is apprehended and understood, and his kingdom is come as in the vision of the Apocalypse—where the corporeal sense of creation was cast out, and its spiritual sense was revealed from heaven—marriage will continue, subject to such moral regulations as will secure increasing virtue. . . Until it is learned that God is the Father of all, marriage will continue. . . Beholding the world's lack of Christianity and the powerlessness of vows to make home happy, the human mind will at length demand a higher affection. There will ensue a fermentation over this as over many other reforms, until we get at last the clear straining of truth, and impurity and error are left

[1] A pastor told the author that when visiting in a Christian Science home he heard a little girl, who was suffering with a severe cold, when asked how she was, gasp out with choking voice, "There is no matter, God is love."

among the lees. The fermentation even of fluids is not pleasant.
An unsettled, transitional stage is never desirable on its own account.
Matrimony, which was once a fixed fact among us, must lose its
present slippery footing, and man must find permanence and peace
in a more spiritual adherence. . . Proportionately as human
generation ceases, the unbroken links of eternal, harmonious being
will be spiritually discerned.

These statements are vague and "slippery," but their
meaning is reasonably clear. Marriage is a legal and moral
temporary provision, which must be tolerated for the
present because we have not yet learned that "God is the
Father of all," and because of our "lack of Christianity,"
but when we attain to this through Mrs. Eddy's "Science"
and know that she herself is the "woman" in the vision
of the Apocalypse,"[1] then "the human mind will demand a
higher affection. . . Matrimony, which was once a fixed
fact among us, must lose its present slippery footing, and
man must find permanence and peace in a more spiritual
adherence." In a word, marriage must go! This "reform"
will be attended with "fermentation" and "fermentation
is not pleasant," but despite the trouble of getting rid of
it, marriage must go! It "was once a fixed fact among
us," but already it is growing fluid and will presently
evaporate into "a more spiritual adherence." It is to
be understood that all this does not refer to any future
spiritual world, but to the world that now is when freed
from "mortal mind" by "Christian Science." Marriage
will then be done with and people will form "a more
spiritual adherence."

It will not be difficult for some of the votaries of this
doctrine to believe that they already know that "God
is the Father of all" and that therefore they are ready to

[1] See page 98.

discard this "once fixed fact among us" and form this "more spiritual adherence." In fact, it is only a step from the belief in this doctrine to the practice of free love. Mrs. Eddy discouraged marriage among her followers, though she practiced it liberally herself, and in spite of the fact that she gives some good advice on the subject of marriage in this chapter, she yet lays the ax at the very root of the tree.

4. CHRISTIAN SCIENCE VERSUS SPIRITUALISM

Of the one hundred and seventeen paragraphs in this chapter only forty-eight can be held to refer even remotely to spiritualism. The first paragraph assures the reader that "the testimony of the corporeal senses cannot inform us what is real and what is delusive, but the revelations of Christian Science unlock the treasures of Truth." The main contention running through all these paragraphs is the wearisome repetition of the obsession that "suffering, sinning, dying beliefs are unreal."

In the fifth paragraph of the chapter Mrs. Eddy attempts to indulge in a little reasoning to support her main contention, something that seldom occurs in these pages of pure dogmatic assertion. The paragraph runs as follows:

Close your eyes, and you may dream that you see a flower—that you touch and smell it. Thus you learn that the flower is a product of the so-called mind, a formation of thought rather than of matter. Close your eyes again, and you may see landscapes, men, and women. Thus you learn that these also are images, which mortal mind holds and evolves and which simulate mind, life, and intelligence. From dreams also you learn that neither mortal mind nor matter is the image or likeness of God, and that immortal Mind is not matter.

Thus Mrs. Eddy confuses and identifies images of the imagination, or images that we "dream," with memory images which are revived impressions made on the senses by external objects, a radical distinction that can be tested and proved and refuses to yield to Mrs. Eddy's claim that all our ideas are wholly the product of "mortal mind."

As to the subject of the chapter, Mrs. Eddy says, "I never could believe in spiritualism," yet that she did both believe in and practice it in her early years is established by indisputable evidence.[1] Her reason for rejecting spirit communications is that spirits could not enter into relations with mortal minds, for this would mix mind and matter, which are irreconcilable, being "opposite dreams." "No correspondence nor communion can exist between persons in such opposite dreams as the belief of having died and left a material body and the belief of still living in an organic, material body." The condition of the dead is repeatedly spoken of in this chapter as being also a "dream" state. The very idea of death is a dream. "When you can waken yourself out of the belief that all must die, you can then exercise Jesus' spiritual power to reproduce the presence of those who have thought they have died—but not otherwise." Here it appears that the dead are still laboring under a delusion, they "have thought they have died."

In the midst of this chapter there are inserted five "postulates" which are equally the postulates of all the chapters of this book and may be taken as the fundamentals of Christian Science. They are as follows:

[1] Page 30.

Certain erroneous postulates should be here considered in order that the spiritual facts may be better apprehended.

The first erroneous postulate of belief is, that substance, life, and intelligence are something apart from God.

The second erroneous postulate is, that man is both mental and material.

The third erroneous postulate is, that mind is both evil and good; whereas the real mind cannot be evil nor the medium of evil, for mind is God.

The fourth erroneous postulate is, that matter is intelligent, and that man has a material body which is part of himself.

The fifth erroneous postulate is, that matter holds in itself the issues of life and death—that matter is not only capable of experiencing pleasure and pain, but also capable of imparting these sensations. From the illusions implied in this last postulate arises the decomposition of mortal bodies in what is termed death.

Let it be noted that mind is God and that there are no substance, life, and intelligence apart from God, and this fact is the fundamental pantheism of Christian Science. We are frequently told that man is only an "idea" or a "reflection" of God and has no existence apart from God. Let it also be noted that "pleasure" as well as "pain" is an experience of "mortal mind" and is a delusion to be got rid of. All knowledge derived through or suggested by our senses is to become "extinct," and the perfect state of Christian Science appears to be one of pure passive unconsciousness in which the human soul is merged in God as raindrops in the sea.

5. ANIMAL MAGNETISM UNMASKED

In this chapter Mrs. Eddy deals with her deepest obsession, the evil power of one "mortal mind" over another, which, developed into a veritable devil in her household and got into her kitchen utensils and stopped up her drain pipes and involved her in ever so many quarrels and lawsuits and became the Satan of her religion.

The brief chapter of seven pages opens with a reference
to "Mesmerism in Germany in 1775," and mixed into it
is the usual proportion of matter that gets off from the
subject as announced in the title and reverts to the perpetual obsession that "in reality there is no mortal mind,
and consequently no transference of mortal thought and
will-power," which is a downright contradiction of the
teaching of the chapter that "mortal mind" is a "murderer." "As named in Christian Science, animal magnetism or hypnotism is the specific term for error, or mortal
mind." Here "animal magnetism" is identified with
"hypnotism" and both of these with "mortal mind."
These definitions are confusing. And anyhow, how can
there be any "animal magnetism" when there isn't any
"animal"? Sometimes one thinks one knows what
"mortal mind" is and then again one is given a jolt and
finds he is wrong. In the "Glossary" of this book "Mortal
Mind" is defined as "Nothing claiming to be something,"
and then follows a series of definitions extending to a dozen
lines in which it is said to be all sorts of things, chiefly
certain "beliefs." Now it turns out to be "hypnotism,"
which is defined by Webster as "a state resembling sleep."
But whatever it is or it is not, "mortal mind" is capable
of doing things, for we are asked: "Is it not clear that the
human mind must move the body to a wicked act?
Is not mortal mind the murderer? The hands, without
mortal mind to direct them, could not commit murder."
It is not clear how all this can be done when both "the
hands" and "mortal mind" are "nothing claiming to be
something."

In this chapter Mrs. Eddy endeavors to make it out that
the courts should exercise jurisdiction over "mortal

mind." "To say that these tribunals have no jurisdiction over the carnal or mortal mind, would be to contradict precedent and to admit that the power of human
law is restricted to matter, while mortal mind, evil,
which is the real outlaw, defies justice and is recommended
to mercy. . . Mortal mind, not matter, is the criminal
in every case." It will be recalled how she was implicated
in bringing suit against Daniel H. Spofford on the ground
that he had exercised the "malicious animal magnetism"
of "mortal mind" against one of her students and thereby
she endeavored to revive the principle and spirit of trial
for witchcraft in Salem, Mass.[1] The judge dismissed
the case "with a smile," but if it had succeeded it would
have been a reversion to one of the most fearful delusions
that ever cursed the world.

6. SCIENCE, THEOLOGY, MEDICINE

This chapter extends to fifty-eight pages and is divided
into three sections with the three title words of the chapter
as subheads, but the divisions have little to do with the
substance of the thought, which runs on in the same
general stream of intermingled and confused ideas.

In this chapter there is a statement of "the fundamental
propositions of divine methaphysics," which Mrs. Eddy
says, "are summarized in the four following, to me, self-
evident propositions. Even if reversed, these propositions
will be found to agree in statement and proof, showing
mathematically their exact relation to Truth. De Quin-
cey says that mathematics has not a foot to stand

[1] Page 45.

upon which is not purely methaphysical." The four propositions are as follows:

1. God is All-in-all.
2. God is good.   Good is Mind.
3. God, Spirit, being all, nothing is matter.
4. Life, God, omnipotent good, deny death, evil, sin, disease—Disease, sin, evil, death, deny good, omnipotent God, Life.

Much is made by Christian Scientists of this "reversion" as a "proof" of these propositions. It is said that they read backward just as well as forward, but this is a mere verbal device and claim and has no logical value. It is one of those neat little rhetorical contrivances that please childish minds. It may also be said that these propositions are not the only sentences in this book that may be read backward as well as forward.

As to the four self-evident propositions, they are dogmatic assertions that appeal to those to whom they appeal. The first one, "God is All-in-all," together with its reversion, "All-in-all is God," is pantheism pure and simple. The second proposition is not strictly reversible, for "good" in the first form is an adjective or attribute, and has to be turned into a noun or substance in the second form. The fourth proposition uses the word "deny" in the sense of "destroy" or "annihilate" "death, evil, sin, disease," and in this sense the proposition, when "reversed," is not true even according to Christian Science, for surely death and sin do not destroy "omnipotent God."

In this chapter is given a more specific statement of how Christian Science heals disease. It is denied in this chapter and throughout the book that this system

heals by mental suggestion or human will power or by any
form of faith cure. "Human will-power is not science.
Human will belongs to the so-called material senses,
and its use is to be condemned. Willing the sick to
recover is not the metaphysical practice of Christian
Science, but is sheer animal magnetism." In the Preface
we may read: "They [mental healers] regard the human
mind as a healing agent, whereas this mind is not a factor
in the principle of Christian Science." Healing is generally attributed to Mind, which word, when capitalized,
always means God. It is the mere knowledge of or
belief in this Mind that heals disease, and not any faith
or action of the human mind itself.

And yet the action of the human mind in healing is
frequently emphasized. The Christian Science practitioner is told to "deny" disease, and the patient is urged to
do the same thing. Healing by "argument" is explicitly
explained on page 412. When a child falls on the carpet
and "thinks she has hurt her face," the mother is told to
say to it, "Oh, never mind! You're not hurt, so don't
think you are." On the same page (153) where this
precious advice is given, we are told: "The human mind
acts more powerfully to offset the discords of matter
and the ills of the flesh, in proportion as it puts less weight
into the material or fleshly scale and more weight into the
spiritual scale." Mrs. Eddy in spite of her denials that
her system is one of faith cure frequently makes statements
and uses illustrations that imply the action of the human
mind and the faith cure principle in the healing of disease.
"It is related," she says, "that Sir Humphrey Davy
once apparently cured a case of paralysis simply by in-
troducing a thermometer into the patient's mouth.

This he did merely to ascertain the temperature of the patient's body; but the sick man supposed this ceremony was intended to heal him, and he recovered accordingly. Such a fact illustrates our theories." It does indeed, and this method is the real principle and virtue of Christian Science.

Mrs. Eddy constantly confuses subjective experiences with objective causes. For example:

> You say a boil is painful; but that is impossible, for matter without mind is not painful. The boil simply manifests, through inflammation and swelling, a belief in pain, and this belief is called a boil. Now administer mentally to your patient a high attenuation of truth, and it will soon cure the boil. The fact that pain cannot exist where there is no mortal mind to feel it is proof that this so-called mind makes its own pain—that is, its own belief in pain.

It is true enough that pain cannot exist where there is no mind to experience it, but there is an objective cause for the pain, and that objective cause is the real boil. It is just at this point that Mrs. Eddy misses and perverts the position of philosophical idealism, as held by Berkeley, and that her system goes to pieces on the rock of objective reality.

7. PHYSIOLOGY

This chapter of thirty-six pages may be summarized in one of its sentences: "Mind has no affinity with matter, and therefore Truth is able to cast out the ills of the flesh," a sentence that equally summarizes all these chapters. The first sentence says that "Physiology is one of the apples from 'the tree of knowledge,' " or forbidden fruit which brought death into our world and all its woe. All through the chapter anatomy, physiology, hygiene, the laws of health, food, "flesh-brush, flannels, bath, diet, exercise, and air," are excommunicated as the real "mortal mind" and the true cause of disease. The usual self-contradictions and amazing assertions are plentiful. "What is termed disease does not exist. It is neither mind nor matter." This is mystifying, for over and over again Mrs. Eddy says that disease is a form or delusion of "mortal mind" and that "mortal mind" is "matter." Now the follower of Christian Science is told that disease is "neither mind nor matter." "Disease does not exist," and yet on the same page is the statement that "sickness is a growth of error," and "what causes disease cannot cure it." What has "no existence" is yet a "growth" and something "causes" it.

Among the contradictions in this chapter is the usual way of speaking of the natural sciences in one place as real and in another place as having no existence. "Through astronomy, natural history, chemistry, music, mathematics, thought passes naturally from effect back to cause," and yet "the so-called laws of matter are nothing but false beliefs," and "treatises on anatomy, physiology, and health, sustained by what is termed material law, are the promoters of sickness and disease." On one page "faith in drugs begets and fosters disease," and on another page "mortal belief is all that enables a drug to cure mortal ailments," which after all admits that a drug can cure.

Marvelous things are brought to light in this chapter. "Our ancestors. . . were innocent as Adam, before he ate the fruit of false knowledge, of the existence of lungs"— they did not know they had any lungs and therefore they really had none! We have them simply because we believe we have them. The blacksmith's strong arm is not due

to his exercise of it, but to "the blacksmith's faith in
exercise." The hammer that he wields "is not increased
in size by exercise," "because nobody believes that mind
is producing such a result on the hammer." If the
blacksmith only believed it, his hammer would grow along
with his muscle! Even horses appear to be subject to
Christian Science principles, for "you can even educate a
healthy horse so far in physiology that he will take cold
without his blanket, whereas the wild animal, left to his
instincts, sniffs the wind with delight. The epizoötic is
a humanly evolved ailment, which a wild horse might
never have." This, however, is but the beginning of
wonders. Mrs. Eddy claimed that she "had caused an
apple tree to blossom in January," one of her followers
reported in the Christian Science Journal that her dog
had been bitten by a rattlesnake and she "was able to
demonstrate over the belief in four days. The dog is
now as well as ever," and another follower was able to
cure a sick horse by saying to it "in an audible voice, 'You
are God's horse. You cannot overeat, have colic, or be
foundered.' At noon he was all right."[1]

It is not simply individual belief but the social belief
of mortal mind that produces disease and evil.

If a dose of poison is swallowed through mistake, and the patient
dies even though physician and patient are expecting favorable
results, does human belief, you ask, cause this death? Even so, and
as directly as if the poison had been intentionally taken. In such
cases a few persons believe the poison swallowed by the patient to be
harmless, but the vast majority of mankind, though they know
nothing of this particular case and this special person, believe the
arsenic, the strychnine, or whatever the drug used, to be poisonous,
for it is set down as a poison by mortal mind. Consequently, the
result is controlled by the majority of opinions, not by the infinitesimal minority of opinions in the sick-chamber.

[1] Milmine, *History*, pp. 186, 320, 372.

The general social mind is thus turned into a collective demon creating disease and sowing the world with evil. It appears from this that healing does not depend on individual faith, even of Christian Scientists, but on a majority vote of the community. It is hard to see how Christian Science is ever to succeed if things are to go on in this democratic way and even infidels according to this faith are allowed to vote.

8. FOOTSTEPS OF TRUTH

This chapter opens with the statement that "the best sermon ever preached is Truth practiced and demonstrated by the destruction of sin, sickness, and death," and our feet are in a familiar path. We learn that "to mortal sense, sin and suffering are real," in spite of the ceaseless iteration that they are "nonexistent," "fiction," "myths," "delusions," and "nothing." How what is nonexistent and nothing can in any sense be "real" passes understanding. At times we find a distinction between "mortal mind" and "matter," and yet we are also told that "matter" is "another name for mortal mind." Although we are told as early as in the Preface of the book that "the human mind as a healing agent" "is not a factor in the principle of Christian Science," yet in this chapter we are warned, "You must control evil thoughts in the first instance, or they will control you in the second," and are assured, "If you believe in and practice wrong knowingly, you can at once change your course and do right"; we are also frequently bidden to "deny" evil.

The eternity of man, which is a principle of pantheism, comes to the surface in this chapter. "Man in Science is

neither young nor old. He has neither birth nor death."
In accordance with this teaching followers are admon-
ished, "Never record ages. Chronological data are no
part of the vast forever. Time-tables of birth and death
are so many conspiracies against manhood and woman-
hood." Man is only an "idea" or a "reflection" of God
and has no existence apart from God.

9. CREATION

In the opening paragraph we read: "The mythical
human theories of creation, anciently classified as the
higher criticism, sprang from cultured scholars in Rome
and in Greece." This indicates that Mrs. Eddy's idea
of "the higher criticism" is peculiar, but she frequently
indulges in these slips of ignorance which her official
censor overlooked. Again the statement is made that
"the belief in a bodily soul and a material mind" "is
shallow pantheism," showing her misconception of pantheism. All the way through her book she thinks that
pantheism is the doctrine of "mind in matter."

In this chapter further light or obscurity is thrown on
Mrs. Eddy's view of the nature of "man" after he has
been stripped of "mortal mind." The "five corporeal
senses" are gone so that "man" no longer sees or hears
or feels either pain or pleasure. "We know no more of
man as the true divine image and likeness, than we know
of God." "Man is deathless, spiritual. He is above sin
or frailty. He does not cross the barriers of time into
the vast forever of Life, but he coexists with God and
the universe."

"The effect of mortal mind on health and happiness is

seen in" the case of an aged actor "who hobbled every day to the theater, and sat aching in his chair till his cue was spoken—a signal which made him as oblivious of physical infirmity as if he had inhaled chloroform, though he was in the full possession of his so-called senses." This is a good illustration of the power of the mind over the body, which is the stock in trade of Christian Science and the principle it has capitalized, however this may be denied.

"Spirit and its formations are the only realities of being," we read. Philosophical idealism makes this same assertion, only by "formations" it means the material world. It is difficult to say what Mrs. Eddy means by the word in this connection, only she cannot mean "matter," for this is her one universal devil and father of all evil. The material universe, which philosophical idealism views as the "formations" or activities of the infinite Spirit, is in her system the one great falsity to be detested and cast out of all thought and life. This distinction marks the deep and impassable gulf between Christian Science and philosophical idealism; the one is a fundamental misunderstanding and perversion of the other.

10. SCIENCE OF BEING

This chapter is the longest in the book, extending to seventy-three pages, but it is only the same confusion confounded. Mrs. Eddy does not use the technical term "ontology" in this chapter or anywhere in her writings, probably because she had not heard of it, for with her love of big swelling words which she did not understand it would surely have been a sweet morsel under her tongue.

"Belief in a material basis, from which may be deduced all rationality, is slowly yielding to the idea of a metaphysical basis." The idea is familiar, after having read it hundreds of times, but how from "a material basis," "may be deduced all rationality" is a new perplexity. Is "rationality" also one of the delusive exercises of "mortal mind"? If so we may be pardoned for thinking that this is one reason why it is so seldom employed in this volume.

All through this book Mrs. Eddy uses familiar words in a peculiar sense, constituting the jargon or slang of Christian Science, although, of course, she inherited this language from Quimby and others of her predecessors. "Science" is one of these terms which is used in a sense very different from its ordinary and accepted meaning. The reader is told, "Deductions from material hypotheses are not scientific. They differ from real Science because they are not based on divine law. Divine Science reverses the false testimony of the senses, and thus tears away the foundations of error." There is indeed "enmity," as Mrs. Eddy says, between this kind of "Science" and the science which all the world knows.

The usual self-contradictions stare us in the face on every page. "Spirit is the only substance and consciousness recognized by divine Science. The material senses oppose this, but there are no material senses, for matter has no mind." If there "are no material senses," how can they "oppose" anything? That "matter has no mind" is announced with all the appearance of a new statement, though it has been asserted thousands of times in this book and is found in one or another form no less than sixteen times on this same page (278).

Mrs. Eddy informs us that "in the Saxon and twenty other tongues 'good' is the term for God," but this etymology is like her other etymologies, a "fiction" of her "mortal mind." Long ago an American humorist said, "It is better not to know so many things than to know so much that ain't so."

Once in a while the reader is launched out on the deep of natural science and is treated to some wonderful opinions. Physicists who are striving day and night to find out what electricity is should consult this book, where they may read: "Electricity is the sharp surplus of materiality which counterfeits the true essence of spirituality or truth—the great difference being that electricity is not intelligent, while spiritual truth is Mind." This is almost as clear as the nature of electricity itself.

Mrs. Eddy hardly ever quotes or refers to Scripture that she does not utterly pervert it to her own purpose, putting on it a sense the Scripture writer never dreamed of. Thus: "Jacob was alone, wrestling with error—struggling with a mortal sense of life, substance, and intelligence as existent in matter with its false pleasures and pains—when an angel, a message from Truth and Love, appeared to him and smote the sinew, or strength, of his error, till he saw its unreality; and Truth, being thereby understood, gave him spiritual strength in this Peniel of divine Science." This is a fair specimen of what Scripture becomes in her hands.

"Matter is made up of supposititious mortal mind force." "Matter" is a wonderfully elusive shadow in Mrs. Eddy's teaching. "Mortal mind" is itself "nothing," and now we have a "supposititious" "nothing," or "nothing" raised to the second degree of nothingness, or a zero of zero. "If Soul could sin, Spirit, Soul, would be flesh instead of Spirit. It is the belief of the flesh and of material sense which sins." But we have been told a thousand times that "flesh," "matter," has no "intelligence" and is "nothing," and here we have "material sense" exercising "belief" so that it "sins."

Of a dead man she says: "The belief of that mortal man that he must die occasioned his departure." If the poor man had not believed he must die he would not have died. Strange that all the devotees of this cult, including Mrs. Eddy herself, who profess that belief in death is nothing, yet die with such unfailing regularity and total unanimity.

"The true idea of God. . . takes away all sin and the delusion that there are other minds, and destroys mortality." That there are "other minds" is also a delusion and thus one is landed in the pit of pantheism. "The divine principle which saves and heals": "Principle" is always treated as a neuter impersonal noun, and thus Mrs. Eddy's very grammar is pantheistic.

"One should not tarry in the storm if the body is freezing, nor should he remain in the devouring flames." Why not since the body is nothing? "Until one is able to prevent bad results, he should avoid their occasion." Christian Scientists do avoid freezing and flames along with other people, though they do so at the expense of their faith in their own doctrine.

This chapter concludes with thirty-two numbered paragraphs which are laid down as the "platform" of Christian Science. The first sentence of the first paragraph reads, "God is infinite, the only Life, substance, Spirit, or Soul, the only intelligence of the universe, including man." The pantheism of this principle is apparent, and the same principle runs through all of these paragraphs. The substance of the entire platform is expressed in the third paragraph: "The notion that both evil and good are real is a delusion of material sense, which Science annihilates." In the tenth paragraph we have a statement of the distinction that Mrs. Eddy makes between "Jesus" as a human person and "Christ" as "the divine idea of God." "Jesus demonstrated Christ; he proved that Christ is the divine idea of God— the Holy Ghost, or Comforter, revealing the divine Principle, Love, and leading into all truth." We have already been told that "the Holy Ghost" or "Comforter" is "Divine Science."

In paragraph twenty-five is this statement: "God is individual and personal in a scientific sense, but not in any anthropomorphic sense." Is this a denial of pantheism? It is not. What is meant by saying that God is personal "in a scientific sense"? The word "scientific" here means a "Christian scientific sense," and an "anthropomorphic sense" is the only sense in which we can understand personality and ascribe it to God.

11. SOME OBJECTIONS ANSWERED

Out of the mass of repetition in this chapter four objections to Christian Science are mentioned. The first is: "It is objected to Christian Science that it claims God as the only absolute Life and Soul, and man to be his idea—that is, his image." The objection is that Christian Science merges man in a pantheistic God. The answer made is: "It should be added that this is claimed to represent the normal, healthful, and sinless condition of man in divine Science, and that this claim is made because the Scriptures say that God has created man in his own image and after his likeness. Is it sacrilegious to assume that God's likeness is not found in matter, sin, sickness, and death?" The answer confuses "idea" and "image." An "idea" of God is a state of his own consciousness, and if man is "an idea of God" then he is part of God and we are landed in pantheism. The Scripture doctrine that man is created "in the image of God" does not make man a part of God but a distinct being and separate personality. When Mrs. Eddy teaches that "man is an idea of God" she is teaching pantheism and the first objection is sustained.

The second objection is: "It is sometimes said, in criticizing Christian Science, that the mind which contradicts itself neither knows itself nor what it is saying. It is indeed no small matter to know oneself; but in this volume of mine there are no contradictory statements— at least none which are apparent to those who understand its propositions well enough to pass judgment upon them." The answer is only a dogmatic denial of the objection and does not remove the abounding self-contradictions in this volume, and the objection stands.

The third objection is: "It is sometimes said that Christian Science teaches the nothingness of sin, sickness, and death, and then teaches how this nothingness is to be saved and healed. The nothingness of nothing is plain; but we need to understand that error is nothing, and that its nothingness is not saved, but must be demonstrated in order to prove the somethingness—yea, the allness—of Truth. It is self-evident that we are harmonious only as we cease to manifest evil or the belief that we

suffer for the sins of others.   Disbelief in error destroys
error, and leads to the discernment of Truth.   There are
no vacuums.   How then can this demonstration be
'fraught with falsities painful to behold'?"   This is a
fine specimen of Christian Science lingo and logic.   "Error
is nothing," yet "disbelief in error |destroys error,"
that is, "disbelief in nothing destroys nothing."   The
absurdity of teaching "the nothingness of sickness,"
and then writing a book of seven hundred pages to explain
how to heal this nothingness is still "painful to behold,"
and this objection still stands.   What Mrs. Eddy really
means by "the nothingness of sickness" is that sickness
is a subjective state of mind and not an objective bodily
reality, but she never succeeds in expressing this idea.
She digged this pit for herself when she started out with
her initial blunder that "matter" is a "delusion" to be
"denied" and cast out of the mind.   There is a sense in
which she believes in the existence of sickness and another
sense in which she does not, but she never makes the
distinction clear to her readers or to herself and therefore
she is constantly involving herself in confusion and contradiction.

The fourth objection is: "It is said by one critic, that
to verify this wonderful philosophy Christian Science
declared that whatever is mortal or discordant has no
origin, existence, nor realness.   Nothing really has Life
but God, who is infinite Life; hence all is Life, and death
has no dominion.   This writer infers that if anything
needs to be doctored, it must be the one God, or Mind.
Had he stated his syllogism correctly, the conclusion
would be that there is nothing to be doctored."   To see
Mrs. Eddy giving a lesson to anybody on stating a "syllo-

gism correctly" is amusing in the extreme. This fourth objection is the same pantheistic objection as the first one, and notwithstanding the lesson on syllogistic logic it still stands.

12. CHRISTIAN SCIENCE PRACTICE

The principle of Christian Science practice is summed up in the statement: "The efficient remedy is to destroy the patient's false belief by both silently and audibly arguing the true facts in regard to harmonious being—representing man as healthy instead of diseased, and showing that it is impossible for matter to suffer, to feel pain or heat, to be thirsty or sick. Destroy fear, and you end fever." This is the principle of faith healing in all its forms, however often Mrs. Eddy may claim that her system is something different. The difficulty, of course, if not the impossibility is to keep on saying you don't "feel pain" when you know you do. Fever "ends in a belief called death," but "destroy the fear, and you end the fever." "When the first symptoms of disease appear, dispute the testimony of the material senses with divine Science." "Suffer no claim of sin or of sickness to grow upon the thought. Dismiss it with an abiding conviction that it is illegitimate, because you know that God is no more the author of sickness than he is of sin."

Mrs. Eddy has a pronounced aversion to hygiene and all its works. "If half the attention given to hygiene were given to the study of Christian Science and to the spiritualization of thought, this alone would usher in the millennium. Constant bathing and rubbing to alter the secretions or to remove unhealthy exhalations from the cuticle receive a useful rebuke from Jesus' precept,

'Take no thought. . . for the body'. . . He who is ignorant of hygienic law, is more receptive of spiritual power
and of faith in one God, than is the devotee of supposed
hygienic law, who comes to teach the so-called ignorant
one." An ignorant immigrant or a savage covered with
filth and vermin "is more receptive of spiritual power"
than one who takes a bath and puts on clean linen at proper
intervals. Bathing a baby is "no more natural or necessary than would be the process of taking a fish out of water
every day and covering it with dirt to make it thrive
more vigorously thereafter in its native element"! Here
is a woman in this enlightened day, after the battle for obedience to the laws of health as against the outrageous
and dreadful treatment of the body in the Dark Ages
has been won at the cost of centuries of struggle with
ignorance and superstition, who would throw overboard
anatomy, physiology, hygiene, pathology, materia medica,
and all the knowledge we have gained that has banished
pestilence and enabled us to heal and save thousands
of men and women and children, and plunge the world
back into the blackest night of savagery. "Realize the
evidence of the senses is not to be accepted in the case
of sickness, any more than it is in the case of sin." Look
on your suffering dear one, mother or wife or darling
child, however the beloved one may scream and writhe
in agony, with a stony heart and never move a hand,
for there is no suffering and only your eyes and ears
are telling you lies. What monsters of cold-blooded
insensibility and cruelty can such a doctrine make out
of human beings! In numerous published and in un-
numbered unpublished instances Christian Science believers and practitioners have refused to accept the evi-

dence of their senses and have stood stolidly by and let die the sick who might have been saved. No wonder that when these facts are known people stand aghast with horror at such inhumanity and that the civil courts interfere to prevent it as a barbarism.

"Not understanding Christian Science the sick usually have little faith in it till they feel its beneficent influence. This shows that faith is not the healer in such cases. The sick unconsciously argue for suffering, instead of against it. They admit its reality, whereas they should deny it." "They should deny it": What is this but exercising faith in the system. The contention that faith on the part of the sick plays no part in their healing is falsified on many a page. "Always support their trust in the power of Mind to sustain the body."

Because failure in surgical cases is too patent and public and because of the law, they are exempt from Christian Science treatment. "Until the advancing age admits the efficacy and supremacy of Mind, it is better for Christian Scientists to leave surgery and the adjustment of broken bones and dislocations to the fingers of a surgeon, while the mental healer confines himself chiefly to mental reconstruction and to the prevention of inflammation. Christian Science is always the most skillful surgeon, but surgery is the branch of its healing which will be the last acknowledged." It is always the most skillful surgeon, yet it is better to leave surgery to the surgeon. The logic is lame, as the author has not "stated her syllogism correctly," but the conclusion is sound.

From a precious passage in this chapter we learn that everyone is crazy except the devotees of Christian Science. "There is a universal insanity of so-called health, which mistakes fable for fact throughout the entire round of the material senses, but this general craze cannot, in a scientific diagnosis, shield the individual case from the special name of insanity.   Those unfortunate people who are committed to insane asylums are only so many distinctly defined instances of the baneful effects of illusion on mortal minds and bodies."   If to be sane is to be in the same state of mind with the author of this confused book, many of her readers would prefer to be crazy.   The reader is told further that "if the reader of this book observes a great stir throughout his whole system, and certain moral and physical symptoms seem aggravated, these indications are favorable.   Continue to read, and the book will become the physician, allaying the tremor which Truth often brings to error when destroying it."   One does, indeed, notice while reading this book that "certain moral and physical symptoms seem aggravated," but they are symptoms of increasing stupor and deep drowsiness making it hard to keep from falling dead asleep.

13. TEACHING CHRISTIAN SCIENCE

Early in this chapter is encountered the fear of animal magnetism which runs through it.   "Also the teacher must thoroughly fit his students to defend themselves against sin, and to guard against the attacks of the would-be mental assassin, who attempts to kill morally and physically."   "A thorough perusal of the author's publications heals the sick.   If patients sometimes seem worse while reading this book, the change may arise either from the alarm of the physician, or it may mark the crisis of the disease.   Perseverance in the perusal of the book has generally healed such cases." The book is thus treated as if it were charged with magic and had the virtue of the fetish of a South Sea islander. There are curious affinities between Christian Science and fetishism, the worship of relics and even devil worship with its mental assassination, and other forms of superstition. The author confesses that he did "sometimes seem worse while reading this book," but in his case the trouble did not "arise either from the alarm of the physician," or from "the crisis of the disease," but it arose from the tangle of confusion and absurdity in the book itself.

Here and there one finds good things in this book. For example: "If patients fail to experience the healing power of Christian Science, and think they can be benefited by certain ordinary physical methods of medical treatment, then the mind physician should give up such cases, and leave invalids free to resort to whatever other systems they fancy will afford relief." This is good advice, and many of Christian Science patients have acted on it with good results. One also reads: "Students are advised by the author to be charitable and kind, not only towards differing forms of religion and medicine, but to those who hold these differing opinions." This also is good advice for all people.

We are told that "it is anything but scientifically Christian to think of aiding the divine Principle of healing or of trying to sustain the human body until the divine Mind is ready to take the case." Does not this mean or imply that it is not in accordance with Christian Science to be "trying to sustain the human body" with food? This is certainly the logic and sometimes is the express teaching of this system, yet on turning the leaf one reads:

"I do not maintain that anyone can exist in the flesh without food and raiment." These self-contradictions abound and are inherent in the system.

Another inconsistency appears in the following: "Usually to admit that you are sick, renders your case less curable, while to recognize your sin, aids in destroying it." Since both sickness and sin are equally unreal and "nothing," why should admitting the one and recognizing the other have such opposite effects?

"Our Master. . . never enjoined obedience to the laws of nature." How absurd is such a statement! Time and again he fed hungry people and when he raised the little daughter of Jairus from the sleep of death "he commanded that something should be given her to eat." Mrs. Eddy would abolish the whole framework of the universe and then she presumes to quote Jesus Christ as sustaining her absurdity.

Obstetrics is a delicate and dangerous point with Christian Scientists. "Teacher and student should also be familiar with the obstetrics taught by this Science. To attend properly the birth of the new child [did anyone ever attend the birth of an "old" child?], or divine idea, you should detach mortal thought from its material conceptions, that the birth will be natural and safe." This kind of "obstetrics" was tried in the early history of Christian Science with terrible results, but the law now has something to say about such practice.

On the last page of this chapter one finds a grave relapse from Christian Science orthodox belief and practice. "If from an injury or from any cause, a Christian Scientist were seized with a pain so violent that he could not treat himself mentally—and the Scientist had failed to relieve him—the sufferer could call a surgeon, who would give him a hypodermic injection, then, when the belief in pain was lulled, he could handle his own case mentally. Thus it is that we 'prove all things; [and] hold fast that which is good.'" It seems that this advice plainly admits the "somethingness" instead of the "nothingness" of pain, especially when it becomes "so violent" that the Christian Scientist is helpless before it. And is it not a rather humiliating confession of having "failed" and an abject groveling before "a surgeon" to run to him for help in such an extremity? In this chapter Mrs. Eddy says that "it should be granted that the author understands what she is saying." One frequently doubts, while reading this book, that she did, and it is certain that often nobody else understands her; and it seems that she must have been nodding when she made this admission and gave this advice. If Christian Science "is always the most skilful surgeon," why ever go back on it and run away from it to such a "nothing" as "a hypodermic injection"? Tell it not in Gath, publish it not in Boston that Christian Science has apostatized from the faith and bowed the knee to the god of matter and to the devil of medicine! Does not this prove that Christian Science practice becomes so impossible that even the high priestess of the cult herself must abjure its orthodoxy and resort to the heresy of medicine and matter? And after this authorization by Mrs. Eddy herself, are we not now all warranted in resorting to "a hypodermic injection" and to "a surgeon" and to all the "ordinary physical methods of medical treatment"? May we not now go further and obey all "the laws of nature"? May we not now not only eat food and wear clothes, but wash our babies and even occasionally take a bath and put on clean linen ourselves? Where are we going to draw the line? If Mrs. Eddy and her followers can resort to the "hypodermic" and the "surgeon" in the dry tree, what may not we do in the green tree? The bars are down and we appear to be free to roam and revel in the nothingness of matter.

14. RECAPITULATION

This chapter recapitulates the few ideas which have already been said many hundreds of times in the book by saying them over again many times more. It consists of questions and answers, and two main threads run through them all: pantheism and the "nothingness" of matter and sickness and suffering and sin. It will not be necessary to do more than give a few illustrations. The whole chapter is saturated with pantheism. God is Principle and "Principle" is always treated as an impersonal noun, as of course it is. The fourth question is, "What are spirits and souls?" The answer is: "To human belief they are personalities constituted of mind and matter, life and death, truth and error, good and evil; but these contrasting pairs of terms represent contraries, as Christian Science reveals, which neither dwell together nor assimilate." Of course this very language contradicts itself, for how can spirits be "personalities constituted" of these "contraries" if they "neither dwell together nor assimilate"? Next one reads: "The term 'souls' or 'spirits' is as improper as the term 'gods.' Soul or Spirit signifies deity and nothing else. There is no finite soul nor spirit. Soul or Spirit means only one mind, and cannot be rendered in the plural." This is Mrs. Eddy's constant teaching that there is no separate human soul or spirit,

but that the only soul is God and man is "an idea" of
God. Man is merged in God, and one is landed in the
pit of pantheism.

As for the nothingness of matter which runs through
this recapitulation, we need only adduce the familiar
statements that "matter is mortal error," and that "sin,
sickness, and death are to be classified as effects of error."

The last question in this chapter is, "Have Christian
Scientists any religious creed?" The answer starts off,
"They have not, if by that term is meant doctrinal beliefs.
The following is a brief exposition of the important points,
or religious tenets, of Christian Science." Then follow
six "tenets," every one of which is a "doctrinal belief,"
and all taken together constitute a "religious creed,"
which it has just been denied that Christian Scientists
have. The first "tenet" is, "As adherents of Truth, we
take the inspired Word of the Bible as our sufficient guide
to eternal life." But it is easily seen how Mrs. Eddy
perverts the Scripture to her own whimsical and often
absurd interpretation and purpose, and this fact nullifies
this first tenet. The other five tenets, which relate to
the "one supreme and infinite God," "forgiveness of sin,"
"Jesus' atonement," "the crucifixion of Jesus and his
resurrection," and prayer are all vitiated and under-
mined by the same absurd system of interpretation.

15. GENESIS

With this chapter begins the appendix to "Science and
Health," which is called "Key to the Scriptures." This
was not in the early editions of the book, for at first Mrs.
Eddy had no thought of starting a religion, and the "Key
to the Scriptures" was an afterthought which was produced

and appended to the book in 1884, after she began to dream of the day when "the church bells would ring out her birthday."

If the reader of "Science and Health" constantly wonders at the type and state of the mind that could have produced such a mass and mess of obscurity and absurdity, literally denying the reality of the world and turning it all into an illusion and delusion and also constantly denying this denial, he will wonder still more at the "Key to the Scriptures," which consists of the irrationality and folly of "Science and Health" raised to the second if not to the nth power. This amazing performance would be truly considered incredible and impossible did not the cold type stolidly and persistently stare one in the face.

For one thing, while it proclaims itself a "Key to the Scriptures," it consists of comments on only a few verses of Scripture, about one hundred in all. These verses consist of the first, second, third, and part of the fourth chapters of Genesis, and a few verses from the tenth, twelfth, and twenty-first chapters of Revelation. In addition the Twenty-third Psalm is appended to the chapter with Mrs. Eddy's interpretation and perversion of it after the manner of her rendition of The Lord's Prayer. It is out of such material as this that parallel interpretations to every part of the Scripture are furnished to be read along with the Scriptures in the Christian Science services; but as parallel lines never meet, so these "parallels" not only do not meet but usually this "Key to the Scriptures" has no more connection with the Scriptures themselves than has a dog with the Dog Star.

It will be unnecessary to do more than give a few il-

lustrations of the manner in which Scripture is unlocked
by this "Key." The "exegesis" of the very first verse
of the Bible consists in denying its plain meaning. Genesis
1:1 reads: "In the beginning God created the heavens
and the earth." The comment begins: "The infinite
has no beginning. This word 'beginning' is employed
to signify 'the only'—that is, the eternal verity and unity
of God and man, including the universe. The creative
Principle—Life, Truth, and Love—is God. The universe
reflects God. There is but one creator and one creation.
This creation consists of the unfolding of spiritual ideas. . .
and the highest ideas are the sons and daughters of God."
The point of all this is to deny that there is any other
being than God, and thus pantheism lies at the root of
this interpretation of the first verse of the Bible, though
the verse itself and the whole Bible deny pantheism
from beginning to end.

The comment now runs along verse by verse, every
verse being turned into an utterly fanciful and false
"interpretation." When "God said, Let the waters under
the heavens be gathered together unto one place, and
let the dry land appear," the "interpretation" is that
"Spirit, Soul, gathers unformed thoughts into their
proper channels, and unfolds these thoughts, even as
he opens the petals of a holy purpose in order that the
purpose may appear."

A marvelous division of the Creation story in Genesis
is introduced at the sixth verse of the second chapter,
which reads, "But there went up a mist from the earth,
and watered the whole face of the ground." We are
then told: "The Science and truth of the divine creation
have been presented in the verses already considered,

and now the opposite error, a material view of creation, is to be set forth. The second chapter of Genesis contains a statement of this material view of God and the universe, a statement which is the exact opposite of scientific truth as before recorded. The history of error or matter, if veritable, would set aside the omnipotence of Spirit; but it is the false history in contradistinction to the true." Following this principle of interpretation, when it is written that "Jehovah God formed man of the dust of the ground, and breathed into his nostrils the breath of life; and man became a living soul," Mrs. Eddy exclaims, "Did the divine and infinite Principle become a finite deity, that he should now be called Jehovah? Is this addition to his creation real or unreal? Is it truth, or is it a lie concerning man and God? It must be a lie, for God presently curses the ground." A more false and blasphemous "interpretation" of Scripture can nowhere be found. Let it not be forgotten or forgiven that this woman, because it does not agree with her theory, dared to write across the account of creation in the second chapter of Genesis the impious statement, "It must be a lie"!

Many remarkable things come to light in the closing pages of this chapter. Mrs. Eddy here and there through her book takes to discussing matters of science and delights in using big scientific and philosophical words as though she were learned and even an authority in these things, and yet she invariably "gives herself away" so that it is evident that she does not know what she is talking about. A page or two are devoted to "embryology" in which we learn some astounding things. We are told that "Agassiz was able to see in the egg the earth's atmosphere, the gathering clouds, the moon and stars, while the germinating speck of so-called embryonic life seemed a small sun." Students of Darwin will be interested in learning Mrs. Eddy's notion of Darwinism. "Briefly, this is Darwin's theory—that Mind produces its opposite, matter, and endues matter with power to recreate the universe, including man." Professors of biology will please make note of this valuable summary.

One of the most astounding things in the book is this: "It is related that a father plunged his infant babe, only a few hours old, into the water for several minutes, and repeated this operation daily, until the child could remain under water twenty minutes, moving and playing without harm, like a fish. Parents should remember this, and learn how to develop their children properly on dry land." The application does not seem to be quite germane, for obviously the logical lesson that should be drawn from the alleged fact is that parents should learn how to develop their children properly under water. The real point, however, that the illustration demonstrates is the monumental credulity of Mrs. Eddy. As she can get her credulous followers to believe any absurd thing that she tells them, so there is nothing so absurd or impossible that is too much for her own boundless gullibility.

16. THE APOCALYPSE

In this chapter the same principle of "interpretation" is applied to about twenty verses picked out of the book of Revelation. Mrs. Eddy has a special fondness for the verses (ch. 12:1–6) in which is mentioned the "woman arrayed with the sun," and we have already seen[1] how

[1] Page 98.

she early began to suggest the identity of herself with this woman. "The Revelator saw also the spiritual ideal as a woman clothed in light. . . The woman in the Apocalypse symbolizes generic man, the spiritual idea of God; she illustrates the coincidence of God and man as the divine Principle and divine idea." "As Elias presented the idea of the fatherhood of God, which Jesus afterwards manifested, so the Revelator completed this figure with woman, typifying the spiritual idea of God's motherhood." The strongly suggested analogy is that as Jesus manifested the fatherhood of God, so the Revelator completed the figure with woman, who was Mrs. Eddy herself, "typifying the spiritual idea of God's motherhood."

It is unnecessary to follow further the incredible vagaries of this "Key" to the Apocalypse. The chapter concludes with the statement: "The writer's present feeble sense of Christian Science closes with John's Revelation as recorded by the great apostle, for his vision is the acme of this Science as the Bible reveals it." Again "this Science" and "the Bible" are classed together as divine revelations, only, as we have learned, the "Science" is a later and fuller revelation than the Bible.

17. GLOSSARY

This chapter purports to give "the metaphysical interpretation of Bible terms, giving their spiritual sense, which is also their original meaning." One hundred and twenty-six words are thus defined, the "metaphysical interpretation" consisting of a string of supposedly synonymous words or phrases, in some instances extending to a full page. A few choice specimens have already been culled from its pages,[1] and only a few more need be adduced. "Adam" is in a very bad way with Mrs. Eddy, for she devotes a page to him in which she calls him all manner of evil names. If he had been living at the time he would have had a good case against her for libel, and any jury would have awarded him heavy damages. The long catalogue starts, "Error; a falsity; the belief in 'original sin,' sickness, and death; evil; the opposite of good," and so on to the end of the page. In addition to all this she made this astonishing discovery: "Divide the name Adam into two syllables, and it reads, 'A dam,' or obstruction." The point of this remarkable etymology, which Webster and all other lexicographers have strangely overlooked, is that Adam was an obstruction to our growth in spirituality. We wish to enter a protest against this personal vilification of Adam and even dare to utter a word in his defense. He has long had to bear a heavy enough burden of odium in connection with the human race without having this terrible catalogue of abusive epithets unloaded on him. Eve has only six lines devoted to her "metaphysical interpretation" as compared with Adam's full page, yet she fares little better, for she is "mortality; error; the belief that the human race originated materially instead of spiritually—that man started first from dust, second from a rib, and third from an egg." Evidently Eve deserves our pity and charity. Mrs. Eddy seems to have some spite against Jacob and his sons, for Jacob himself is "a corporeal mortal embracing duplicity, repentance, sensualism," while Benjamin is "a physical belief as to life, a false belief," Issachar is "a corporeal belief, envy; hatred; self-will; lust," and poor

[1] Pp. 90, 91.

Dan is that dreadful demon, "Animal magnetism." One often wonders what might be the "spiritual sense" of the river Gihon, but now comes the information that it is "the rights of woman acknowledged morally, civilly, and socially." It will be admitted that the genius that gave the river this name was gifted with long foresight and was a remarkable prophet. "Matter," of course, is "another name for mortal mind; illusion," and so on, ending with "that which mortal mind sees, feels, hears, tastes, and smells only in belief." "Mortal Mind" is a familiar friend, "Nothing claiming to be something, error creating other errors," and many other grave offenses, ending in "sin; sickness; death." "Red Dragon" appropriately means "animal magnetism." "Divine Science" is found symbolized under many names, including "Dove," "Gad," "Elias," "New Jerusalem," and the rivers "Euphrates" and "Hiddekel"!

All these "metaphysical interpretations" are seriously given as the "original meaning" of these terms. This egregious "Glossary" may be viewed as a literary curiosity and monstrosity, or as a pitiful display of ignorant conceit, or as a painful exhibition of sacrilegious trifling with Scripture, or as a symptom of incipient egotistic insanity, a kind of lexical madhouse; but it may be summed up by saying that it is a conglomeration of arrant nonsense and fatuous folly without a rival, so far as is known, in the English or any other language.[1]

[1] We would find the nearest approach to this performance in the "allegorizing" of some of the ancient Hebrew rabbis and the medieval Cabalists. "The Cabalists were searching out the sacred inner meaning of the Bible; they proceeded slowly, starting with 'in the beginning,' and stopping at every word, every letter, and found in every word and every letter a mine of secrets." Viktor Rydberg, *The Magic of the Middle Ages*, p. 144.

18. FRUITAGE

The final chapter of the book consists of eighty-four letters, republished from The Christian Science Journal and Christian Science Sentinel, giving the experiences "of people who have been reformed and healed through the perusal or study of this book." The consideration of such cures will be taken up in a later chapter.

However, for the present, the author wishes to point out two strange features that are obvious to the most casual non-Scientist reader of these letters; two self-contradictions that are written all over them and woven into every line of them.

The first is this: Since we have been told countless times all the way through this book that disease is nothing and nonexistent because "Man is incapable of sickness," how in the world does there come to be so much of it? And why all this pretense and pother of curing it? Since disease is only the imagination of "mortal mind," which is itself "nothing," it seems there is an awful fuss made over getting rid of something that does not really exist, or is only the fiction of a fiction. Having "denied" the body and shed it as only a bad dream, why bother so much about it? Since there really is no matter, how can there be anything the matter with it? This puzzle constantly stares us in the face as we read these letters that are saturated and dripping with diseases that these persons were "incapable" of having.

And the second strange thing is stranger still and it is this: The readers of this book and the writers of these letters have been taught that the senses are utterly false and not to be believed on any subject. They have been assured that "the testimony of the corporeal senses cannot inform us what is real and what is delusive," that "health is not a condition of matter, but of Mind; nor can the material senses bear reliable testimony on the subject of health," that "corporeal sense defrauds and lies," that "the evidence of the senses is not to be accepted in the case of sickness," and that "the so-called senses receive no intimation of the earth's motions or of the science of astronomy." If the senses cannot tell any truth about such big and plain things as astronomy and the motions of the heavenly bodies how much less can they be trusted to tell anything about anatomy and the motions of our organs? Yet the writers of these letters all appeal to their senses, first, to show what diseases they did have, and, second, to prove that they don't have them now and never did have them. How did they know that they had these broken arms and fibroid tumors and cataracts in their eyes? They say that they saw these things, but such testimony "is not to be accepted in the case of sickness" and is branded as fraudulent and "lies" in the book. Having thrown the senses out of court as prevaricators, how can they now bring them back in again to prove both their diseases and their cures?

The ways of the Christian Science mind are past finding out. Yet the writers of these letters never seem to be aware of these self-contradictions and absurdities. It is only a step or a slip from idealism or spiritualism into materialism, and these two contradictions illustrate the fact that Mrs. Eddy and her followers, with all their affirmation of "Mind" as the only reality and in spite of all their denial of and aversion to "matter," are yet deeply mired in materialism, and in all their teaching and practice they are constantly struggling with this "too,

too solid flesh," which will not melt and vanish at their bidding.

Some additional opinions of this book by other students of it are here appended in conclusion to this chapter. The author has already referred to and quoted from "The Interpretation of Life," by Gerhardt Mars, who strongly supports Mrs. Eddy's claims, and yet he writes as follows:

The first reading of her chief work, "Science and Health with Key to the Scriptures," leaves the impression, in spite of much that is strikingly beautiful and true, that there is a prevailing tone of incoherence, contradiction, illogicality, and arbitrary, dictatorial assertion, with no regard for evident fact either in the realm of objective nature or history.

Robert Hugh Benson, a Roman Catholic dignitary, wrote as follows:

It is impossible to describe the confusion of mind that falls upon the student of "Science and Health". . . . The quasiphilosophical phraseology of the book, the abuse of terms, the employment of ambiguous words at crucial points, the character of the exegesis, the broken-backed paradoxes, the astonishing language, the egotism —all these things and many more end by producing in the mind a symptom resembling that which neuritis produces in the body, namely a sense that an agonizing abnormality is somewhere about, whether in the writings or in the reader is uncertain.[1]

Stephen Paget, M. D., in his book "The Faith and Works of Christian Science," quotes the opinions of several writers of which a brief extract follows:

Dr. Polk, Dean of the Medical Department, Cornell University: Take "Science and Health," separate yourself from disturbing surroundings, open its pages with a mind even somewhat prejudiced, set yourself seriously to the task of comprehending its various iterations and reiterations, its statements backward, its statements forward, its statements sidewise, and every other wise, of its initial

[1] *The Dublin Review*, July, 1908, reprinted in his *Book of Essays*.

proposition, throughout its 569 pages, and I know there are many of you who, long before you had fathomed its depths, would find yourself in a state of mental vacuity fit for the action of "suggestion."

Dean Hart, of the University of Denver: I have found that "Science and Health" is the best mode of inducing the mesmeric sleep I have ever experienced. The repetition of senseless sentences, with constantly changing signification of words, whose new meanings have to be gleaned from the context, produces a strange maze which dazes the mind and produces a mesmeric condition.

Rev. P. C. Woolcott: What really happens when you attack these tiresome monotonous pages, is this: you struggle at first to master the difficulties and get at the meaning. If you become convinced that it is not worth the effort, you dismiss the matter from your mind, and that is the end of it. But. if you force yourself to the task, and pore over the pages, you soon fall into a condition of mental dizziness or vertigo. The reasoning faculties are benumbed, your critical judgment is lulled to sleep, and suggestion dominates the intellect.

M. Carta Sturge, "after ten years' study of the book," says:

I have met with extraordinary difficulty to get a connected idea of the contents of "Science and Health," owing to one of its most striking characteristics, namely, its entire want of sequence, both in thought and in expression. It abounds in contradictions, not only to be found on the same page, the same paragraph, the same sentence, but often between two words used consecutively. We have never read a book which attempted to be a scientifically sound system which is so full of glaring contradictions, and in which the conclusions were so absolutely disconnected from the premises. Unfortunately their rendering of truth has been given with such an entire want of sense and logic that when read in the light of ordinary intelligence it reads as entire nonsense, and a beautiful ideal and a great truth has been rendered ridiculous, whilst the minds of Christians in general have been shocked.[1]

Such a consensus of opinions from competent judges, which might be indefinitely extended, is strong evidence as to the unreadableness and irrationality of this queer book.

[1] *The Truth and Error of Christian Science*, pp. viii, ix.

CHAPTER VII

CHRISTIAN SCIENCE TEACHING

On the basis of the contents of "Science and Health" as it has been summarized and as supplemented by the other writings of the same author, we may now state and examine the main points of Christian Science teaching.

1. ITS FUNDAMENTAL DENIALS

Christian Science is based, first on the denial of matter, sickness, suffering, pleasure, sin, and death. These denials expressed in the most unequivocal and positive terms are found on almost every page of Mrs. Eddy's writings and are repeated wearisomely an incredible number of times. The author has estimated, on the basis of the average number of reiterations on each page, that in one or another form this denial occurs in "Science and Health" at least three thousand times; and in all her writings it may be asserted not less than ten thousand times. One writer, giving his impression of this endless repetition, says that Mrs. Eddy has made this denial "for the millionth time." It is her obsession and her demon and it never leaves her for one moment.

(1) Denial of Matter. "Matter" in Christian Science is another name for "mortal mind" and is declared to be a "myth," a "delusion," and "nothing." This is not the doctrine of philosophical idealism, as held by Berkeley, Lotze, Paulsen, Bowne, Royce, and many other

thinkers from Plato down to our day. Mrs. Eddy herself says: "Those who formerly sneered at it as foolish and eccentric now declare Bishop Berkeley, David Hume, Ralph Waldo Emerson, and certain German Philosophers, or some unlearned mesmerist, to have been the real originators of Mind Healing." She, however, disclaims this origin and she is right in this. She proceeds: "Emerson's ethics are models of their kind; but even that good man and genial philosopher partially lost his mental faculties before his death, showing that he did not understand the Science of Mind Healing as elaborated in my 'Science and Health'; nor did he pretend to do so." It is certainly amusing to see Mrs. Eddy thus patronize Emerson, and she is entirely correct when she says that he did not "pretend" to understand her "Science."

Philosophical idealism holds to the objective reality of matter as a divine idea and mode of activity, but it does not at all declare it is "nonexistent" and "nothing." Berkeley believed in the existence of the objective world as much as anybody, only he conceived it as being mental or spiritual in nature and having its source and seat in the divine Mind. "I have never doubted," he says, "that fire is hot and that ice is cold." Of him it has been said: "No man ever delighted less to expatiate in the regions of the abstract, the impalpable, the unknown. His heart and soul clung with inseparable tenacity to the concrete realities of the universe."[1] But Christian Science absolutely denies the existence of the objective world except as a baseless delusion of "mortal mind," which is itself another equally baseless delusion. It

[1] Professor James F. Ferrier, quoted in the article on Berkeley in Hastings' *Encyclopedia of Religion and Ethics.*

abolishes the whole framework of nature and boldly declares that "there are no vertebrata, mollusca, or radiata." This contradicts the plain testimony of the senses and the universal experience of mankind, falsifies the mental faculties, and annihilates the material universe at a blow and with a breath. How can Christian Scientists keep up this denial of the objective world and endlessly repeat this monstrous untruth? It shakes confidence in their sincerity and sanity.

Mrs. Eddy evidently had in her mind a confused notion of the psychological and philosophical distinction between subjective experience and objective reality, and she probably meant to make matter a purely subjective idea in the mind and deny it any extramental reality. If she had clearly grasped this distinction and consistently stuck to it she could have carried her scheme through.[1] But unfortunately for her system she upset it and dug a miry pit for herself by making this idea in the mind an "illusion" and "delusion" of "mortal mind" and then making "mortal mind" itself a "delusion," so that she left no reality for matter either out of the mind or in it but reduced it to "nothingness," and thus she made her whole system a delusion of a delusion and threw it into confusion worse confounded. It was at this point that she misunderstood and perverted philosophical idealism, and it was this initial blunder that wrecked her whole scheme and involved her in endless contradictions.

(2) Denial of Sickness. There is no such thing as rheumatism, hernia, tumor, insanity, epilepsy, cataract,

[1] On this point see Mrs. A. D. T. Whitney's thoughtful little book, *The Integrity of Christian Science*, pp. 13–16.

heart disease, cancer, tuberculosis, Bright's disease, neurasthenia, diseased eyes, stomach trouble, dyspepsia, deafness, diseased lungs, rupture, liver complaint, dropsy, kidney disease, diseased bowels, eczema, catarrh, spinal disease, asthma, yet these are the names of diseases found in the headings of the letters on "Fruitage" in "Science and Health," from which their writers claim to have been cured. And yet these diseases are also declared to be "delusions" and "nothing." To say in one breath that they had these "delusions" and base the proof of this fact on the evidence of their senses and then in the next breath affirm, "nor can the material senses bear reliable testimony on the subject of health," gives no logical jolt or sense of contradiction to Christian Scientists.

(3) Denial of Pain and Pleasure. Pain is constantly declared to be a "delusion" of "mortal mind" and "nothing," and pleasure is consigned to the same "nothingness." It is true that at times admission is made that pain and pleasure exist as states of "mortal mind," but none the less is the reality of these states denied, and those who experience them are urged to "deny" them and refuse to believe that they have them. The patient is told that he has no pain, but only thinks that he has. The little child, having injured itself, is told that it does not hurt, and thus a falsehood is almost literally crammed down its throat or forced into its consciousness. That we should be told and asked to believe that we have no pain when agony may be sweeping through the soul like flames of fire, or that we are experiencing no pleasure when we are eating delicious food or quenching intense thirst, or are thrilled with the beauty of a poem or a symphony or

a sunset, or with the joy of love, is to try get us to contradict our immediate consciousness and surest knowledge and believe a lie, and is incredible except when viewed as the delusion of an insane mind or wild fanatic.

(4) Denial of Sin.   Deeper still in falsity is the Christian Science denial of sin.   This also is declared to be mere "myth" and "nothing."   It is said that "man is incapable of sin," for he is an "idea" or "reflection" of God and is as sinless and impeccable as God himself.   "To hold yourself superior to sin," says this false prophetess, "is true wisdom."   This contradicts the individual conscience of every normal person and the universal consciousness and conscience of mankind.   That "all have sinned, and fall short of the glory of God" is not only the express teaching of Scripture from Genesis to Revelation, but it is also written just as plainly in all the histories and stamped upon all the races and classes and upon all the human conduct and character of the world.   "If we say that we have no sin, we deceive ourselves, and the truth is not in us," "and we make" God "a liar."   That any man or woman, however blinded by bigotry or partisan purpose, should stand up before the sorry spectacle of this world, with all its vice and crime and wickedness and woe, and declare that there is no sin and that man cannot sin, passes belief; and yet Christian Scientists are doing this incredible thing every time they read their textbook and express confidence in the founder of their faith.

(5) Denial of Death.   The Christian Science denial of death may strike us as the extremest absurdity of all the irrationalities of this cult, but Mrs. Eddy asserts it calmly and boldly without once losing her composure or moving a muscle of her face.   If she had any sense of

humor we might think she was not meaning to be taken too seriously, but she is always dead in earnest; and her followers do not balk or blink at anything she says. It is true that all her husbands and relatives and students died in due order and she herself followed them in committing this act of mortal belief and delusion, but this does not affect her followers. They still unflinchingly say that death is a "mortal belief" and that if we were only not so foolish as to believe it and were to "deny" it resolutely, there would be no great enemy to fear and no death to die. But as long as Christian Scientists die so regularly and so unanimously we may be permitted to "deny" their theory.[1]

(6) Moral Tendencies of These Denials. Nothing enters more deeply into life than one's philosophy. However subtle and remote from practical affairs it may seem, yet if it be planted as a real belief in the mind and heart it will inevitably work its logical tendencies out into life. "The most practical and important thing about a man," says Mr. G. K. Chesterton, "is still his view of the universe. . . We think the question is not whether the theory of the cosmos affects matters, but whether, in the long run, anything else affects them."

What is the practical tendency of these denials of Christian Science? They first undermine the trust-

[1] Some Christian Scientists actually hold that Mrs. Eddy did not die. After her death the authorities of The Mother Church published a selection of editorials from various newspapers, commenting on her death. Whereupon Mrs. Augusta E. Stetson, of New York, wrote an indignant letter in which she said that such admissions were contradictory and disloyal to the Christian Science teachings and declared in italics, "Mary Baker Eddy never died." See her book *Give God the Glory*, in which she repeatedly makes this assertion.

worthiness of the human mind as an organ of knowledge. They turn the senses, pains, and pleasures into false reports of a false world and thereby overthrow the most familiar and necessary beliefs and turn the whole material universe into a monstrous lie.   Nothing in the objective world is true as we see and experience it, and our very souls are not persons but only reflected ideas of a principle which is an impersonal pantheistic mind.

What effect will trying to believe this have on one's sense of truth and life?   The logical result of it will be to pervert one's intellectual conscience.   When Christian Scientists teach little children to say that they are not hurt when their own consciousness asserts they are suffering pain, what effect do they think such teaching will have on children's sense of truth?   And how can Christian Scientists keep on stultifying their senses and their most vivid experience of reality in suffering and sin, and not blunt their conscience and blur the deepest and sharpest distinctions between truth and error?   There is such a thing as people so saturating their souls with deceit and subverting their very sense of truth that "God sendeth them a working of error, that they should believe a lie" (II Thess. 2:11).   Such a fundamental and pervasive falsity as lies at the root of Christian Science must pervert all the intellectual processes of the mind.

But the denial of matter and of sin cuts much deeper into the moral tissues of life.   It is antinomian in principle and in fruit.   This denial is a very ancient doctrine and its consequences are well known in history.   Among the Gnostic sects of the early Christian centuries were the Manichæans who held that the spiritual being of man was unaffected by the action of matter, and their morals were loose, and there were also the Nicolaitans (Rev. 2:6) who were antinomian libertines. If the flesh is an illusion and sin is nothing the dividing line between virtue and vice grows thin to the vanishing point, and it is then easy to slip from the one into the other. If one really holds to the theory of the nonreality of sin it will not be difficult for his conscience to confuse the flesh and the spirit and to lose all sense of difference between them; and, indeed, there is no difference if "Good is all, and all is good." This doctrine has been a menace to the world both outside and inside the Church in all ages. Let a man once be obsessed with the belief that sin has no reality and is a myth, and there is no sin, however sensual and shocking, that he may not commit without any compunction of conscience or sense of guilt, for he can say, with Browning's "Johannes Agricola in Meditation,"

> I have God's warrant, could I blend
> All hideous sins, as in a cup,
> To drink the mingled venoms up;
> Secure my nature will convert
> The draught to blossoming gladness fast.

As to the followers of this cult, we doubt not that they are generally people above reproach. But we are dealing with the logical tendency of their faith, and their denial of the reality of matter and of sin has an ancient history and its record is not good. It has been prolific of evil and it is still a menace to right thinking and good living.

2. THE PANTHEISM OF CHRISTIAN SCIENCE

Mrs. Eddy repeatedly denies and her followers repeat the denial that her system is pantheistic. But her denials cannot save her from her self-contradictions on this as on other points. She is laboring under a misunderstanding of what pantheism is, owing to her ignorance of the correct meaning of many terms which she uses and to her lack of learning in general. She thinks that pantheism is the theory that matter is intelligent, "mind in matter," as she says countless times. But of course this is not pantheism, which is the doctrine of one infinite, eternal, impersonal substance which is the totality of being. The pantheistic God, therefore, has no consciousness and will in itself, but only such consciousness as appears in men, who are parts of the infinite substance or Absolute, related to it as waves and spray and foam are related to the sea, eternally thrown up out of it and falling back into it. This one substance may be material or spiritual in nature, and Mrs. Eddy's identification of pantheism with "mind in matter" or with "corporeality" is an error.

Now Mrs. Eddy's teaching is pantheistic in the true sense of the term in spite of her denial. The evidence of this runs through the entire web and woof of her writings. "God is supreme: is Mind; is Principle, not person: includes all and is reflected by all that is real and eternal; is Spirit, and Spirit is infinite, is the only substance; is the only life. Man was and is the idea of God; therefore mind never can be in man." This language from one of the earlier editions of "Science and Health" is as pure pantheism as could be expressed in words. Her favorite name for God is "Principle," which is a neuter noun and which she always treats as an impersonal term, never using the personal pronoun "who" but always the impersonal pronoun "which" in relation to it. Her doctrine of prayer is pantheistic, for she denies that prayer has any effect on God but has only subjective influence on us. "To address Deity as a Person impedes spiritual progress and hides Truth." Her doctrine of the nature of man is pantheistic, for she repeatedly declares that man is an "idea" and "reflection" of God and denies that he has any existence separate and apart from God. Her doctrine of sin is pantheistic, for she denies its reality. Her fundamental principle that "God is all in all, and all in all is God," this being her famous "reversible" statement that reads as well backward as forward, is pantheism; in fact this statement is a classical philosophical definition of pantheism. It merges God and the world into one being, which is the sum total of the universe in which man has no enduring personality and is only a drop in the infinite ocean and has no more freedom and responsibility than a wave or the wind. Occidental pantheism, whether it regards the one Substance of the totality of being as materialistic or spiritualistic, does not deny the reality of the objective world, whereas Oriental pantheism resolves the objective world into deceitful appearance or unreal illusion. It is obvious that Mrs. Eddy's pantheism, with its denial of the reality of matter as being a mere illusion, belongs to the Oriental type of pantheism, especially to that of India.

We have not only Mrs. Eddy's written teaching on this point, but also the testimony of her students as to her private and more explicit instruction. In the suit that she brought against Charles Stanley, a student whom she had dismissed from her class, for unpaid tuition, Richard Kennedy testified:

I had nothing to do with the instructions—she told me that she had expelled Mr. Stanley from the class—of his incompetency to understand her science—that it was impossible to convince him of the folly of his times—that his faith in a personal God and prayer was such that she could not overcome it—She used the word "Baptist" in connection with him because he was a Baptist—but it was the same with all the other creeds. So long as they believed in a personal God and the response to prayer, they could not progress in the scientific religion—I performed the manipulation of Mr. Stanley as follows: Mrs. Eddy requested me to rub Mr. Stanley's head and to lay special stress upon the idea that there was no personal God, while I was rubbing him. I never entirely gave up my belief in a personal God, though my belief was pretty well shaken up.[1]

The moral tendency of pantheism is to dull conscience and relax all sense of obligation and virtue, for it denies sin and annuls freedom and responsibility and obliterates all distinction between good and evil as being equally determined and necessary; and whenever pantheism saturates the thought and life of a people, as in India, it leads to unspeakable moral degradation.

3. CHRISTIAN SCIENCE AND MARRIAGE

We have already seen that in "Science and Health" Mrs. Eddy sets forth her peculiar views on marriage in unmistakable terms. Marriage is merely a temporary arrangement to be regarded only as long as we believe in "mortal mind." "The human mind will at length demand a higher affection," and "there will ensue a fermentation over this as over many other reforms." Her various statements are sugar-coated with asseverations that "in Christian Science the gospel of marriage is not without the law, and the solemn vow of fidelity," but these cannot sweeten her express teachings which contain a deadly poison to the marriage problem. The author supplements the dangerous views already quoted with

[1] Milmine, *History*, p.145.

even more explicit teaching as found in her "Miscellaneous Writings" as follows:

Until time matures human growth, marriage and progeny will continue unprohibited in Christian Science. We look to future generations for ability to comply with absolute Science, when marriage shall be found to be man's oneness with God—the unity of eternal Love. At present, more spiritual conception and education of children will serve to illustrate the superiority of spiritual power over sensuous, and usher in the dawn of God's creation, wherein they neither marry nor are given in marriage, but are as the angels. To abolish marriage at this period, and maintain morality and generation, would put ingenuity to ludicrous shifts; yet this is possible in Science, although it is to-day problematic. The time cometh, and now is, for spiritual and eternal existence to be recognized and understood in Science. All is Mind. Human procreation, birth, life, and death are subjective states of the human erring mind; they are the phenomena of mortality, nothingness, that illustrate mortal mind and body as one, and neither real and eternal.[1]

Let it not be overlooked that while it is admitted that "to abolish marriage at this period" would result in "ludicrous shifts," nevertheless it is declared without qualification that "yet this is possible in Science," and it is further declared that "the time cometh, and now is" when this possibility should be "recognized and understood in Science." What is this but teaching that marriage might and ought to be "abolished" now by those that recognize and understand it in Science?

Mrs. Eddy holds that "generation rests on no sexual basis," and says: "The propagation of their species by butterfly, bee, and moth, without the customary presence of male companions, is a discovery corroborative of the Science of Mind, because it shows that the origin and continuance of these insects rests on Principle apart from

[1] *Miscellaneous Writings*, p. 286.

material conditions." Alleging that in the birth of Jesus "the Science of being overshadowed the sense of the Virgin mother, with a full recognition that Spirit is the basis of being," she calls "His birth what everyone's should be." She says that "I never knew more than one individual who believed in agamogenesis; she was unmarried, a lovely character, was suffering from incipent insanity, and a Christian Scientist cured her." "It is well authenticated, however, that one of Mrs. Eddy's disciples some years back took Mrs. Eddy's words at face value and calmly announced to a wonder-struck world the immaculate conception and birth of a son."[1]

The extremest and most offensive statement on the subject of marriage was made by Mrs. Eddy at the dedication of her Boston church. Mr. Peabody gives the following account of it:

The most impressive and conspicuous incident in Christian Science history was the dedication in June, 1906, of the "Mother Church" in Boston, a beautiful building that cost upwards of two million dollars. In order to get her views regarding marriage before the faithful, in the most impressive manner, Mrs. Eddy incorporated them in her message which was read at the church dedication ceremonies. She took the bit in her teeth, as it were, and notwithstanding efforts to dissuade her or induce her to modify her statement, insisted upon getting her views before her following in their most extreme and obnoxious form, characterizing marriage as "synonomous with legalized lust." It has been denied by Mrs. Eddy's press agents that she gave utterance to this opinion of marriage; but it will be found in her dedication message as published in the Christian Science Sentinel for June, 1906, and the Christian Science Journal for July, 1906.[2]

That any respectable man or woman should publicly stigmatize the holy relation of marriage as "synonomous

[1] Marsten, *The Mask of Christian Science*, p. 133.
[2] *Masquerade*, p. 165.

with legalized lust" is an offense against one of the most sacred and vital institutions of the world.

In accordance with her teaching that "generation rests on no sexual basis," Mrs. Eddy declares that there is no hereditary transmission of traits from parents to children. In the chapter on "Questions and Answers" in her "Miscellaneous Writings" she asks, "Does Christian Science set aside the law of transmission, parental desires, and good or bad influences on the unborn child?" and answers:

Whatever is real is right and eternal; hence the immutable and just law of Science, that God is good only, and can transmit to man and the universe nothing evil, or unlike himself. For the innocent babe to be born a lifelong sufferer because of his parents' mistakes or sins, were sore injustice. Science sets aside man as a creator, and unfolds the eternal harmonies of the only living and true origin, God. According to the beliefs of the flesh, both good and bad traits of the parents are transmitted to their helpless offspring, and God is supposed to impart to man this fatal power. It is cause for rejoicing that this belief is as false as it is remorseless.[1]

Yet in direct contradiction with this teaching she affirms, in her textbook, parental propensities are inherited:

The offspring of heavenly minded parents must inherit more intellect, better balanced minds, and sounder constitutions. If some fortuitous circumstance places spiritual children in the arms of gross parents, these beautiful children early droop and die, like tropical flowers born amid Alpine snows. If perchance they live to become parents, in their turn they may reproduce in their own helpless little ones the grosser traits of their ancestors. What hope of happiness, what noble ambition can inspire the child who inherits propensities that must either be overcome or reduce him to a loathsome wreck.

This is only one among many positive self-contradictions that are found in these writings.

[1] *Miscellaneous Writings*, pp. 71, 72.

This teaching on the subject of marriage is not without its practical effect among Christian Scientists. When Mrs. Eddy asks, "Is marriage nearer right than celibacy?" and answers, "Human knowledge inculcates that it is, while Science indicates that it is not," this cannot fail to have some influence upon her devotees, and there are painful facts bearing on this point. To quote from Mr. Peabody:

Mrs. Eddy, having been married three or four times, now emphatically disapproves of marriage, and a marriage between Christian Scientists is decidedly objectionable. There has never been a marriage in the Christian Science church. There is no Christian Science ceremony and no Christian Science official authorized to perform a marriage. The marriage relation, as such, is regarded as sensuous and impure, and the marriage of an official of the church in any part of the country would mean instant loss of power and influence together with his office and its emoluments. . . With this objection to marriage goes also the objection to children, so that the birth of children in Christian Science families is of rare occurrence and is regarded as evidence of unspiritual living and is decidedly discrediting. "Sensual and mortal beliefs, material suppositions of life," Mrs. Eddy calls children. The effects of this teaching are shown in the difference between Christian Science Sunday schools and Christian Sunday schools. The membership of the Methodist, Baptist, and Presbyterian Sunday school is about the same as their church membership; while in Christian Science Sunday schools there is but one child for every five members.[1]

Dr. Powell also asks: "Why has not The Mother Church in Boston, with its seating capacity of five thousand and its resident membership doubtless much larger, made provisions for a larger Sunday school than one of two hundred and fifty members?"[2]

[1] *Masquerade*, pp. 163, 164.
[2] *Christian Science*, p. 212. In the United States Census of 1906 the Christian Scientists reported 82,332 members and only 16,116 Sunday-school scholars. See H. K. Carroll's *Religious Forces of the United States*, p. LVIII.

What is the effect of such teaching on domestic relations in the home? The author here quotes from Dr. L. P. Powell, who is one of the most thoroughly informed and most impartial writers on the whole subject of Christian Science as he made a wide investigation of it and is always quick to see and acknowledge the good that is in it. In immediate connection with the testimony which follows he says: "I know that some families have been blessed by the conversion of their members to Christian Science. I know that a new conception of the dignity and spiritual value of self-control has been lodged in many a mind. I know that many a husband has been reclaimed from dissipation, many a wife from frivolity, by the call of the spiritual which in spite of all its errors does echo from 'Science and Health,'" One who writes in this spirit can be trusted when he testifies as follows:

I could give instances—for I have made inquiries far and wide—in which families that have for long years known only happiness and concord have suddenly become the prey of discord and division, in which the love of husbands for wives and fathers for children has dissolved into an unfortunate aloofness, in which wives have ceased, except in name, to live as wives, and mothers have come to think of children as millstones round their necks, in which daughters have ceased to be daughters except before the world, and sisters have separated for all time from sisters who declined to go with them into Christian Science, in which lovers have broken their engagement and friends have given up their lifelong friendship for no reason save a difference in the point of view concerning what is nothing after all except a problem in pure metaphysics.[1]

The doctrine that marriage is "synonomous with legalized lust" and that in this world "the human mind will at length demand a higher affection" and "man must

[1] *Christian Science*, pp. 204, 205.

find permanence and peace in a more spiritual adherence" may at first sight seem to lend itself to purity and be a reënforcement in the battle of the spirit against the flesh. But flesh and spirit lie close together and it is but a slip from the one into the other. Human experience bears abundant witness that all theories of "perfection" and "entire sanctification" are attended with the danger of lapse into sensuality. "Wherefore let him that thinketh he standeth take heed lest he fall." The early Christian churches were plagued and scandalized with various Gnostic sects that proclaimed the "nothingness" of matter and of sin and then practiced the grossest immorality. The Christian Science doctrine of marriage has in it this poisonous germ. People that believe that the marriage relation should be displaced by "a higher affection" and "a more spiritual adherence" will not find it difficult to believe that they are so far advanced in "Science" that they can make the substitution. In plain truth, "a more spiritual adherence" may easily slip into free love.

Mrs. Josephine Curtis Woodbury, who was once a leader in the Christian Science movement and "emerged," to use her own words, "from the toils after many years of close association with the head of the new church," referring to marriage in her article in the Arena for May, 1899, says: "One may well hesitate to touch on this delicate topic in print, yet only thus can the immoral possibilities and the utter lack of divine inspiration in 'Christian Science' be shown."

The author closes the study of the Christian Science doctrine of marriage by quoting the view of Dr. Francis E. Marsten, a careful and conscientious student of the system:

Call the flesh an "illusion" if you please, call the life of earth a dream life, all its most sacred relations only phantoms and shadows, educate the young into the belief that sin is nothing, and when the moving pictures of the sensuous life enter with the lusts of the carnal nature, it will be nothing strange if the dream of the Nicolaitans of the first century is dreamed over again in this twentieth century. These doctrines touching on marriage promulgated by the "Mother" are so subtle and insidious that they constitute a formidable menace to social well-being. They strike not at a human, but at a divine institution.[1]

4. CHRISTIAN SCIENCE AND CHRISTIAN DOCTRINES

Christian Science, though it started only as a method of mind healing, rapidly developed into a religion with a church and a creed and an elaborate system of theology. It is also professedly a form of the Christian religion, and, indeed, it proclaims itself to be a later and completer and even the final and perfect form. It apparently accepts the Bible and Christ and God after the Christian manner, and an uncritical reader of the textbook and bible of this new religion in his unsophisticated innocence might think that it is only another if not improved form of Christianity, only one Christian denomination more. Do not Christian Scientists read the Bible and pray in their churches? And is it not, then, sectarian narrowness and bigotry on the part of Christian churches that they do not recognize Christian Science churches as being of the same faith?

But there is abundant reason for the fact that Christian churches do not recognize Christian Science churches as being in any true sense Christian. This is not at all an attitude and spirit of bigotry and uncharity, but is only an honest recognition of a plain fact. Mrs. Eddy herself repudiates the historical form of Christianity as

[1] *The Mask of Christian Science*, p. 130.

utterly bound up with "mortal mind" and therefore false, and she and her church will have no part or lot with it. Christians and Christian Scientists cannot walk together because they do not agree in any distinctively Christian doctrine. The whole Christian system is accepted by these two parties in fundamentally different senses that are utterly exclusive of each other. In a word, Christian Science drives a dislocating plowshare through the Bible from Genesis to Revelation and leaves it a different book in every word and idea. It is not simply a variant form of historic Christianity, but it is another and antagonistic religion as far removed from Christianity as is Buddhism, with which, indeed, it has close affinities. Christian Science really denies every Christian fact and perverts and falsifies every Christian doctrine, in the sense in which these facts and doctrines have universally been and still are understood by the Church catholic and the Christian world. This has already been seen in detail, and the author will now only briefly recapitulate its teaching on these fundamental doctrines.

(1) Its doctrine of God is pantheism, for it denies the personality of God, declaring "God is not person" but "God is Principle," a name as impersonal, to use Mrs. Eddy's own analogy, as "the principle of mathematics," merging God with the totality of being or the universe, and rendering him inaccessible to prayer; and thus God is lost in a pantheistic world and religion is cut up by the roots.

There is usually an element of truth lurking behind Mrs. Eddy's confused statements, and the truth in her oft-repeated assertion that "God is infinite, the only Life, Substance, Spirit, or Soul, the only intelligence in the

universe, including man," is that God is the only absolute
One who has existence in himself.   But he has also created
the universe and finite spirits, who have relative being
dependent on him; yet they are separate from him and
are not to be included or merged in him.

(2) Its doctrine of creation is pantheistic. It represents the whole creation as being simply an unfolding
of God. "This creation consists of the unfolding of
spiritual ideas and their identities, which are embraced
in the infinite Mind and forever reflected.   These ideas
range from infinitesimal to infinity, and the highest
ideas are the sons and daughters of God." Man is the
"idea" and "reflection" of God, and he "is incapable of
sin."

How, then, did "matter" arise in this purely divine
universe and how did "mortal mind" originate in man
who is an idea of God?   We are asked to believe that
the second chapter of Genesis "contains a statement
of this material view of God and the universe;" and this
statement "is a lie"!   "There went up a mist from the
earth," and this mist is the origin of "matter" and of
"mortal mind."   But even granting this dogmatic assumption, how did the "mist" originate in a world that was
simply the "unfolding of spiritual ideas," or of God?   Mrs.
Eddy tells us that matter, sickness, suffering, sin, and
death are all "delusions" that arise out of "mortal mind":
but how did "mortal mind" arise, especially in a world
in which "God is all" and "all is good"?   "Where the
spirit of God is, and there is no place where God is not,
evil becomes nothing."   Then how in such a world or
rather in such a God did "mortal mind" get started?
Mrs. Eddy does not tell us.   Here is an unplumbed

mystery in her system of interpretation on which she throws no light and of which she does not appear to be aware. She cannot fall back upon the Scriptural doctrine that "God made man upright; but they have sought out many inventions" (Eccl. 7:29), for in her scheme man in his pristine purity was an idea of God "incapable of sin." How original man ever got this dreadful thing she calls "mortal mind" and just what its relation to man is, are insoluble puzzles in her system that must be left in the same heap with her other self-contradictions.

(3) Its doctrine of man is also pantheistic, for it reduces man to an idea or reflection of God and denies that man has any personality and existence apart from God. Though Mrs. Eddy denies that she is a pantheist, because she ignorantly confuses pantheism with "a belief in the intelligence of matter," yet she is just as certainly a thoroughgoing pantheist as Spinoza himself.

(4) Its doctrine of Christ is a strange dualism, unheard of in all the heresies of Church history, according to which Jesus is "the highest human corporeal concept of the divine idea," apparently meaning God, incarnated in "mortal mind," and Christ is "the divine manifestation of God, which comes to the flesh to destroy incarnate error." Such a "concept" leads us to suspect that she has taken away our Lord and we know not where to look for him.

(5) Its doctrine of the Holy Spirit is grotesque and abhorrent, for it identifies the Holy Spirit with "Divine Science."

(6) Its doctrine of matter, sickness, suffering, sin, and death is an utter denial of the reality of these things except as pure delusions or false beliefs of "mortal mind"

which is itself a false state of belief, and thereby it falsifies our senses and our most primary intuitions and surest forms of knowledge and blows the universe into nothingness with a single breath of denial. Such a monstrous absurdity is contradicted not only by all our philosophy, science, psychology, and ethics, but also by the express and implied teachings of the Bible from the first verse to the last. On this theory sin is only a bad dream and all we need do to get rid of it is to stab ourselves broad awake. This doctrine of the nothingness of matter and of sin is of ancient Gnostic lineage and it has lost none of its antinomian tendency. It is allied to the pantheistic doctrine of illusion that saturates the Orient and is so productive of immorality. This denial of the very possibility of sin logically sweeps away all barriers against the flesh and opens the gates for sensuality to flood the soul. If Christian Scientists do not give way to this tendency it is because they are better than their doctrine.

(7) Its doctrine of prayer reduces prayer to a state of silent meditation which cannot affect God but only influences man. "God is not influenced by man." Such a prayer is only a soliloquy and becomes impossible after the secret of its true nature is once discovered. One cannot really pray to "Principle" any more than to "the principle of mathematics," or to the precession of the equinoxes.

(8) Its doctrine of the atonement is a purely moral influence theory, declaring that "the atonement of Christ reconciles man to God, not God to man." Such an atonement makes no real provision for the divine forgiveness of sin, and there appears to be no such forgiveness

in Christian Science, for "to remit the penalty due for sin, would be for Truth to pardon error." "Sin is not forgiven; we cannot escape its penalty. . . Suffering for sin is all that destroys it." Even in The Lord's Prayer the petition, "Forgive us our debts," is bleached into the colorless sentiment, "Love is reflected in love." And so there is no real gospel in Christian Science, no good news of an atoning Saviour and a forgiving Father.

(9) Its doctrine of ordinances rejects baptism and wounds and insults the Founder of Christianity by setting aside the Last Supper which he instituted with his disciples and commanded all his followers, "This do in remembrance of me," the most precious ordinance of the Christian Church, and presumes to substitute for it the celebration of the "morning breakfast" at which Jesus was present with his disciples on the shore of Galilee. But even this parody of a "Communion Service" was discontinued by Mrs. Eddy in her Mother Church in Boston in 1908. It was, indeed, an ordinance better honored in the breach than in the observance.

(10) Its doctrine of marriage discredits this union as a temporary condescension to an infirmity of "mortal mind," which is really to be gotten rid of as soon as possible as being "synonomous with legalized lust" and to be replaced by those who are versed in "Science" with "a higher affection" and "a more spiritual adherence"; a doctrine which is logically subversive of the holy relation of marriage and tends to moral laxity.

(11) Its doctrine of the Bible is that it is to be inpreted in "a metaphysical sense" according to which everything means something wholly different from what the words naturally mean and from what the entire

Christian world has always believed and ever will believe they do mean, and which turns all the sense and sanity of the book into absurdities as false and grotesque as the absurdities of Christian Science itself.

(12) Its doctrine of healing is that mind, meaning the mind of God, destroys disease as a mere illusion or nothing. This is a form of mind cure which will be considered in a later chapter.

(13) Its doctrine of eschatology. "Eschatology" is another word we have not found in Mrs. Eddy's writings, and if she had lighted on it, it would surely have been another sonorous polysyllable in her vocabulary as delectable to her as "the blessed word Mesopotamia" was to Mrs. Partington. But though she knows not the word yet she has the thing, and her eschatology is as peculiar and pantheistic as the rest of her scheme. As regards this world, she looks forward to a time when marriage will be superseded by "a more spiritual adherence," when children will be produced without sexual union, and when death itself will cease to act as a fatal delusion of mortal mind.

As regards the other world or final state, Mrs. Eddy says that the corporeal senses and all sense knowledge and pleasure and pain will vanish along with the bad dream of the body and the spirit will survive as an idea of God, having no personality or existence apart from God. What sort of existence this would be we cannot tell, but it would appear that it cannot have any consciousness and certainly no personality. All things will dissolve into their original Principle, the clouds and mist and raindrops will go back into the eternal sea out of which they came, pantheism will have its perfect work and end, or rather it will keep up its eternal round of impersonal and fatalistic change.

Such is the way Christian Science perverts Christian doctrines and gives us for bread a stone, and for fish a serpent. Probably few people outside of the Christian Science churches know what a destructive and absurd system of doctrine it is, innocently thinking it is only a harmless vagary; and it must be the fact that many people in the Christian Science churches are but little better informed as to the true teaching of the system, not having read for themselves or really understood their obscure and mystifying textbook.

This is the cult that is called "Christian Science," the "so-called Christian Science" which Professor G. T. Ladd brands as "an almost equally grotesque mixture of crude pantheism, misunderstood psychological and philosophical truths, and truly Christian beliefs and conceptions."[1] If all the vocabularies of all languages had been ransacked for a name, two more inappropriate words could not have been found to be applied to this system; and it is a pity and scandal that two of the most significant and noblest words in the English tongue should have been prostituted to the ignoble use of naming this false religion and scientific monstrosity. As Voltaire said of the "Holy Roman Empire" that it was not an empire and was not Roman and was not holy, so must it be said of Christian Science that it is not science and it is not Christian.

[1] *Philosophy of Religion*, vol. I, p. 167.

CHAPTER VIII

THE CHRISTIAN SCIENCE CHURCH

When Mrs. Eddy began to teach her system of mind cure she had no thought of founding a religion and a church. The title of her book "Science and Health" shows this, the addition "With Key to the Scriptures" being an afterthought which was added in 1884, several years after she began to dream of the day when the church bells would ring in her honor. She not only had no thought of a church, but she expressly declared against such an institution.

It is true, however, that she began to organize her work at an early date, for she was farseeing enough to know that it could not grow and last unless it had an organized form.

1. FOUNDING OF THE CHURCH OF CHRIST SCIENTIST

In June, 1875, eight of Mrs. Eddy's students met together under the name of "the Christian Scientists" and subscribed money to have her address them each Sunday, and in July of the next year they formed "The Christian Scientists' Association." These loose associations, however, did not meet the needs of Mrs. Eddy and her students. Her followers were practically all from Christian churches, and they found the air of a mere metaphysical association too thin and cold to supply their emotional and religious demands. Mrs. Eddy, who was always an opportunist and was quick to see and adapt herself to new situations, responded with alacrity to the call of the hour. In fact, this turn of affairs gave her a new idea and one that dominated her whole after life.

In 1879 she founded her first church organization, naming it "The Church of Christ, Scientist," a charter being applied for on August 6 of that year. All these proceedings were conducted secretly so as not to come to the knowledge of the "mesmerists" Spofford and Kennedy, even care being taken to select a notary before whom the papers could be signed who could be vouched for by one of the members as having no affiliation with these dangerous people.[1] The purpose of the corporation was stated to be "to carry on and transact the business necessary to the worship of God," Boston was named as the place where the church was to be located, and there were twenty-six charter members.

For sixteen months the church had no regular place of meeting and services were held in the homes of various members in Lynn and Boston. The minutes of the meetings show that attendance at these early services was very small, sometimes falling as low as four or five. The service consisted of silent prayer or Mrs. Eddy's interpretation of The Lord's Prayer and readings from "Science and Health" and from the Scriptures. Mrs. Eddy usually delivered an address, her subject frequently being "mesmerism." The record for September 5, 1880, reads as follows:

[1] The facts as to the founding of the Christian Science Church are mostly taken from Milmine, *History*, ch. XIV, and from Mrs. Eddy's "Historical Sketch" found in the *Manual of the Mother Church*.

Meeting opened by Mrs. Damon in the usual way. Mrs. M. B. G. Eddy, having completed her summer vacation, was present and delivered a discourse on Mesmerism. Whole number in attendance, twenty-two.

The record shows that the subject on the following Sunday was again "Mesmerism." On December 12, 1880, the Christian Scientists began to hold their services in Hawthorne Hall on Park Street, Boston, and the following passage from Miss Milmine's "History" gives an interesting picture of these meetings:

Mrs. Eddy usually preached and conducted the services, though occasionally one of her students took her place, and now and again a minister of some other denomination was invited to occupy the pulpit. In spite of the fact that she was always effective on the rostrum, Mrs. Eddy seemed to dread these Sunday services. The necessity for wearing glasses embarrassed her. When she sometimes wore glasses in her own home, she apologized for doing so, explaining that it was a habit she often rose above, but that at times the mesmerists were too strong for her. She believed that the mesmerists set to work upon her before the hour of the weekly services, and on Sunday morning her faithful students were sometimes called to her house to treat her against Kennedy, Spofford, and Arens, until she took the train for Boston.

After her formal removal from Lynn to Boston in 1882, "she constantly learned from her new associates, even to the extent of resolutely breaking herself of certain ungrammatical habits of speech—no mean achievement for a woman above sixty." It certainly is an astonishing fact that this woman who had passed her sixtieth birthday and was yet utterly unknown outside of a little circle in and around Boston and was generally regarded with pitying amusement or contempt as a visionary with a queer obsession, afterwards became and now is one of the most widely known women in the world and to-day is the religious leader of a considerable body of people.

Mrs. Eddy became "pastor" of her church in 1881. "When others preached," writes Mrs. Josephine C. Woodbury, who was once one of her closest associates, "she occasionally attended the church whereof she was nominally pastor, and took some part in the service. Once she held a baptismal service without water, though her memory failed her in repeating the formula prepared by herself; and sometimes there was a communion service, without water or wine. Most Sundays, however, she worshiped God in the privacy of her own home. If wonder was expressed at her absence, the adoring disciples replied, 'How could she, the divinely inspired, bear to hear ordinary preaching.' "[1]

The place of meeting of the Christian Science Church was removed from Hawthorne Hall to Chickering Hall and finally to its permanent location on Falmouth Street in the fashionable Back Bay district. The purchase of this location was itself a complicated and curious transaction in which Mrs. Eddy played a characteristic part, finally getting the lot entirely into her own hands by what she herself called "a circuitous, novel way" and giving her absolute control of the church property.[2] On this lot was built the original "Mother Church," a gray granite structure seating 1100, which was dedicated on January 6, 1895. Eleven years later in 1906 there was dedicated the splendid marble church called the "Annex" which seats 5000, the whole property costing more than $2,000,000. The twenty-six charter members of 1879 had grown by 1894 to 2978 as reported at the second annual

[1] *The Arena*, May 1899, pp. 564, 565.
[2] The full story of this affair is told by Miss Milmine, *History*, pp. 399–406.

business meeting held in that year. Money to build the original "Mother Church" with its imposing "Annex" had flowed into the treasury in copious streams and the Christian Science Church was at the high tide of prosperity.

2. DISSENSIONS IN THE CHRISTIAN SCIENCE CHURCH

The course of Church history never did run smooth, and Christian Science has had its full share. Dissensions among the followers of Mrs. Eddy began early. Her peculiar temperament, jealous and irritable, dictatorial and intolerant, left small room for other personalities of any individuality and independence and no room for opinions different from hers. We have already seen how she became involved in quarrels and lawsuits with student after student in her early years in Lynn, and this unhappy disposition and fate plagued her to the end. Many of her most prominent and efficient followers and workers withdrew from her fellowship and church, some of them going off to start rival healing movements. Christian Science has given birth to a surprising number of sects or "denominations." "Disgruntled Christian Scientists," says Miss Milmine, "usually went off and started a church of their own, and there were by this time (1896) almost as many 'reformed' varieties of Christian Science as there were dissenters. Mrs. Gestefield taught one kind in Chicago, Mrs. Crosse another kind in Boston, Frank Mason another in Brooklyn, Captain Sabin was soon to teach another in Washington, while nearly all the students who had quarreled with Mrs. Eddy or broken away from her were teaching or practicing some variety of mind cure."

The first serious dissension in Mrs. Eddy's church and withdrawal from it occurred in 1881 when eight prominent members signed the following statement:

We, the undersigned, while we acknowledge and appreciate the understanding of Truth imparted to us by our Teacher, Mrs. Mary B. G. Eddy, led by Divine Intelligence to perceive with sorrow that departure from the straight and narrow road (which alone leads to growth of Christlike virtues) made manifest by frequent ebullitions of temper, love of money, and the appearance of hypocrisy, cannot longer submit to such Leadership; therefore, without aught of hatred, revenge or petty spite in our hearts, from a sense of duty alone, to her, the Cause, and ourselves, do most respectfully withdraw our names from the Christian Science Association and Church of Christ (Scientist).

> S. DURANT,
> MARGARET J. DUNSHEE,
> DORCAS B. RAWSON,
> ELIZABETH G. STUART,
> JANE L. STRAW,
> ANNA B. NEWMAN,
> JAMES C. HOWARD,
> MIRANDA M. RICE.

21st October, 1881.

These resignations came to Mrs. Eddy as a complete surprise, and no wonder she was filled with indignation, for it must have shocked "the Discoverer and Founder" of this new faith to find herself charged with heresy, bad temper, the love of money, and hypocrisy. But she quickly recovered her poise and, instead of accepting the eight resignations, notified the resigning members that they were liable to expulsion and summoned them to appear at a church meeting. They refused to appear, but at the meeting two more members, including the secretary of the church, resigned, stating that they "could no longer entertain the subject of Mesmerism which had lately been made uppermost in the meetings and in Mrs. Eddy's talks." Mrs. Eddy was left with scarcely a dozen students in Lynn, and this first schism was a blow to her church in that city from which it has not recovered to this day. The secession of 1881 was followed by a more serious division in 1888. Trouble had been brewing for several years over a variety of causes. Some of Mrs. Eddy's students were disillusionized, including Mrs. Sarah Crosse, editor of the Journal. The chief trouble, however, arose over a notorious case in obstetrics. One of her students, Mrs. Abbey H. Corner, had attended her own daughter in childbirth, and both mother and child had died. The case aroused wide indignation, action was brought against Mrs. Corner, and then Mrs. Eddy completely repudiated her own student, though the Christian Scientists' Association stood by Mrs. Corner and paid her attorney out of its treasury. A stormy meeting of the association followed and thirty-two members resigned from it. However, they found themselves confronted and blocked by one of Mrs. Eddy's by-laws, which read:

Resolved, That everyone who wishes to withdraw without reason shall be considered to have broken his oath.
Resolved, That breaking the Christian Scientists' oath is immorality.

Members had already been expelled for this "immorality." The dissenting faction got hold of the books of the association and refused to surrender them until Mrs. Eddy signed the letters of dismissal as president of the association. The withdrawal of these thirty-two from less than two hundred members again seriously weakened Mrs. Eddy's church. But she always quickly rallied after these losses and smoothed over the secession of

1888 by writing in the Journal of September in that year: "The late much ado about nothing arose solely from mental malicious practice, and the audible falsehood designed to stir up strife between brethren, for the purpose of placing Christian Science in the hands of aspirants for place and power." But she was always expert at keeping beyond the reach of the law and it was at this juncture that she secured the service of Dr. E. J. Foster as "assistant in obstetrics," and announced in the Journal: "Doctor Foster will teach the anatomy and surgery of obstetrics, and I, its metaphysics. The combination of his knowledge of Christian Science with his anatomical skill, renders him a desirable teacher in this department of my college. In twenty years' practice he has not had a single case of mortality at childbirth."

Whenever anyone, especially a woman, became prominent in the Christian Science Church and appeared to be looming up as a rival of its "Discoverer and Founder," this exalted personage soon found a way of removing her. One of her students who was overtaken by this unhappy fate was Mrs. Josephine Curtis Woodbury, who had been associated with Mrs. Eddy as one of her foremost teachers and healers since 1879. She it was who gave birth to a son in 1890, as the result, as her followers believed, of an "immaculate conception," the possibility of which had been taught by Mrs. Eddy herself. The child was named "The prince of peace" and was often called "Little Immanuel." By the time of its birth, however, strained relations had arisen between the two women, and Mrs. Eddy promptly branded it "an imp of Satan." Mrs. Woodbury had imagination and was a woman of much greater culture than Mrs. Eddy and was able to give to

Christian Science "an emotional coloring which was very distasteful to Mrs. Eddy herself." She had preached and lectured east and west and had conducted a school of her own in Boston, and all this was viewed with jealousy by Mrs. Eddy, and she soon found a way of excluding and then excommunicating her dangerous rival. Mrs. Woodbury now renounced Christian Science and all its works and especially its "Discoverer and Founder" in an article in the Arena of May, 1899, in which she says, "the writer has emerged from the toils after many years of close association with the head of the new church." Mrs. Eddy promptly retaliated the next month in her annual message to the Mother Church in which she used language which disclosed what fountains of rage and bitterness were hidden in the heart of her whom Christian Scientists are fond of characterizing as "a sweet-spirited and gentle woman." Mrs. Woodbury's husband died almost immediately after the appearance of her article in the Arena, and this fact turns some of Mrs. Eddy's words into daggers. "In language," says Mr. Peabody, "seldom or never before equaled for cruelty and brutality, Mrs. Eddy assailed Mrs. Woodbury. Pretending, herself, to be 'the woman arrayed with the sun,' spoken of in the book of Revelation, Mrs. Eddy denounced Mrs. Woodbury as the Babylonish woman there referred to." We give only a few sentences from this address which was read from the pulpit of the Mother Church in June, 1899:

The doom of the Babylonish woman referred to in Revelation is being fulfilled. This woman, drunken with the blood of the saints and with the blood of the martyrs of Jesus, drunk of the wine of her fornication, would enter even the church and retaining the heart of the harlot and the purpose of the destroying angel. . . poison such as drink of the living water. . . Double unto double, according to

her work: in the cup which she hath filled, fill to her double.   For
she saith in her heart I am no widow. . .   Therefore shall her plague
come in one day, death, mourning and famine: for strong is the Lord
who judgeth her.   That which the revelator saw in spiritual vision
will be accomplished.   The Babylonish woman is fallen: and who
shall mourn over the widowhood of lust, of her that hath become
the habitation of devils, and the hold of every foul spirit and the
cage of every unclean bird.[1]

Christian Scientists would be glad to forget and especially to have the public forget this odious language,
but it was published in the Christian Science Sentinel
where it can be read to this day.

As Christian Science churches were founded in other
cities than Boston they began to acquire influence and their
pastors became leaders and attained prominence.   Mrs.
Augusta E. Stetson was pastor of a specially strong church
in New York, Mrs. Ewing was pastor of such a church
in Chicago, Mrs. Leonard in Brooklyn, Mrs. Williams in
Buffalo, Mrs. Norcross in Denver, and Mrs. Steward in
Toronto.   Mrs. Eddy began to scent danger of rivalry
and of the possible beginning of differing creeds and cults
and budding denominations in these churches, and she
took prompt and effective measures to cut short any
such tendencies.   In the Journal of April, 1895, she announced without warning that there were to be no more
pastors or preachers, but instead a First and a Second
Reader and that the Sunday sermon was to consist only
of extracts from the Bible and from "Science and Health."
Her first arrangement was that the First Reader would
read from the Bible and then the Second Reader would
follow with the selection from her own book, but she
soon reversed this order, and now it is the Second Reader

[1] *Masquerade*, pp. 10–14.

that reads from the Bible and the First Reader that reads
from "Science and Health." This order emptied at one
fell swoop every Christan Science pulpit of its pastor.
"In 1895 I ordained the Bible and 'Science and Health'
with 'Key to the Scriptures,' as the Pastor, on this
planet, of all the churches of the Christian Science denomination." "Did anyone expect such a revelation,
such a new departure would be given?" humbly wrote
one of the deposed pastors in the August Journal. "No,
not in the way it came. . . Such disclosures are too
high for us to perceive. To One alone did the message
come." Mrs. Eddy thus made it certain that there would
be no successor to herself as "Pastor" of The Mother
Church and no more "pastors" anywhere in the Christian
Science churches, for she had made the Bible and her
own book "the Pastor on this planet" for all time.

The order to retire from the pulpit as pastor fell with
special hardship on Mrs. Stetson in New York. She
also, like Mrs. Woodbury, was a woman of finer fiber and
broader culture than Mrs. Eddy, and she had built up a
flourishing and influential church in the metropolis. She
had, however, become altogether too conspicuous and was
filling too large a place in the public eye. It was also
being rumored that she was in training to succeed Mrs.
Eddy as the head and leader of Christian Science, and
this in itself was a mortal sin. She bowed to the decree
to retire from the pulpit of her own church and wrote a
letter to Mrs. Eddy, addressed to "My precious Leader,"
in which she protested her loyalty in nauseating terms,
which yet made the impression that she was protesting altogether too much. She had announced the plan of building a new and magnificent church on the fashionable

Riverside Drive in New York which was to "rival in beauty of architecture any other religious structure in America." Such a project looked too much like a rival to the two million dollar Mother Church in Boston, and Mrs. Eddy promptly put her foot on it. It was announced in her church organ that Mrs. Eddy was not pleased "with what purport to be plans of First Church of Christ Scientist of New York City, for she learned of this proposed rival to The Mother Church for the first time, in the daily press." The editorial further stated that "three leading facts remain immortal in the history of Christian Science," namely:

1. This Science is already established, and it has the support of all true Christian Scientists throughout the world.

2. Any competition or any rivalry in Christian Science is abnormal, and will expose and explode itself.

3. Any attempt at rivalry or superiority in Christian Science is unchristian; therefore it is unscientific. The great Teacher said: "As ye would that men should do to you, do ye."

But still Mrs. Stetson loomed large in New York, and Mrs. Eddy could endure no rival priestess and altar anywhere. At length the New York leader was summoned to appear before the directors of The Mother Church in Boston where she was subjected to a kind of court-martial trial. She was found guilty of the following charges as summarized by Miss Milmine:

"Erroneous teaching of Christian Science; the exercise of undue influence over her students, which tended to hinder their moral and spiritual growth; turning the attention of her students to herself away from divine principle; teaching and practicing contrary to 'Science and Health;' and finally, that 'Mrs. Stetson attempts to control and injure persons by mental means, this being utterly contrary to the teachings of Christian Science.'" She was officially deprived of her rank as a healer and as a teacher and forbidden to teach or practice Christian Science and "placed on a three years' probation, at the conclusion of which, if her conduct has been exemplary and if she has met Mrs. Eddy's requirements as to loyalty, she may, if Mrs. Eddy sees fit, again be permitted to teach and practice."

The dictator's despotic hand is plainly visible in these terms. Mrs. Eddy's personal will determined everything. The same autocratic condemnation also fell upon sixteen practitioners and eight of the nine trustees of the First Church of New York who were supporters of Mrs. Stetson. The outcome of this celebrated case was that Mrs. Stetson was expelled from The Mother Church in Boston, but she still claims to be loyal to Mrs. Eddy's teachings and is conducting the "New York City Christian Science Institute."[1]

The lawsuits that swarmed around Mrs. Eddy in her life have pursued and plagued her church since her death. When she transferred her large property to trustees she sowed the seed of a new crop of lawsuits. Both the directors and the trustees of The Mother Church have had internal dissensions. In 1919 the directors removed one of their number, who then appealed to the court for reinstatement and the decision was in his favor. A clash arose between the two boards. The directors claimed authority over the trustees, removed one of their number on the ground that he had "allowed a sense of self-interest to interfere with the interests of Christian

---

[1] A full history of this case is given in *Vital Issues in Christian Science*, a large volume issued by Mrs. Stetson in 1914. Charges of "animal magnetism" and other malicious practices fly back and forth between Boston and New York, and the volume throws interesting light into the medieval beliefs and autocratic star chamber proceedings and warring factions and inside troubles of Christian Science.

Science," and also endeavored to interfere with the control
of the trustees over the publishing house of the church.
In March, 1919, the trustees brought suit to have the
directors restrained from interfering with their conduct
of the Publishing Society's affairs. The trustees con-
tended that the directors' power was limited and that
they had no right to remove any member of the Board
of Trustees. The decision of the court was rendered
in December, 1919, and it established the contention
of the trustees that they are in no way subordinate to
the directors and that the directors have no legal power
to control or remove members of the Board of Trustees.
The case was then referred by the court to a master, and
on March 6, 1920, he rendered his decision confirming
the decision of the court.

This litigation over millions of dollars of trust funds
and involving the supreme power of control in the church,
accompanied with much bitter personal animosity, has
rocked the Christian Science organization from top to
bottom. It caused dissension and disruption in the
Seventh Church of Christ, Scientist, in New York. At
a meeting of this church on February 22, 1920, the following resolutions were adopted·

This is a very crucial moment in the growth of our beloved cause
and also in that of the Seventh Church. Disloyalty to the Manual
of the Mother Church and to the Directors of The Mother Church
seems rampant throughout the field. This disloyalty has tried to
gain a footing in the Seventh Church. Loyalty to a disloyal student
of Christian Science is considered disloyalty in itself.

The resolutions then demanded that no persons in the
church be permitted to hold office who refused to declare
publicly in favor of the directors and against the trustees

in the Boston lawsuit. The First Reader of the church refused to sign this declaration and was then removed from his office, and he and about one third of the congregation, who also refused to sign the resolutions, went off and formed another church.

The case in Boston still goes to the Supreme Court of the State, further lawsuits are threatened in New York, and the end is not yet.

3. ORGANIZATION OF THE CHRISTIAN SCIENCE CHURCH

The first organization of the "Church of Christ, Scientist," which was effected in 1879, continued until 1890, when Mrs. Eddy abolished it by one fell decree. The members continued to meet and hold services as before, but there were no more business meetings. The reason given in the Journal for this revolutionary and arbitrary action was that "the bonds of the church were thrown away so that its members might assemble themselves together to 'provoke one another to good works' in the bond only of love." As usual, however, there was method in Mrs. Eddy's apparent madness, and it was seen in due time that she was playing a deep game by which she was planning to get the church in its whole organization and property completely in her own hands so that there would be no more rebellions and rivals in it. It was during this interval of disorganization that she obtained possession, in her "circuitous, novel way," of the lot on Falmouth Street and then conveyed it to her own self-chosen directors in a deed which provides that "Whenever said directors shall determine that it is inexpedient to maintain preaching, reading, or speaking in said church in accordance with the terms of this deed, they are authorized to reconvey forthwith said lot of land with the building thereon, to Mary Baker G. Eddy, her heirs and assigns forever, by a proper deed of conveyance." She thus secured an unbreakable grip on this property, which with its costly building is worth more than $2,000,000 and to which she contributed only $5000.

This notable deed bears the date of September 1, 1892. The ground was now cleared for a new organization of her church, and on September 23, 1892, three weeks and one day after the date of the deed, the church was reorganized. Mrs. Eddy herself appointed the officers and also twelve "charter members," who had the power of admitting new members by ballot, a device by which she was able to keep out of the new church such members of the old organization as did not suit her. The new organization now became The Mother Church and head of all other Christian Science churches throughout the world, which are branches of it, many of the members of the branch churches also being members of The Mother Church in Boston. The twelve "charter members" with certain others became "First Members," and these by a by-law adopted March 17, 1903, became "Executive Members," and these disappeared by the repeal of this by-law on July 8, 1908.[1]

The Mother Church is governed by the "Manual of The Mother Church, By Mary Baker Eddy," which contains "the Church Tenets, Rules, and By-Laws, as prepared by Mrs. Eddy," and is published by the Christian Science Publishing Society and is now in its eighty-ninth edition. This little book of 139 pages is almost as important in the history and doings of Christian

[1] *Manual*, p. 18.

Science as "Science and Health" itself. It is really the hub of the whole organization out of which run spokes to every point on the circumference. It is a master-piece of despotic origination and control out of which every trace of democracy and initiative and individuality has been carefully erased. In nothing has Mrs. Eddy shown her dominating and domineering spirit and her deep-rooted suspicion and jealousy of rivalry and re-bellion and disloyalty and her cunning in guarding every point and keeping everything in her own hands and in the hands of "her heirs and assigns forever" as in this little book. Her hand has written or dictated every line of it and every line bears the impress of her authorship and design. It was a growth, and she was able to meet every emergency with a new "rule" or "by-law" that put some enemy out of business or secured some personal end. No kaiser or Russian czar ever wielded such ar-bitrary power as she clothed herself with as with a purple robe in this "Manual" and ruthlessly exercised. Bismarck would have envied the genius that conceived it. Machia-velli would have marveled at it as a masterpiece. The pope himself is a pale specter as compared with Mrs. Eddy and has no such ecclesiastical authority as is em-bodied in this little book. Yet Christian Scientists in democratic America meekly submit to it and have "no more voice in the management of the church than has the audience in the management of a theater."[1]

---

[1] Mark Twain devotes a considerable part of his book *Christian Science* to a sarcastic exposition and ridicule of this Manual. "In 1895, she wrote a little primer, a little body of autocratic laws, called the *Manual of The First Church of Christ, Scientist*, and put those laws in force, in permanence. Her government is all there; all in that deceptively innocent-looking little book, that cunning

The preface to the book is a quotation from a letter of Mrs. Eddy's in "Miscellaneous Writings" and is as follows:

The Rules and By-Laws in the Manual of The First Church of Christ, Scientist, Boston, originated not in solemn conclave as in ancient sanhedrin. They were not arbitrary opinions nor dictatorial demands, such as one person might impose on another. They were impelled by a power not one's own, were written at different dates, and as the occasion required. They sprang from necessity, the logic of events—from the immediate demand for them as a help that must be supplied to maintain the dignity and defense of our Cause; hence their simple, scientific basis, and detail so requisite to demonstrate genuine Christian Science, and which will do for the race what absolute doctrines destined for future generations might not accomplish.

This preface bears all the marks of Mrs. Eddy's fine hand—the mock modesty ("not arbitrary opinions nor dictatorial demands"), the claim of divine inspiration ("impelled by a power not one's own"), and the bland assumption of legislating "for the race." But in spite of this denial these rules are emphatically "arbitrary opinions" and "dictatorial demands," and there was never a truer word said than the admission that these "Rules and By-Laws" "were written at different times, and as the occasion required"; and "the occasion required" very often and in connection with the most trivial point or incident, especially when the occasion touched Mrs. Eddy herself in the slightest way. When she found that her rival in New York, Mrs. Stetson, was still teaching in her church, it was quickly written in Article XXIII that "Teachers and practitioners of Christian Science

little devilish book, that slumbering little brown volcano, with hell in its bowels. In that book she planned out her system, and classified and defined its purposes." Pp. 343–344.

shall not have their offices or rooms in the branch churches, in the reading rooms, nor in rooms connected therewith," and Mrs. Stetson at once retired with her classes to her own home. When she found that she was being annoyed by people loitering around her house and along the road in the hope of seeing her she stopped the impertinence by what is rather strangely called "The Golden Rule" and which declares: "A member of The Mother Church shall not haunt Mrs. Eddy's drive when she goes out, continually stroll by her house, or make a summer resort near her for such purpose." When Mark Twain ridiculed her assumption of the title "Mother," she changed Article XXII in an astounding manner. This article originally read:

The Title Mother. In the year 1895 loyal Christian Scientists had given to the author of their textbook, the Founder of Christian Science, the individual, endearing term of Mother. Therefore, if a student of Christian Science shall apply this title, either to herself or to others, except as the term for kinship according to the flesh, it shall be regarded by the Church as an indication of disrespect for their Pastor-Emeritus, and unfitness to be a member of The Mother Church.

After Mark Twain's ridicule of this particular bit of conceit and silliness, the article was changed to read as it now stands:

The Title of Mother Changed. In the year eighteen hundred and ninety-five, loyal Christian Scientists had given to the author of their textbook, the Founder of Christian Science, the individual, endearing term of Mother. At first Mrs. Eddy objected to being called thus, but afterward consented on the ground that this appellative in the Church meant nothing more than a tender term such as sister or brother. In the year nineteen hundred and three and after, owing to the public misunderstanding of this name, it is the duty of Christian Scientists to drop this word "mother" and to substitute "Leader," already used in our periodicals.

The contradictory statements in these two forms of this article need no comment. The name "Leader," however, having been appropriated by Mrs. Eddy, instantly became sacred and restricted to her, and any other member "shall not be called Leader by members of this Church."

Nothing is too trivial to escape Mrs. Eddy's eye and hand and every slightest detail is fixed in this "Manual." For example, Article XXIII designates the title of The Mother Church as "The First Church of Christ, Scientist," and then adds: "but the article 'The' must not be used before titles of branch churches, nor written on applications for membership in naming such churches." And thus "that imperial word THE," says Mark Twain, "lifts The Mother Church away up in the sky" along with "the Milky Way, the Bible, the Earth, the Equator, the Devil. . . and by clamor of edict and By-Law Mrs. Eddy gives personal notice to all branch Scientist Churches on this planet to leave that THE alone." As another instance of meticulous supervision of trivial details, "The Mother Church shall not. . . enter into a business transaction with a Christian Scientist in the employ of Rev. Mary Baker Eddy, without first consulting her on said subject and adhering strictly to her advice thereon."

Extraordinary care is taken to guard the sovereignty and dignity and feelings of Mrs. Eddy, and her simple word is enough to convict a member of an offense. Article XI, on "Complaints," has 13 sections, and they are mostly concerned with Mrs. Eddy. To quote from this Article as follows:

Any member who shall unjustly aggrieve or vilify the Pastor Emeritus or another member, or who does not live in Christian fellowship with this Church, shall either withdraw from the Church or be excommunicated. . . If a member of this church shall, mentally or otherwise, persist in working against the interests of another member, or the interests of our Pastor Emeritus and the accomplishment of what she understands is advantageous to this Church and to the Cause of Christian Science, or shall influence others thus to act, upon her complaint or the complaint of a member for her or for himself, it shall be the duty of the Board of Directors immediately to call a meeting, and drop forever the name of the member guilty of this offense from the roll of Church membership. . . If a member of this Church were to treat the author of our textbook disrespectfully and cruelly, upon her complaint that member should be excommunicated. If a member, without her having requested the information, shall trouble her on subjects unnecessarily and without her consent, it shall be considered an offense. . . If the author of "Science and Health" shall bear witness to the offense of malpractice, it shall be considered a sufficient evidence thereof. . . If a member of The Mother Church publishes, or causes to be published, an article that is false or unjust, hence injurious, to Christian Science or to its Leader, and if, upon complaint by another member, the Board of Directors finds that the offense has been committed, the offender shall be suspended for not less than three years from his or her office in this Church and from Church membership. . . If a member of this Church, either by word or work, represents falsely to or of the Leader and Pastor Emeritus, said member shall be immediately disciplined, and a second similar offense shall remove his or her name from membership of The Mother Church. . . A member of The Mother Church and a branch church of Christ, Scientists, shall not report nor send notices to The Mother Church, or to the Pastor Emeritus, of errors of the members of their local church; but they shall strive to overcome these errors.[1]

It will be seen from these personal rules relating to Mrs. Eddy, and these instances might be multiplied, how dangerous it was in her lifetime to be a member of the Christian Science Church. A single word from her

[1] It is of this "Pastor Emeritus," whose "personality" is so sedulously guarded and extravagantly exalted all through this *Manual*, that an official Christian Science publication says: "No human being in modern times was farther removed from a desire to perpetuate a sense of personality than Mary Baker Eddy, the Discoverer and Founder of Christian Science." *The Christian Science Quarterly*, February, 1920.

could send any member into outer darkness. And her despotic power was rendered infinitely more dangerous by reason of the fact that she claimed she could read the minds of people and infallibly discern their very thoughts and motives. "I possess," she declared, "a spiritual sense of what the malicious mental practitioner is mentally arguing which cannot be deceived; I discern in the human mind thoughts, motives, and purposes; and neither mental arguments nor psychic power can affect this spiritual insight."[1]   What priestly inquisitor or pope ever had such power as this?   It was by the swift stroke of this sharp sword that the heads of Kennedy and Spofford and Mrs. Woodbury and Mrs. Stetson and many other members and leaders metaphorically fell into her basket.

With this fateful Manual in hand, let us look into the government and administration of the Christian Science Church. Article I, Section 1, says: "The Church officers shall consist of the Pastor Emeritus, a Board of Directors, a President, a Clerk, a Treasurer, and two Readers." How are all these officers elected? "The Christian Science Board of Directors shall consist of five members. They shall fill a vacancy occurring on that Board after the candidate is approved by the Pastor Emeritus. A majority vote or the request of Mrs. Eddy shall dismiss a member. Members shall neither report the discussion of this Board, nor those with Mrs. Eddy." Did Bismarck or any pope or secret conclave ever dream of anything like that? She makes the board, fills vacancies, and by a mere request can dismiss any member of it! This Board of Directors is the highest governing body of the church, and Mrs. Eddy holds it right in her hand. It

[1] *Christian Science History,* by Mary B. G. Eddy, p. 16.

dare not do one thing displeasing to her, for she can dismiss the whole body with a single stroke of her pen and start all over again with a new board of her own appointment. Now that she is gone, we suppose this board fills its vacancies without being subject to any veto power, but as long as she had a breath in her body it had no independent will and power whatever.

Now let us see what this Board of Directors can do, always subject to the approval and control of Mrs. Eddy. The Church, as we have seen in Article I, Section 1, has officers consisting of a President, Clerk, Treasurer, and two Readers. How are they elected? "The President shall be elected, subject to the approval of the Pastor Emeritus, by the Board of Directors." The clerk and the treasurer are elected "at the annual meeting held for this purpose, by a unanimous vote of the Christian Science Board of Directors and the consent of the Pastor Emeritus in her own handwriting." Mrs. Eddy always had a special care for financial matters and therefore the election of the treasurer must not only have her consent, but this consent must be given in writing and "in her own handwriting" at that. It will be recalled that Article XXI forbids The Mother Church to "enter into any business transaction with a Christian Scientist in the employ of Rev. Mary Baker Eddy without first consulting her on said subject and adhering strictly to her advice." She was a masterly financier and took no chances with any treasurer or business transaction.

The Board of Directors has a Finance Committee consisting of three members who "shall be appointed annually by the Christian Science Board of Directors and with the consent of the Pastor Emeritus"; and it also has a Committee on Business of three members, "who shall transact promptly and efficiently such business as Mrs. Eddy, the Directors, or the Committee on Publication shall commit to it," and before being elected to this committee the names of the candidates "shall be presented to Mrs. Eddy for her written approval."

The two readers are important officers in the Christian Science Church. How are they elected? "Every third year Readers shall be elected in The Mother Church by the Board of Directors, which shall inform the Pastor Emeritus of the names of the candidates before they are elected; and if she objects, said candidates shall not be chosen."

But how are readers and officers in branch churches controlled? This "Manual" of rules is only for The Mother Church, and branch churches are forbidden to adopt or even copy it. "Each Church of Christ, Scientist, shall have its own form of government." It is amusing to read that "In Christian Science each branch church shall be distinctly democratic in its government, and no individual, and no other church shall interfere with its affairs," after every trace and tincture of democracy has been wiped and washed out of this "Manual." The branch churches, however, with their readers are not out of the control of The Mother Church and the omnipresent and omnipotent "Pastor Emeritus"; for it takes at least sixteen members to organize a branch church, "four of whom are members of The Mother Church," and every reader in a branch church must be a member of The Mother Church, and this provision puts all these members and readers in Mrs. Eddy's power; for by Article XI "upon her complaint" the Board of Directors must "drop

forever" any member who works against "what she understands is advantageous to this Church and to the Cause of
Christian Science." By this long arm Mrs. Eddy could
reach across the continent and around the world and
remove any reader in any branch church.

This provision by which the branch churches must have
members and readers who are also members of The Mother
Church is the centralizing agency and long and powerful
arm and hand by which the branch churches are kept under
control of the directors and pastor emeritus. This supreme and sacrosanct sovereignty of The Mother Church is
the reason why no branch church can use the article
"The" in its title. "In its relation to other Christian
Science churches, in its By-Laws and self-government, The
Mother Church stands alone; it occupies a position that
no other church can fill. Then for a branch church to
assume such a position would be disastrous to Christian
Science. Therefore, no Church of Christ, Scientist,
shall be considered loyal that has branch churches or
adopts The Mother Church's form of government, except
in such cases as are specially allowed and named in this
Manual." These special "cases" are the apron strings
by which the branch churches are kept closely tied to
and under the control of "The Mother Church."

In addition to the Board of Directors, there is a "Board
of Trustees," whose appointment is "subject to the approval of the Pastor Emeritus," who "hold and manage
the property conveyed" in Mrs. Eddy's Deed of Trust
of 1898, "and conduct the business of 'The Christian
Science Publishing Society' on a strictly Christian basis,
for the promotion of the interests of Christian Science."
"The Christian Science Board of Directors shall have

the power to declare vacancies in said trusteeship, for such reasons as to the Board may seem expedient," only as to any vacancy "the Pastor Emeritus reserves the right to fill the same by appointment." This relation between the two boards has resulted in the lawsuit between them, which is threatening to disrupt the Christian Science organization to which reference has already been made.[1]

Mrs. Eddy has taken the utmost precaution and pains to control, not only the literature of her church, but even what her followers shall buy and read and even what bookstores they shall patronize. Article VIII enjoins: "A member of this Church shall neither buy, sell, nor circulate Christian Science literature which is not correct in its statement of the divine Principle and rules and the demonstration of Christian Science. . . A departure from the spirit or letter of this By-law involves schisms in our Church and the possible loss, for a time, of Christian Science. . . A member of this Church shall not patronize a publishing house or bookstore that has for sale obnoxious books." This is a rigid censorship over what Christian Scientists shall buy and read and even what bookstores they shall enter that surpasses that of the "Index Librorum Prohibitorum" or of any other religious censorship in the world. Mrs. Josephine C. Woodbury, one of her associates for many years, says that Mrs. Eddy "bids her followers abjure books, papers, magazines, or anything literary except the Bible and her own book."[2] This reveals the fear she had of modern

[1] Pp. 186 — 188.
[2] *Arena* for May, 1899. For a still more zealous "war against heresy" that was "carried on too zealously at last," see Milmine, *History*, p. 362. "The *Journal* also instructed Mrs. Eddy's loyal students to burn all forbidden literature."

learning and light, and this fear was well-grounded, for our whole system of education from the kindergarten to the university and all our science and literature and all the libraries in the world are in direct contradiction to her teaching. Christian Science tries as far as possible to keep its followers immune from the world's literature and to supply them with its own literature, even to a daily newspaper.

All the editors and managers of the Publishing Society are elected "by a unanimous vote, and the consent of the Pastor Emeritus given in her own handwriting." This strangle hold of her own consent on the control of her Publishing Society is drawn still tighter so as to include in her grip the humblest janitor or office boy in Article XXV, which provides: "A person who is not accepted by the Pastor Emeritus as suitable, shall in no manner be connected with publishing her books, nor with editing or publishing The Christian Science Journal, Christian Science Sentinel, Der Herold der Christian Science, nor with The Christian Science Publishing Society."

There is "a Board of Education, under the auspices of Mary Baker Eddy, President of the Massachusetts Metaphysical College, consisting of three members, a president, vice-president, and teacher of Christian Science. Obstetrics will not be taught." The enforcement of the law following disastrous cases of malpractice put this last provision in this Manual. "The teacher shall be elected every third year," "subject to the approval of the Pastor Emeritus."

There is further "a Board of Lectureship, the members of which shall be elected, . . subject to the approval of the Pastor Emeritus." Until 1898 any Christian

Scientist could give public lectures on Christian Science, but this privilege and duty was then restricted to lecturers duly appointed with Mrs. Eddy's approval. "It is the duty of the Board of Lectureship to include in each lecture a true and just reply to public topics condemning Christian Science, and to bear testimony to the facts pertaining to the life of the Pastor Emeritus. Each member shall mail to the clerk of this church copies of his lectures before delivering them." These lecturers are able men, gifted and trained in the art of rhetoric and elocution, and are paid very large salaries, but it will be noticed that they are not trusted to say a word without submitting it to the clerk of The Mother Church who is under Mrs. Eddy's eye and control. The writer has listened to these lecturers with much interest and no little amusement as he has heard them smoothing over the absurd and abhorrent things in Christian Science with discreet silence and plausible speech and especially as they bore "testimony to the facts pertaining to the life of the Pastor Emeritus," when their "facts" were so carefully selected and subjectively colored and there are so many undoubted facts to which they did not bear testimony. If Article XXXI of their Manual is enforced, no newspaper reporter or war correspondent was ever more carefully and ruthlessly censored than are these lecturers.

There is a Committee on Publication "which shall consist of one loyal Christian Scientist who lives in Boston, and he shall be manager of the Committees on Publication throughout the United States, Canada, Great Britian and Ireland. He shall be elected annually by a unanimous vote of the Christian Science Board of Directors and the consent of the Pastor Emeritus." "It shall be the duty of the Committee on Publication to correct in a Christian manner impositions on the public in regard to Christian Science, injustices done Mrs. Eddy or members of this Church by the daily press." Arrangements are made for appointing a similar Committee on Publication in each State, Mrs. Eddy having the right to name the candidate for the office. "Or if she shall send a special request to any Committee on Publication, the request shall be carried out according to her direction." Practically every newspaper and periodical is kept under the surveillance of this Committee, and when an article reflecting on Christian Science, especially if it contains "injustices done Mrs. Eddy," appears in a paper, the editor of it quickly receives a reply or a visit from the "Committee" and is pestered to "correct" the "imposition." The author has had a large experience in this matter.

Although the election of each officer, trustee, president, clerk, treasurer, reader, editor, lecturer, manager, and employee is subject to the consent of Mrs. Eddy in the proper article, yet to make assurance doubly sure there is a blanket provision in Article XXII, Section 3, which declares that "It shall be the duty of the officers of this Church" and of the editors and members of various boards "promptly to comply with any written order, signed by Mary Baker Eddy, which applies to their official functions. Disobedience to this By-Law shall be sufficient cause for removal of the offending member from office." Any vacancy thus caused "shall be supplied by a majority vote of the Christian Science Board of Directors, and the candidate shall be subject to the approval of Mary Baker Eddy." Thus a Damocles sword, "suspended by a single hair," hangs over the head of every officer, editor, member of the Committees on Publication, trustee of the Publishing Society, or of the Board of Education of the Christian Science Church, and at the signal of the pastor emeritus the hair is severed. All of these provisions, depending on the personal consent "in her own handwriting" of Mrs. Eddy, ended, of course, with her life. The supreme authority of the Christian Science Church now rests in or between the two Boards of Directors and of Trustees, and they are now fighting out the question of which is supreme between themselves.

The members of The Mother Church have no voice in its affairs. "The regular meetings of The Mother Church shall be held annually, on Monday following the first Sunday of June. No other than its officers are required to be present. These assemblies shall be for listening to the reports of Treasurer, Clerk, and Committees, and general reports from the field." The business of the meeting appears to be confined to "listening." The clerk can call a special meeting, but he must inform the directors and pastor emeritus of its purpose and have their consent before calling it.

It is not easy to become a member of The Mother Church. A complicated process of application and indorsement must be passed through, and the blanks to be filled out look like an application for life insurance. There is only one way of getting in, but there are thirteen ways of getting out by excommunication.

One of the strictest requirements in the Manual relates to announcing the name and author of "Science and Health" in the Christian Science service. Like some other important points, it is repeated several times and appears near the beginning, the middle, and the end of the book.   Article I enjoins that "The Readers of 'Science and Health with Key to the Scriptures' before commencing to read from this book, shall distinctly announce the full title of the book and give the author's name. Such announcement shall be made but once during each lesson." This requirement is extended to all of Mrs. Eddy's books and reasons given for it in Article XV as follows: "To pour into the ears of listeners the sacred revelations of Christian Science indiscriminately, or without character-izing their origin and thus distinguishing them from the writings of authors who think at random on this subject, is to lose some weight in the scale of right thinking. Therefore it is the duty of every member of this Church, when publicly reading or quoting from the books or poems of our Pastor Emeritus, first to announce the name of the author.   Members shall also instruct their pupils to adopt the aforenamed method for the benefit of the Cause."   The mass of confused and muddy stuff in "Science and Health," which we have already waded through, is thus characterized as "sacred revelations"; and for Mrs. Eddy to speak with an air of lofty condescen-sion of "the writings of authors who think at random" and of losing "some weight in the right scale of thinking," is a delicious instance of her utter lack, not only of a proper literary and logical sense, but also of a sense of humor.

Prayer in the Christian Science service is limited to silent prayer and The Lord's Prayer with Mrs. Eddy's interpretation, but in Article VII we read this peculiar pro-vision: "The prayers in Christian Science churches shall be offered for the congregations collectively and exclusively." Does this mean that Christian Scientists pray only for those found in Christian Science congregations?

Sunday-school scholars shall not "remain in the Sunday school of any Church of Christ, Scientist, after reaching the age of twenty," and they "shall be taught the Scriptures, and they shall be instructed according to their understanding or ability to grasp the simpler meanings of the divine Principle that they are taught." "The instruction given by the children's teachers must not deviate from the absolute Christian Science contained in their textbook." This means that children are taught perverted and often absurd interpretations of Scripture from Genesis to Revelation.

Abundant warnings against mental malpractice and heresy are scattered through the Manual. "It shall be the duty of every member of this Church to defend himself daily against aggressive mental suggestion." "Members will not intentionally or knowlingly mentally malpractice." "If a member of this Church shall depart from the Tenets . . . the offender's case shall be tried and said member exonerated, put on probation, or excommunicated." The Board of Directors, no other persons being present, "has power to discipline, place on probation, remove from membership, or to excommunicate members of The Mother Church." As we have already noted, there are thirteen offenses which may be punished with excommunication, some of them very trivial, such as annoying Mrs. Eddy.

A peculiar provision that probably arose out of experience is that "If the Clerk of this Church shall receive a communication from the Pastor Emeritus which he does not fully understand, he shall inform her of this fact before presenting it to the Church and obtain a clear understanding of the matter—then act in accordance therewith." If at a meeting of the church doubt or disagreement arises "as to the signification of the communications of the Pastor Emeritus to them, before action is taken it shall be the duty of the Clerk to report to her the vexed question and to await her explanation thereof." No doubt many a "vexed question" had to be referred back to her for elucidation.

Another peculiar provision is that "Christian Scientists shall not report for publication the number of members of The Mother Church, nor that of branch churches. According to the Scripture they shall turn away from personality and numbering the people." They shall turn away from every "personality" except one, and that pervades this book from cover to cover. In accordance with this same provision as to undue emphasis upon "personality" is the provision that "As a rule there should be no receptions nor festivities after a lecture on Christian Science." Every care seems to be taken that no "personality" shall ever loom up into conspicuous comparison with the pastor emeritus.

Article XXXV, the last article in this precious book, is devoted exclusively to the Manual and fastens it on The Mother Church without the possibility of amendment forever. Section 1 states that "It stands alone, uniquely adapted to form the budding thought and hedge it about with divine Love. This Manual shall not be revised without the written consent of its author." Section 2 says that the members of the Board of Directors, Committee on Bible Lessons, and Board of Trustees "shall each keep a copy of the Seventy-third Edition and of subsequent editions of the Church Manual." And Section 3 and the last word in the book declares that "No Tenet or By-Law shall be adopted, nor any Tenet or By-Law amended or annulled, without the written consent of Mary Baker Eddy, the author of our text-book, 'Science and Health'." Now that she is gone, there is no power on earth that can give this "written consent," and these by-laws stand unchangeable and inviolate to the end of time, or to the end of The Mother Church. She affected to believe that she was legis-lating "for the race," and left no room for any son or daughter of Adam to tamper with her work. Not even an angel from heaven could change a syllable of it. This is the "dead hand" raised to the highest power, and it can never be relaxed. Boston culture may breed skepti-cism and doubt of the finality of some of these "Tenets," emergencies may arise in some far distant year that would call for revision of some of these "By-Laws," Boards of Directors and Trustees may grow angry and furious with these iron-bound fetters, the right of private judgment and the spirit of American democracy might be born in the minds and souls of the members and officers of this Church and rebel fiercely against these bonds, but all their doubts and difficulties would beat against the fixed and final prison bars of this Manual in vain.

> The Moving Finger writes; and having writ,
> Moves on; nor all your Piety nor Wit
>   Shall lure it back to cancel half a Line,
> Nor all your Tears wash out a Word of it.

This is the way the matter stands as left by Mrs. Eddy. We have little doubt that since her death the officers of this church do find some tolerable way of meeting emergencies and getting along. But in so far as they disregard any syllable of the Manual they defy her authority; and their organization is still a highly centralized, self-perpetuating, despotic autocracy and secret conclave from which the members of the church are absolutely excluded and against the injustices of which they have not the slightest redress.

What is the practical working of this autocratic system? Does the American spirit of democracy and justice never arise in Christian Scientists and rebel against it? It certainly does. There is much evidence and many cases to show that the system is attended with a great deal of unrest and strife and bitterness, at times breaking into open defiance and rebellion, to be promptly followed by excommunication. The various early secessions from Mrs. Eddy sprang from this spirit of revolt against her autocracy. The celebrated case of Mrs. Stetson in New York throws a fierce searchlight into the working of the system, and she herself uttered this warning:

Adherents to the scientific conception of Christian Truth, as represented in branch churches throughout the world, should be made aware of the peril which we are persuaded has come to the Cause through the overriding of spiritual freedom by ecclesiastical self-assertion tending to stamp out a conviction of Truth as enduring as the consciousness of man's oneness with God.[1]

A more recent case of this kind occurred in the First Church of Christ, Scientist, of St. Louis, of which Mr. and Mrs. Leon Greenbaum were members and officers. They revolted against the despotism of the Manual as

[1] *Vital Issues in Christian Science*, p. 3.

administered by The Mother Church in Boston and quickly had their names removed from its roll and from membership in the St. Louis church. Mr. Greenbaum wrote to the Boston authorities: "The despotic interpretation and application of the Church Manual . . . is the invisible root cause of the fratricidal strife in The Mother Church and its offspring (the branch churches) here and elsewhere." The whole case is set forth in Mr. Greenbaum's book and he affirms that the same trouble is causing strife "elsewhere."[1]

We must not, however, attach much significance to these dissensions as a means of undermining Christian Science, for all churches have been subject to strife and division. The Christian Science Church has more to fear from the peaceful penetration of the light and logic of truth as it gently and imperceptibly permeates its members. The blow of a hammer can shatter ice into a thousand pieces, but every piece is still ice. Only sunshine can melt it into sweet water.

4. CHRISTIAN SCIENCE CHURCH SERVICE

Did the reader ever attend a Christian Science church service? The author would not recommend it as a regular and permanent means of grace, but he has attended such services in pursuance of this study. He did not go in any spirit of disrespect, much less of ridicule, for he would not in such a spirit enter a Mohammedan mosque or a Chinese pagoda. He doubts not that God is in a Christian Science service, for he is in all places and has some blessing for every sincere worshipper, Christian or

[1] *Follow Christ.*

pagan, however mistaken and blinded such worshipper may be.

On entering a Christian Science church one is quickly impressed with the air of quietness and reverence in the place. The people enter noiselessly and sit in silence, and late comers, entering while some exercise is going on, are shown to a rear seat until there is a proper place in the service for them to go forward. The Christian Scientists emphasize the value of silence and meditation and practice these exercises more than most other people. At their headquarters in each city they have a "Silent Room" where anyone can enter and sit in silence and read Christian Science literature or engage in meditation. We are in danger of losing these fine means of grace in this noisy, hurrying age, and the followers of this faith set us a good example in this respect. The congregation in a Christian Science church appears to be composed of well-to-do people, and it is known that nearly all of them have come out of the orthodox churches, for Christian Science wins few converts out of what is known as "the world." Some of these members from orthodox churches, however, having made trial of Christian Science, have returned to their former faith and fellowship.

The "Order of Service," consisting of fourteen exercises, was arranged by Mrs. Eddy herself and is part of the inviolable legacy she left in the Manual. This order with its readings for each Sunday is binding on The Mother Church and all branch churches the world around, and the service held in the morning is exactly repeated in the evening. There is a very similar order for the Wednesday evening meeting and also for the Sunday school, and there is a slightly different order for Thanksgiving Day and another for the "communion services in the branch churches," the communion service having been abolished by Mrs. Eddy in The Mother Church. The ordinance of communion itself, if such it may be called, consists merely in kneeling "in silent communion," "concluded by the audible repetition of The Lord's Prayer."

The references to the readings from the Scriptures and "Science and Health" are selected for three months and published in The Christian Science Quarterly. These selections constitute the sermon for the services and must be used in all Christian Science churches.

The first order of exercise is the singing of a hymn, the singing being accompanied by an organ and led by a soloist who is usually a good singer. Christian Scientists as a class are people of sensitive nerves if not of esthetic sensibilities, and everything about their church buildings and services is artistic and "done decently and in order," except the literary style of the readings from "Science and Health" and the "poetry" of some of their hymns. The Christian Scientists are wealthy, and whatever money can buy they can have; but there are some things money cannot buy.

The Christian Science hymn book is a literary curiosity. The classical psalms and hymns of Christianity, in their lofty aspiration and nobility of thought and beauty of literary expression, are one of its most precious fruits and proofs, and any religion can be judged by its hymns. Tried by this test, Christian Science fares badly. It has few hymns of its own production, and these fall painfully below the level of Christian hymns. In the Christian Science hymn book there are five hymns by Mrs. Eddy, but their quality is poor, both in poverty of thought and commonplace, unpoetic expression. Dr. T. G. Moulton characterizes these hymns as "the dreariest doggerel sung to noble tunes."[1] The tunes, of course, are appropriated along with the hymns, for Christian Science appears to be as barren of musical genius as of literary taste.

Having few of its own, Christian Science has boldly laid hands on many of our classical hymns, prostituting them to a sense and use which their authors would have abhorred. It is unjust to the memory of Watts and Wesley and Whittier, Toplady and Newman and other honored hymn writers, to drag them into the company of Mrs. Eddy and force them unwittingly to serve at her strange altar.

It is admitted in the Preface to this book that these hymns do not properly express Christian Science ideas, which, of course, they were never meant to and cannot honestly be made to do, and so they are put through a process of adaptation, which is often a surgical operation of sad mutilation and sometimes of grotesque perversion. The hymns are also usually abridged to two or three or at the most to four or five verses, and this abbreviation is not altogether a fault as it helps to shorten the service. In fact, brevity is a virtue of the whole service, for Christian Scientists are always sensitive to their own comfort and are careful to avoid fatigue, although, of course, there is no such thing and it is only a form of the "nothingness" of "mortal mind."

As an example of the way in which Christian Scientists tamper with our Christian hymns we give Toplady's "Rock of Ages" as it appears in their hymn book:

[1] *An Exposure of Christian Science*, p. 17.

Rock of Ages, Truth, Divine,
Be Thy strength forever mine;
Let me rest secure in Thee,
Safe above life's raging sea.

Rock of Truth, our fortress strong,
Refuge from the shafts of wrong,
When from foes of sense I flee,
Let me hide myself in Thee.

Truth of Christ, asylum sure,
On this rock we are secure;
Cure is there for every ill,
Peace is there our life to fill.

This is only a parody and a very poor one at that on one of the noblest hymns in the English language, and everyone with any poetic sense must feel the outrage it commits. We devoutly wish that the Christian Scientists would keep their hands off our Christian hymns and prayers and write their own.

The second order of the service is "Reading a Scriptural Selection," which is read by the First Reader.

The third order is "Silent Prayer, followed by the audible repetition of The Lord's Prayer with its spiritual interpretation." No audible prayer is offered in the service, with the exception noted, for Mrs. Eddy condemned such prayer, as has already been seen, and, indeed, cut up the real roots of all prayer by declaring that "God is not influenced by man." We would suppose that silent prayer is subject to the same limitation.

The readers alternately render the petitions of the prayer and its interpretation. The Manual provides that these readers shall be "a man and a woman" and they are to be "exemplary Christians and good English scholars." The author does not know about their English scholarship and can only hope that it is better than that of

Mrs. Eddy herself, but he can testify that as many of them as he has heard are good readers, rendering the text with admirable voice and modulation, distinctness and purity of tone, so that their reading is beautiful elocution; and in this fine art they are models for all preachers and readers.

The Second Reader, who is the woman, reads each petition of The Lord's Prayer, and then the First Reader reads "its spiritual interpretation." Formerly this order of the readers was the reverse, but Mrs. Eddy changed it to the present order and thereby seems to have indicated her estimate of the relative values or importance of the two forms. The Manual says that "It shall be the duty of the First Reader to conduct the principal part of the Sunday services." This "spiritual interpretation," has already been given[1] which at first had a very different form, but like Mrs. Eddy's book was subject to any degree of change and finally was given its present shape. Of all the offenses of "the Founder" and the followers of Christian Science this is the worst, unless it be her travesty of a "communion service." It perverts the prayer at every point and is an exegetical and literary outrage which justly excites the indignation of Christians the world over. That this illiterate and uncultivated and morbidly egotistical and madly presumptuous woman should dare to lay her vandal hands on these simple and noble words that fell from the lips of our Lord and that in their lofty devotion and literary beauty are one of the most sacred and precious treasures of the world in every land and language is a shame that Christian Scientists should blush to recognize and honor in their services.

[1] P. 104.

The fifth order is another hymn, and then follows "Announcing necessary notices." The emphasis falls on the word "necessary" in this notice, for the Manual orders that the readers "shall make no remarks explanatory of the Lesson sermon at any time, but they shall read all notices and remarks that may be printed in the Christian Science Quarterly." Mrs. Eddy was always extraordinarily watchful and suspicious of every word spoken or written by anybody except herself. Hence outside of the local notices expressed in the fewest words there is not a word said in a Christian Science service except what has been dictated and printed for the readers. If one of them were to offer a word of extempore prayer or of comment on the "Lesson sermon," it would shock the congregation as an unheard-of, forbidden, and scandalous thing. It is remarkable to what extent Mrs. Eddy, being dead, yet speaks.

The sixth order is a "solo." "The solo singer," says the Manual "shall not neglect to sing any special hymn selected by the Board of Directors." "The Board of Directors" is, or was, Mrs. Eddy.

The seventh order is "Reading the explanatory note on first leaf of quarterly." This note reads as follows:

Friends.—The Bible and the Christian Science textbook are our only preachers. We shall now read Scriptural texts, and their correlative passages from our denominational textbook—these comprise our sermon. The canonical writings, together with the word of our textbook, corroborating and explaining the Bible texts in their spiritual import and application to all ages, past, present, and future, constitute a sermon undivorced from truth, uncontaminated and unfettered by human hypotheses, and divinely authorized.

The eighth order is "Announcing the subject of the Lesson-Sermon, and reading the Golden Text."

The ninth order is "Reading the Scriptural selection, entitled 'Responsive Reading,' alternately by the First Reader and the congregation." This responsive reading is printed in the quarterly.

The tenth order is "Reading the Lesson-Sermon. (After the Second Reader reads the Bible references of the first Section of the Lesson, the First Reader makes the following announcement: 'As announced in the explanatory note, I shall now read correlative passages from the Christian Science textbook, "Science and Health with Key to the Scriptures," by Mary Baker Eddy.')"

The lesson sermon for January 4, 1920, consisted of six groups of selections, arranged in parallel columns, the Bible references on the left side and the references to "Science and Health" on the right side of the page. One or two of these selections will illustrate the appositeness of the "correlative passages." One Scripture reference is II Sam. 23:1–4, which reads as follows:

> Now these are the last words of David.
> David the son of Jesse saith,
> And the man who was raised on high saith,
> The anointed of the God of Jacob,
> And the sweet psalmist of Israel:
> The spirit of Jehovah spake by me,
> And his word was upon my tongue.
> The God of Israel said,
> The Rock of Israel spake to me:
> One that ruleth over men righteously,
> That ruleth in the fear of God,
> He shall be as the light of the morning, when the sun riseth,
> A morning without clouds,
> When the tender grass springeth out of the earth,
> Through clear shining after rain.

The "correlative passage" set over against this is

"Science and Health," p. 469, lines 13–21, which reads
as follows:

Mind is God. The exterminator of error is the great truth that
God, good, is the only Mind, and that the supposititious opposite of
infinite Mind—called devil or evil—is not Mind, is not Truth, but
error, without intelligence or reality. There can be but one Mind,
because there is but one God; and if mortals claimed no other Mind
and accepted no other, sin would be unknown. We can have but
one Mind, if that one is infinite. We bury the sense of infinitude,
when we admit that, although God is infinite, evil has a place in
this infinity, for evil can have no place, where all space is filled with
God.

A Scripture passage from the New Testament is Acts
17:24–27, which reads as follows:

The God that made the world and all things therein, he, being
Lord of heaven and earth, dwelleth not in temples made with hands,
as though he needed anything, seeing he himself giveth to all life,
and breath, and all things; and he made of one every nation of men
to dwell on all the face of the earth, having determined their appointed seasons, and the bounds of their habitation; that they should
seek God, if haply they might feel after him and find him, though he
is not far from each one of us.

The "correlative passage" from "Science and Health"
is p. 542, beginning with line 29 and is as follows:

The sinful misconception of Life as something less than God,
having no truth to support it, falls back upon itself. This error,
after reaching the climax of suffering, yields to Truth and returns
to dust; but it is only mortal man and not the real man, who dies.
The image of Spirit cannot be effaced, since it is the idea of Truth
and changes not, but becomes more beautifully apparent at error's
demise.

These are the kind of "correlative passages" which are
indicated in the forty pages of this quarterly for the first
three months of the year 1920. Has the reader detected
the slightest connection between the Scripture passages

and the "correlative passages" that give their "spiritual import and application to all ages, past, present, and future"? Would not selections from a Patent Office Report or from "Mother Goose" have as much relation to these verses of Scripture as these "correlative passages"? Does it not show a woeful lack of logical sense and literary taste and is it not sacrilegious to put such confused and inane thought and tawdry rhetoric as these selections from Mrs. Eddy's book in comparison with these noble and beautiful passages of Scripture? One can only wonder at the education and culture of the people who week after week sit and listen to this "Lesson-Sermon."

The eleventh order is a "collection." This collection is for their own support, as the Christian Scientists do not maintain hospitals or schools or carry on any charitable or philanthropic work.[1] It would not be logical for them to do anything that would recognize disease or poverty or any physical condition as a reality. The cry of the poor and the suffering does not reach them for their cure for these things is to deny and forget them.

The twelfth order is a hymn, and then while the people are standing follows the thirteenth order which is "Reading 'The scientific statement of being,' and the correlative Scripture according to I John 3:1-3." This "scientific statement of being" is the following:

There is no life, truth, intelligence, nor substance in matter. All is infinite Mind, and its infinite manifestation, for God is all in all. Spirit is immortal Truth, matter is mortal error. Spirit is real and eternal; matter is the unreal and temporal. Spirit is God, and man is His image and likeness; hence man is spiritual and not material.

[1] "The Christian Science Benevolent Association," for the benefit of its own members was opened by The Mother Church in Boston in October, 1919.

During the whole service one idea and utterance is being constantly dingdonged into the ear, in one or another form: "There is no matter," "matter is nothing," "all is Mind." It becomes as monotonous to the ear and as deadening to the interest of the mind as the continual sawing on one string of a violin or as the constant dropping of water. After all this iteration and reiteration for possibly the hundredth time comes this final "scientific statement of being" in which the eternal assertion that "matter is mortal error" is emphasized one more time, or rather half a dozen times more. The last order is "Pronouncing the Benediction," which consists of a verse of Scripture.

Then, with the echo ringing in our ears that "matter is mortal error" we escape into God's out of doors and rejoice with exceeding joy that we are back again in the world of reality with its green grass and blue sky and singing birds and shining sun and healthful food and drink and work and rest, of the faces of our friends and the play of children, in God's world of common sense.

5. WHAT IS THE MEMBERSHIP OF THE CHRISTIAN SCIENCE CHURCH?

When one sees the large and costly churches Christian Scientists have erected in many of our cities, the impression is received that they are a large and wealthy body; and it would be a mistake to think that they are a feeble folk, although few of the influential people of a city are found among them. When we endeavor, however, to find out their real number, we are blocked. The author personally applied to a high Christian Science official for the facts on this point and was told that they were not giving out such information and that he himself did not know.

In the federal census of 1890 the Christian Scientists reported 221 churches and 8724 members, an average of 40 members to each church. In the census of 1906, the next census that gathered statistics of the churches, they reported 82,332 members and 16,116 Sunday-school scholars.[1] This is an astonishing rate of growth, being tenfold or 1000 per cent in 16 years. This was the fruitful springtime and youthful heyday of Christian Science.

But after the census report of 1906 something happened. Up to and including this census the Christian Scientists made their reports along with all other churches, but after the 1906 census they stopped making such reports and have ever since refused to make any, or give out any information as to their numbers. Mrs. Eddy wrote this sudden and peculiar change of policy into her Manual in Article VIII, Section 28, which reads as follows:

Numbering the People. Section 28. Christian Scientists shall not report for publication the number of the members of The Mother Church, nor that of the branch churches. According to Scripture they shall turn away from personality and numbering the people.

Why was this by-law adopted and why does not the Christian Science Church give out its statistics like other churches? The reason given is that Christian Scientists "according to Scripture shall turn away from personality and numbering the people," but this sounds insincere. Why, then, did they give out statistics up to 1906? Was not this "personality" and "numbering the people"? Mrs. Eddy was not averse to "personality" when it was her own personality, and she appears to have taken satis-

[1] These figures are taken from Dr. H. K. Carroll's *Religious Forces of the United States,* revised edition of 1912. He does not give the number of Christian Science churches for 1906.

faction in "numbering the people" as long as her people were increasing. This change of policy creates the suspicion that the rapid rate of increase that was so marked up to 1906 soon thereafter began to slow down and approach a standstill, and that it was this fact that stopped the publication of "numbering the people." Dr. Carroll, who is our highest authority on religious statistics, in a personal communication to the author gives it as his opinion that decrease in growth was the real reason for this change, and they refused to make a report to the federal religious census of 1916.

But though Christian Scientists will not tell, yet there is a way of making a fairly accurate estimate of their numbers. They do officially publish in the Journal one important basis of calculation and that is a complete list of all their churches and societies in the world. The author has made a careful count of these lists in two issues of the Journal sixteen months apart. In the issue of August, 1918, there is a total of 1576 organizations, 1386 in the United States and 190 in foreign countries. Of these organizations in the United States 789 are churches and 597 are societies, a society being a group not yet incorporated into a church. Of the organizations in foreign countries 89 are churches and 101 are societies. In the issue of December, 1919, there is a total of 1702 organizations, 1504 in the United States and 198 in foreign countries. In the United States there are 840 churches and 664 societies, and in foreign countries there are 122 churches and 76 societies. During the sixteen months between these two issues the total number of organizations increased eight per cent, the churches in the United States increased six and one-half per cent, and the societies eleven per cent. This is a tremendous falling off in the rate of increase from the 1000 per cent increase between the censuses of 1890 and 1906. If this rate had been maintained during the 16 months the increase would have been 83 instead of 8 per cent. We are well aware that the growth of a body slows down as it grows older and larger, but this falling off is ominously large and rapid.

On the basis of the number of churches and societies can we estimate the present membership of the Christian Science church? What is the average membership of the 962 churches in the world? Of course some of them have a large membership running up toward a thousand. The Mother Church, according to the secretary's report in June, 1907, had 43,876, but many of these were also members of the branch churches. Many Christian Science churches are very small; many of them do not have church buildings, but meet in halls or other rented places. We would think that an average membership of 100 each would not be far wrong, and this would yield 96,200 members. There are also 740 societies, and as these are mostly small unincorporated groups of people we would suppose they do not average above 25 members each, and this would give 18,500 members: a total for the world of 114,700 Christian Scientists. If this number is seriously wrong, only the Christian Science officials are to blame for it. Let them come out with their statistics as other churches do. "He that doeth the truth cometh to the light."

Such competent judges as Dr. H. K. Carroll and Dr. Horatio W. Dresser think that Christian Science has about reached its flood and that its tide will soon turn.

CHAPTER IX

MIND HEALING AND CHRISTIAN SCIENCE CURES

Christian Science was at first purely a method of mental healing, as was indicated in the title of Mrs. Eddy's book "Science and Health" before she turned her system into a religion and added to her book the "Key to the Scriptures." Mental healing is still the stronghold of Christian Science, and we shall now examine this part of its claim and work. Our general attitude toward this feature of Mrs. Eddy's system is not that of wholesale denial but rather that of discrimination and explanation.

1. MIND HEALING IN GENERAL

The practical interaction of the soul and the body is one of the most familiar experiences of life. The soul expresses itself through the body. The mind utters its thought through language, feature, and movement. Joy wreathes the face in smiles, grief drenches it with tears, modesty dyes it with a crimson blush, and fear blanches it white.

All the emotions of the heart paint themselves on the face. The will moves every voluntary muscle and nerve to do its work, and the unconscious mind pervades and animates the whole organism. The soul pours through the body, as the sap circulates in the tree and exudes in every leaf and blossom, and thus manifests its whole inner life. Not only the tongue speaks, but the eye is eloquent, the flushed face is charged with meaning, and every feature blabs. So, also, the body acts upon the soul, exciting in it sensation and thought, stirring up its feelings, moving its will, causing it to leap with joy or cry out in pain, and thus flooding it with stimulating influences. Knowing how the soul and body are thus closely connected as causes or signs of each other's condition, from the state of the one we can infallibly infer the state of the other. From seeing the face we can tell the state of the soul, and from the state of the soul we can describe the features of the face. It is true that the ultimate nature of the relation of the soul and the body is unknown to us and is one of the unsolved problems and deepest mysteries of philosophy.[1] We may not know where the psychical leaves off and the physiological and the physical begin, or whether they are of diverse or of the same fundamental nature. But we do know that they powerfully affect each other. The mind under a great stroke of sorrow may whiten the hair and blast and wither the body in a single night, and a flood of great joy may revive and rejuvenate it, so that the body seems like wax in the flame of the mind. The "stigmata" of the saints, in which the mind burnt right through the body, are supported by weighty evidence.[2] "It is quite impossible," says a high authority, Dr. Albert Moll, "to assign any limit to the influence of the mind upon the body, which is probably much more potent and far-reaching than we are usually prepared to admit."[3]

[1] For a discussion of this problem, see the author's *The World a Spiritual System; an Outline of Metaphysics*, pp. 116, 117, 226–233. See also H. R. Marshall's *Mind and Conduct*, pp. 215–230.
[2] See Carpenter's *Mental Physiology*, p. 689.
[3] Quoted by R. H. Hutton in his *Aspects of Religious and Scientific Thought*, p. 161.

The mind thus masters matter, melts down its "too, too solid flesh," so to speak, and casts it in its own mold.

The mind in some degree controls the body by its voluntary will as is the case in all our speech and behavior; and the voluntary will can go further and raise or depress the spirits, affect the action of the heart, and exert a pronounced influence over the general condition and health of the body. But the far greater and deeper control of the mind over the body is exercised by the subconscious mind, the unconscious deep in the soul which appears to be the greater and even vastly the greater part of its life. It is this "underground" region of the soul, which may be compared to the basement and cellar of a great building, in which are stored all our past thoughts and actions and out of which ancestral and racial instincts and personal habits and memories and impulses emerge into our conscious life; and it is this unconscious mind that acts through the sympathetic nervous system to operate and control the organic activities of the body. This subconsciousness is reached in hypnotism and by other forms and means of suggestion, and can thus be turned to exercise its influence and control over the body so as to affect its health in both causing and curing disease.

The action of the mind on the body in connection with health and disease has been known and used from ancient times. In Proverbs, ch. 17:22 we read, "A cheerful heart is a good medicine." Celsus, a Roman medical writer of the first century, A.D., wrote, "It is the mark of a skilled practitioner to sit awhile by the bedside with a blithe countenance." And Cassiodorus, of the sixth century, wrote, "To give joy to the sick is natural healing;

for once make your patient cheerful, and his cure is accomplished."

In modern times this agency in curing disease has come into wide use. An extensive literature has already grown up and is rapidly increasing in this field. Dr. A. T. Schofield, an English medical authority, has published seven or eight volumes on the subject, of which the one entitled "The Force of Mind; or, The Mental Factor in Medicine," is one of the best for lay readers. It is packed with facts and quotations from medical authorities and gives a list of more than a hundred books and articles on the subject. These authorities maintain that functional diseases can be cured or helped by mental means, and some of them admit that at least some organic diseases can be helped or cured by the same means. The two kinds of diseases run into each other so that no sharp line of distinction can be drawn between them. Dr. Schofield quotes the English medical authority, Dr. Daniel Hack Tuke, as saying that "mental therapeutics without hypnotism can cure toothache, sciatica, painful joints, rheumatism, gout, pleuro-dynia, colic, epilepsy, whooping cough, contracted limbs, paralysis, headaches, neuralgias, constipation, asthma, warts, scurvy, dropsy, intermittent fever, alcoholism, typhoid fever, and avert impending death." Other authorities, such as Dr. Weir Mitchell and Dr. Woods Hutchinson, regard such statements as exaggerations, but they all admit that the mind has a wide field and is a great power as a curative agent. At the least it is admitted that the depressed condition of the mind may lower the vitality and resisting power of the body to the point where it falls a prey to diseases of all kinds.

It is not asserted that the mind can cure disease by a sheer act of will, though it can often do much and sometimes work wonders in this way, but that the general state and action of the mind furnish the conditions in which disease may disappear and health be restored. Hypnotic suggestion, by which suggestions counteracting disease are planted in the subconscious mind, plays an important part in the theory and practice of some mental healers; and however it may be got into the mind, the suggestion of health is undoubtedly a powerful antidote to disease. Since the mind under an overwhelming belief or emotion may strike right through the body as though it were a physical force, whitening the hair, raising blisters, causing blood to exude through the skin at particular points, there is no limit we may set to what it may do in resisting disease or even in killing its germs. No doubt excessive claims have been made, especially by faith healers and quacks, for the curative power of the mind in disease, but that it is a vital factor in the matter is emphasized by medical authorities and is receiving increased attention in all quarters.

This power of the mind over the body is the root of all the various forms of mind healing and is the secret and stock in trade of numerous quacks that play on the credulity of people. Dr. Schofield enumerates eight kinds of mental healing as follows:

1. There is the prayer and faith cure at Lourdes; which is based upon the faith in God and the Virgin, perhaps mostly on the latter. 2. Relic cures of all sorts; where the basis is faith in the holy emblems, seen or touched. 3. Evangelical faith cures; based upon external divine power. 4. Mind cures; effected by the realization of the power of mind over matter, or by the conscious effect of the mind of the healer on the patient. 5. Christian Science cures; based on

the unreality of disease, and the direction of the mind to the Divine. 6. Spiritualistic cures; effected by faith in departed spirits. 7. Mesmeric cures; effected by a supposed fluid or magnetic influence passing from healer to patient. 8. Direct faith healing; effected by faith healers, in whom the patient has confidence and who heal on the spot.[1]

The stories told of the manifold and marvelous cures effected by this general means are well known, and many are the healers and healing resorts that can show a remarkable collection of crutches and other paraphernalia that have been left behind by those who were healed. John Alexander Dowie, once prominent as a faith healer in Chicago, had a large hall of which the walls were lined with such mementos and proofs of his healing power. That many of these cures are genuine is an undoubted fact, admitted by medical authorities themselves. The fact that many of them are also spurious does not touch the reality of the genuine ones.

Physicians, it need not be said, understand this principle of healing and use it in their practice. The faith they inspire in their patients by their medicines and perhaps even more by their personality and reputation is a vital factor in their healing power. Many a physician by his contagious optimism begets a like spirit in his patient that has its effect in quickening the vital energies of the whole body. It is also well known that physicians give medicines, such as "bread pills," which they know will have no other virtue than the power of arousing the faith and hope of the patient.

It makes no difference what is the nature of the means by which such faith is excited, if it produces the faith it will do the work. On this account the fetish of the savage

[1] *The Force of Mind*, p. 202.

and all the absurd arts and means of faith healers are effective. The following example is from George Barton Cutten's "Psychological Phenomena of Christianity":

Let me refer to a monthly publication called Unity. The copy which I have in hand is that for February, 1906. One of the leaves of this publication is of red paper, and in addition to elaborate instructions for its use given by the editor, the sheet has printed on it the following: "This sheet has been treated by the Society of Silent Unity, after the manner mentioned in Acts 19: 11, 12. Disease will depart from those who repeat silently, while holding this in hand, the words printed thereon." In addition to these instructions we find these words: "Affirmation for Strength and Power. February 20th to March 20th. (Held Daily at 12 M.) The Strength and Power of Divine Mind are now established in the Midst of Me; and shall go no more out. Affirmation for Prosperity. (Held Daily at 12 M.) The Riches of the Lord-Christ are poured out upon Me, and I am supplied with every good Thing." Near the end of the publication are some testimonials to the value of such suggestions. I choose three of them. "While holding the Red Leaf between my hands it caused vibrations through my whole system, and rheumatic pains that I was troubled with disappeared as if by magic.—M. T. R." "Your Red Sheet of November, I used in treatment of my sister for appendicitis, and also for myself for sore throat. With the December one I treated myself for sore throat and bronchitis, with wonderful results in both and in all cases.—L. V. D." "Your treatments for prosperity have done us so much good, and we are feeling more prosperous, which will open the way to our receiving more. Since our treatments our chickens have laid better, the food goes further, and our whole living seems easier.—A. M. L." It is to be expected that so long as the chickens and people respond so readily to the most naïve and crass forms of suggestion, there will always be found those willing to give the suggestions consideration.[1]

It will be recalled that Mrs. Eddy says in "Science and Health" that persons have been healed while reading this book. "The perusal of the author's publications heals sickness constantly." The thing is credible: the sheet does not always need to be red.

While the power of the mind over the body in the healing of disease is freely admitted and used by medical

[1] Pp. 220, 221.

authorities, yet they restrict it within more or less definite limits. The distinction between functional and organic diseases, while more popular than scientific, yet is of practical use, and it is within the former field that mind healing does its best if not its only work. "Potent as is the influence of mind on body," says Sir William Osler, "and many as are the miracle-like cures which may be worked, all are in functional disorders, and we know only too well that nowadays the prayer of faith neither sets a broken thigh or checks an epidemic of typhoid fever."[1] Dr. Schofield says that "with the exception of mental and functional nerve diseases, the part the mental factor plays is exceedingly small, and often very obscure and ill defined," though "it may be a predisposing cause, and exciting cause, an aggravating or a modifying accompaniment; it may act as a poison, or therapeutically as a medicine."[2]   When alleged cases of the healing of organic diseases by mental means are investigated, they are nearly always if not invariably found to be not based on fact; either the diagnosis was not correct or the cure was not effected.[3]

Among functional diseases also the failures to cure by mental means far outnumber the successful cases. As usual in such matters, the "hits" are remembered and exploited and the "misses" are forgotten.   John Alexander Dowie in his newspaper, "Leaves of Healing," declared, "I pray and lay my hands on seventy thousand people in a year," yet in the two and a half years immediately

[1] Quoted by B. B. Warfield in *Counterfeit Miracles*, p. 229.

[2] *The Force of Mind*, p. 69.

[3] The story of a typical celebrated case of this kind, involving the immediate healing of a broken bone, is told by Dr. J. M. Buckley in his *Faith Healing*, pp. 54, 55.

preceding the date of this statement he reports only seven hundred cures, which is only one success in every two hundred and fifty trials.[1] Such meager results would ruin the reputation of any regular physician.

2. HAVE MIRACULOUS CURES CEASED?

At this point we are confronted with the question, Have the miraculous cures of the Bible, especially of Jesus, ceased? Christian Scientists and many other faith healers give an emphatic negative to this question, and declare that they are doing just what Jesus did and commanded his disciples to do. Mrs. Eddy is especially bold in flinging this challenge in the face of her opponents and she frequently quotes and appeals to the promise: "And these signs shall accompany them that believe; in my name shall they cast out demons; they shall speak with new tongues; they shall take up serpents, and if they drink any deadly thing, it shall in no wise hurt them; they shall lay hands on the sick, and they shall recover." But unfortunately for this contention this passage is found in the spurious appendix to the Gospel of Mark and, being no part of the canonical gospel, cannot be quoted in support of this doctrine.

Several other passages are adduced in behalf of this claim. "And he cast out the spirits with a word, and healed all that were sick: that it might be fulfilled which was spoken through Isaiah the prophet, saying, Himself took our infirmities, and bare our diseases" (Matt. 8:16, 17). This passage refers only to the healing works of Jesus and contains no promise that the same power would be extended to his disciples through the ages.

[1] B. B. Warfield, in *Counterfeit Miracles*, p. 196.

The same principle applies to the power of healing committed by Jesus to the Twelve (Luke 9:1) and to the Seventy (Luke 10:9) as he was commissioning them and sending them forth: they were given such power as his official apostles and not to all believers through all time. "Verily, verily, I say unto you, He that believeth on me, the works that I do shall he do also; and greater works than these shall he do; because I go unto the Father" (John 14:12, 13). The context shows that Jesus was specially speaking at this time of his spiritual works in manifesting the Father, and no one thinks that he meant to extend to every believer miraculous power to still stormy seas and raise the dead. "These 'greater works' were the spiritual effects accomplished by the disciples, especially the great novel fact of conversion" (The Expositor's Greek Testament). "Is any among you sick? let him call for the elders of the church; and let them pray over him, anointing him with oil in the name of the Lord: and the prayer of faith shall save him that is sick, and the Lord shall raise him up" (James 5:14, 15). In this passage the use of the medical means employed in that day is commanded, and this makes it an unfortunate Scripture to be appealed to by those who reject the use of such means. No passage can be quoted that shows that strictly miraculous powers were to be extended beyond Jesus and his apostles who used them as signs of divine authority. The use of medical means is sanctioned all the way through the Scriptures. The Bible is a common-sense book that builds on the broad base of universal natural law and human experience, and it cannot be enlisted in the service of irrational ways of dealing with disease, or with anything else.

Christians of almost all schools believe in prayer for the sick and that God can and does answer such prayer in accordance with his wisdom, but they also believe that he works through means, including medical skill. God is in all the processes of nature and of human art, and no one is more ready to acknowledge this than the Christian physician. "In the healing of every disease of whatever kind," says Dr. Henry H. Goddard, "we cannot be too deeply impressed with the Lord's part of the work. He is the Operator. We are the coöperators. More and more am I impressed that every patient of mine who has ever risen up from his sick bed on to his feet again has done so by the divine power. Not I, but the Lord, has cured him." But such divine part in healing, however supernatural it may be, is not to be confused with a miracle in the Scripture sense of a sign wrought to certify the deity of our Lord and the authority of his apostles.[1]

3. CHRISTIAN SCIENCE CURES

Christian Science is one form of mind cure. Mrs. Eddy was anxious to make the impression that her system had no connection or affinity with the various forms of faith healing. "They regard the human mind as a healing agent," she says in the Preface to "Science and Health," "whereas this mind is not a factor in the Principle of Christian Science." Her theory is that disease and matter and all forms of "mortal mind" are

[1] This subject is fully discussed in Benjamin B. Warfield's *Counterfeit Miracles*. He quotes with approval a writer in the Edinburgh Review: "In point of interpretation, the history of Protestantism is a uniform disclaimer of any promise in the Scriptures that miraculous powers should be continued in the Church."

"nothingness," and that the understanding of truth destroys these delusions. She distinguishes between mind-cure and Mind-cure, capitalized Mind in her vocabulary being the infinite Mind which is the "allness" that includes all things, the knowledge of which leaves no room for the "nothingness" of matter and disease. Nevertheless, there is no escaping the fact that her system is a form of mind cure, for she urges the patient to "deny" disease and all the delusions of "mortal mind," and thereby adopts and uses the fundamental principle of all forms of mental healing. The only difference between her system and other systems and the distinctive feature of her theory is the bad and absurd philosophy that she adopted as the cause and explanation of her method of healing; but this false philosophy has little or no necessary connection with the concrete working of her method.

Chapter XVIII in "Science and Health," entitled "Fruitage," consists of eighty-four letters giving accounts of alleged cases of healing by Christian Science, which are presented in illustration and proof of the system. It is open to anyone to inspect these cases and endeavor to form some judgment of them. Each one has a heading giving the name of the disease that has been cured and is signed with the initials and address of the writer although the addresses are useless for purposes of investigation when only the initials of the writers' names are given. The list looks impressive as one glances through it and notes that every case is reported as cured and that almost every kind of disease is found in it. In the headings there appear such announcements as "Rheumatism Healed," "Astigmatism and Hernia Healed," "Substance of Lungs Restored," "Fibroid Tumor Healed in a Few Days," "Insanity and Epilepsy Healed," "A Case of Mental Surgery," these being the titles of the first six letters.

The writer does not doubt that many of these persons were healed, or that they got well of whatever ailments they had. The cures of Christian Science are as numerous and real as those of other forms of mental healing, and no one disputes this fact. We also admit that these writers were sincere and honest in the accounts they gave of their diseases and their cures as they understood them. But the real question is whether these accounts are correct, and not whether their authors thought they were so.

On closer examination of the letters our suspicion is aroused when we note that no instance of failure is included in these eighty-four cases. What does this mean? Does it mean that there are no failures whatever with Christian Science healers, or that these cases were winnowed out of a larger number from which the failures were omitted? Or does it mean that only those who think they are healed write such testimonies, and others that failed to receive such healing are not heard from? Our doubts as to the trustworthiness of these testimonies are further strengthened by the fact that without exception they were written by nonmedical persons who had no technical knowledge of the diseases and symptoms and cures which they undertake to describe. Not one of them is written by a physician, or is accompanied with the certificate of a physician. Space here permits only several typical extracts from them, as they are usually long and contain much irrelevant matter.

One correspondent writes: "For seventeen years I had suffered with indigestion and gastritis in the worst form, often being overcome from a seeming pressure against the heart. I had asthma for four years, also had worn glasses for four years. It seemed to me that I had swallowed every known medicine to relieve my indigestion, but they only gave temporary benefit. I purchased a copy of 'Science and Health,' and simply from the reading of that grand book was completely healed of all physical ailments in two weeks' time." Another writes: "I pursued the study [of Christian Science] carefully and thoroughly, and I have had abundant reason since to be glad that I did, for through this study, and the resulting understanding of my relation to God, I was healed of a disease with which I had been afflicted since childhood and for which there was no known remedy." And another writes: "Through reading 'Science and Health' and the illumination which followed, I was healed of ulceration of the stomach and kindred troubles, a restless sense of existence, agnosticism, etc."

Now when one considers how difficult it often is to diagnose disease and how often even experienced physicians make mistakes in this part of their art and how easy it is for one suffering with any bodily disturbance to imagine that he has almost any disease, the value of these testimonies as to diseases cured becomes very small. Even when some of these persons say that one or more physicians told them they had these diseases and "gave them up," such testimony, without necessarily being dishonest, is untrustworthy, because it is easy to misunderstand or misreport these physicians and we would like to know what they really did say. In very many instances such alleged reports of physicians have been run down and have been proved to be incorrect.

Over against these testimonies of Christian Scientists who claim they were healed of almost all ailments, including organic diseases and surgical cases, we can put the proved facts as to many notable cases that were total failures and the testimony of eminent medical authorities. As to notorious cases of failure and disaster and death, they have been recorded in such numbers and with such proofs as must stagger the faith of even the most devoted and credulous Christian Scientists.[1]

It is not to be forgotten that Mrs. Eddy herself dropped out of her therapeutics surgery, obstetrics, and infectious diseases. "Until the advancing age admits the efficacy and supremacy of Mind, it is better for Christian Scientists to leave surgery and the adjustment of broken bones and dislocations to the fingers of a surgeon, while the mental healer confines himself chiefly to mental reconstruction and to the prevention of inflammation." "Obstetrics is not Science, and will not be taught." "Mrs. Eddy advises, until the public thought becomes better acquainted with Christian Science, that Christian Scientists decline to doctor infectious or contagious diseases."[2] She further wrote: "Christian Scientists should be influenced by their own judgment in taking a case of malignant disease, they should consider well their ability to cope with the case—and not overlook the fact that there are those lying in wait to catch them in their sayings;

[1] For such cases see Milmine's *History*, pp. 324–326, 354–356; Peabody's *Masquerade*, pp. 103–120; *The New Church Review*, 1908, vol. XV, p. 419; Paget's *Faith and Works of Christian Science*, pp. 130–190.

[2] *The Christian Science Journal*, December, 1902.

neither should they forget that in their practice, whether successful or not, they are not specially protected by law." It was because the hand of the law was laid on Christian Science practitioners that these admonitions and limitations were imposed upon them; and they were embodied in a by-law that "if a member of this church has a patient that he does not heal, and whose case he cannot lawfully diagnose, he may consult with an M. D. on the anatomy involved." These three classes of cases from which the practitioners of this faith are warned away, surgery, obstetrics, and infectious and contagious diseases, cut a wide swath through the field of the disease healing art and are a tremendous limitation upon the power and the claims of Christian Science. In the presence of these admitted limitations, what becomes of Mrs. Eddy's claim that "Christian Science is always the most skillful surgeon," and her boast in the Preface of "Science and Health," that "thousands of well-authenticated cases of healing" "have proved the worth of her teachings," "cases" which "for the most part have been abandoned as hopeless by regular medical attendants"? A "regular medical attendant" who was a general practitioner and would not touch a case of surgery, obstetrics, or infectious or contagious disease would be a curiosity in his profession and would not have much to do.

Time and again Mrs. Eddy and other Christian Scientists have been challenged to submit cases of their healing to medical inspection, but no such challenge has been accepted. Luther T. Townsend, professor of theology in Boston University, submitted this proposition to Mrs. Eddy: "If you or the president of your college, or your entire college of doctors, will put into place a real case of hip or ankle dislocation, without resorting to the ordinary manipulation or without touching it, I will give you one thousand dollars. Or if you or your president, or your entire college, will give sight to one of the inmates of the South Boston Asylum for the Blind, that sightless person having been born blind, I will give you two thousand dollars." The following reply to this appeared in the Christian Science Journal: "Will the gentleman accept my thanks due to his generosity, for if I should accept his bid he would lose his money. Why, because I performed more difficult tasks fifteen years ago. At present I am in another department of Christian work, where 'there shall no sign be given them,' for they shall be instructed in the principles of Christian Science that furnishes its own proof."

Richard C. Cabot, M. D., professor in the Harvard Medical School, in McClure's Magazine for August, 1908, had an article entitled "One Hundred Christian Science Cures." The cases he examined were gathered out of The Christian Science Journal, and he gives evidence to prove that the accounts of the cases had been "doctored" by the editor of the Journal or by some other Christian Science authority, and the same editing is evident in many of the cases reported by Christian Science officials, including those in the chapter on "Fruitage" in "Science and Health." Of these one hundred cases Dr. Cabot found that seventy-two were "functional," seven were "cases of what appears to be organic," eleven were "cases very difficult to class," and ten were "cases regarding which no reasonable conjecture can be made." His conclusions with respect to them were, "first, that most Christian Science cures are probably genuine; but, secondly, they are not cures of organic disease." "I have never found," he says, "one in which there was any good evidence that cancer, consumption, or any other organic disease had been arrested or banished." He had "followed up" many alleged cures of such diseases, but "the diagnosis was never based upon any proper evidence." He further says: "Of the classical methods of psychotherapeutics, namely, explanation, education, psychoanalysis, encouragement, suggestion, rest-cure and work-cure, the Christian Scientists use chiefly suggestion, education, and work-cure, though each of these methods is colored and shaped by the peculiar doctrines of the sect."

One of the most extensive, thoroughgoing, authoritative, and convincing investigations of the cures of Christian Science was made by Stephen Paget, M. D., an eminent English medical authority, and the results were published in his book entitled "The Faith and Works of Christian Science," 1909. He took "two hundred consecutive Testimonies of Healing, from her weekly journal, the Christian Science Sentinel," and published them in his book, filling twenty-nine pages. He adds footnotes to some of the cases, pointing out their ambiguities and telling us that he wrote to some of the patients and in no instance did he receive a satisfactory answer. He then passes judgment on these two hundred cases, but space here permits only a few of his statements:

The vast majority of these testimonies are not worth the paper on which they are printed. . . These are not testimonies, but testimonials; every advertisement of a new quack medicine publishes the like of them. . . What is the good of proclaiming that Christian Science heals diseases which get well of themselves? Time heals them. Here is a girl with a cold in her head: she is healed "through the realization of the omnipresence of Love." Was there ever such an insult offered to the name of Love? . . . Let us apply a fair and mild test to these two hundred cases. Let us show them to any doctor; and let us ask him what he thinks of them. He will laugh at them: he will say, "What is the good of such cases? Why don't they report them properly? Why don't they give details? What do they mean by spinal trouble, and all the other troubles?"

Dr. Paget gives an account of the alleged cure of a case of leprosy; he wrote to the patient and he shows that there is no good ground for believing that he ever had this disease. He gives the experience of and quotes from a number of eminent medical authorities, including Dr. John B. Huber, Professor in Fordham University Medical School, New York, William A. Purrington, University Lecturer on Medical Jurisprudence, New York, Henry H. Goddard, Lecturer on Psychology of Mental Defectives, New York University, Dr. Albert Moll, of Berlin, and Dr. R. C. Cabot, of Boston. The following is a quotation from Mr. Purrington:

In the record of deaths resulting from the treatment of Christian Scientists, Faith Curers, Peculiar People, *et id genus omne,* a large proportion are those of neglected children suffering from acute inflammation of the lungs, diphtheria, pneumonia, and like complaints. One horrible and typical case in Brooklyn was brought to public notice by an undertaker called in by a Faith Curer to bury the latter's child, six years of age, dead from diphtheria. Two other children, one about eight, the other less than two years old, were found suffering from the same disease. The father explained his failure to call in medical aid by saying he did not believe in doctors, since he believed in Christ.[1]

Dr. Paget gives a quotation from Dr. J. M. Buckley's "very careful paper in the North American Review, July, 1901," which is as follows:

[1] For the legal case against Christian Science, see Mr. Purrington's book *Christian Science; An Exposition.*

The failures of Christian Science are innumerable. Twenty years ago I collected vital statistics of various communistic institutions which refuse medical aid, and compared them with the tables of life insurance companies; and on the basis of the results of the comparison, I predicted that, should Christian Science at any time begin to spread rapidly, or should antimedicine, faith-healing institutions be largely increased, the number of deaths would attract attention, and public indignation be excited by failures to heal maladies which ordinarily yield to medical or surgical treatment. This prediction is now being fulfilled every day. Many who have been vainly treated by Christian Scientists are now dead. None of their failures is mentioned by the healers, and few of the living victims, who are usually silenced by shame. One I met in an insane asylum, muttering all day long, "God can never be sick."

Dr. Paget collected and printed in his book sixty-eight cases of alleged cures by Christian Scientists which were shown to be unfounded and worse by physicians who sent them to Dr. Paget for the book. He says of these cases: "They display (1) the great liking which Christian Science has for the very worst sort of 'surgical cases'; (2) the cruelty or brutality which naturally goes with her terror of pain and of death; (3) the element of madness which is in her faith; (4) the vanity or self-conceit which approves and adopts a bastard philosophy, not merely for its own sake, but for the sake of opposition to authority." The twenty-eight pages filled with these cases are verily terrible reading and give one a sense of the appalling suffering and brutality and death that result from this system. There is space for only two reports which come from American physicians. The first one is as follows:

I am sending you the following two cases where the patients were treated by Christian Science, and were worse, and died after the treatment; and the third case, one of "miraculous conception." The first was a man in middle life, who had a mild attack of nephritis, and was told by a Christian Science healer to eat and drink as he pleased, and to go ahead with his business, for "he only thought he was sick." He soon developed uræmic convulsions, and died. The second was a man with a small epithelioma of tongue, who was told by a Christian Scientist that it didn't amount to anything, and that their treatment would soon make it disappear. He died of its ravages while receiving treatment from them. The third case which came to my knowledge, was one of conception, and the delivery of a child at term, in a Christian Scientist, who declared she conceived by thought, as taught in their creed, and that no man entered into the case.

The other case is from a Boston physician and is as follows:

Boston is a hotbed of Christian Science, and we see a great many patients who are treated by those who practice it. I have seen a patient dying of strangulated hernia, who had been treated from first to last by Christian Science until the period of operability had passed. I have seen one or two patients dying of hemorrhage who had been treated by Christian Science. I should say I had seen about a hundred cases, in which the only chance for cure had been lost through Christian Science treatment.

Dr. Paget sums up his investigations of this system thus:

These short notes, put here as I got them, give but a faint sense of the ill working of Christian Science. It would be easy to collect hundreds more. Of course, to see the full iniquity of these cases, the reader should be a doctor. But everybody, doctor or not, can feel the cruelty, born of fear of pain, in some of these Scientists— the downright madness threatening not a few of them, and the appalling self-will. They bully dying women, and let babies die in pain; let cases of paralysis tumble about and hurt themselves; rob the epileptic of their bromide, the syphilitic of their iodide, the angina cases of their amyl nitrite, the heart cases of their digitalis; let appendicitis go on to septic peritonitis, gastric ulcer to perforation of the stomach, nephritis to uræmic convulsions, and strangulated hernia to the *miserere mei* of gangrene; watch, day after day, while a man or a woman bleeds to death; compel them who should be kept still to take exercise; and withhold from all cases of cancer all hope of cure. To these works of the Devil they bring their one gift, willful and complete ignorance; and their "nursing" would be a farce, if it were not a tragedy. Such is the way of Christian Science,

face to face, as she loves to be, with bad cases of organic disease. . .
In a rage, Common-sense cries, "For God's sake leave the children
alone. It doesn't matter with grown-up people; they can believe
what they like about Good and Evil, and germs, and things. But
the children; they take their children to these services. Why can't
they leave the children out of it?". . . The corner stone of her
church is not Jesus Christ but her own vanity. She is cruel to
babies and young children; she is worse than close-fisted over her
money; she despises Christianity, and is at open war with experience
and common sense. . . We examine her testimonials, and find them
worthless. We are told that she is Christ come again, and we can
see that she is not. We listen to her philosophical talk, and observe
that she is illiterate, and ignorant of the rudiments of logic. We
admit, and are glad, that she has enabled thousands of nervous
persons to leave off worrying, and has cured many "functional
disorders;" but she has done that, not by revelation, but by suggestion. The healed, whom she incessantly advertises, are but few,
compared with them that are whole, . . and a thousand brave and
quiet lives, the unnamed legion of good non-Scientists. They bear,
not deny, pain; they confess, not confuse, the reality of sin; they
face, not outface, death.

The author could add from personal knowledge cases of
the failure of Christian Science treatment, especially one sad
case ending in death, but it is better to rest the matter on
the authoritative judgment of medical men; and such
adverse judgments could be multiplied indefinitely.

"By their fruits ye shall know them." By this prag-
matic test the "fruitage" of Christian Science in all cases
of surgery and organic disease and in many other cases is
proved false and injurious, and sometimes it needlessly
and cruelly insures death. It already has to carry a
load of infamy that should condemn it beyond recovery
of any public confidence and respect. The law has laid
its hand on it and restricted it in some degree, but it is
still a dangerous delusion. That an illiterate woman,
utterly ignorant of the most elementary scientific knowledge of the human body and its treatment in disease,
should have been able to overthrow, for many people,

the first principles of medical science, which is the growth of centuries, and get them to trust and practice this false and disastrous theory, is one of the marvels of our day, almost shaking our faith in human rationality; but it is partially explained by the fact that in no other field are people more easily deluded and led astray by impostors and quacks than in medicine. In their eager desire for cure and health they will wildly catch at any straw floating on the stream in which they are struggling.

All this is said while acknowledging that Christian Science as a system of mind cure does succeed in giving relief in many cases of a functional kind. People of a nervous temperament with all kinds of functional derangement gravitate to it by an affinity that is not wholly mistaken, and by the change wrought in their minds do experience temporary relief and often permanent benefit. Let full credit be given to it for such work, which it accomplishes in common with and by the same general means as other forms of mind healing. But when it sets itself up as a system of curing all disease and makes claims of such "fruitage" as is given us in "Science and Health" and is constantly being published in the Christian Science Journal, it is a delusion and menace whose falsity and evil works must be exposed.

4. THE MERCENARY ASPECT OF CHRISTIAN SCIENCE

Mrs. Eddy early developed a keen instinct for money and turned her religion and church into a business concern which in thorough organization and masterly management and in extraordinary success and huge profits rivaled some of our great corporations. She is the only founder of a religion known to history who deliberately set about making money from her cult. She was a prophet out for profit. Jesus in sending out his twelve disciples said unto them: "And as ye go, preach, saying, The kingdom of heaven is at hand. Heal the sick, raise the dead, cleanse the lepers, cast out demons: freely ye received, freely give. Get you no gold, nor silver, nor brass in your purses; no wallet for your journey, neither two coats, nor shoes, nor staff: for the laborer is worthy of his food" (Matt. 10:7–10). They were to charge no price for their healing and to take nothing for the grace of God. But Mrs. Eddy charged for everything and took all she could get, "supposing that godliness is a way of gain" (I Tim. 6:5). When Simon the sorcerer wanted to buy of Peter the gift of the Holy Spirit that he might make money out of it, the apostle pronounced a grave judgment upon him, declaring that he was still "in the gall of bitterness and in the bond of iniquity" (Acts 8:18–24); but Mrs. Eddy stood in no fear of any such retribution. Isaiah cried out, "Ho, every one that thirsteth, come ye to the waters, and he that hath no money; come ye, buy, and eat; yea, come, buy wine and milk without money and without price" (ch. 55:1); but Christian Science healing comes high, and whoever would receive it must come liberally supplied with money. The freeness of the grace of God is proclaimed all the way through the Scriptures and is one of its glories, but whoever would partake of the promised blessing of Mrs. Eddy's gospel must pay for it and pay well. After struggling through years of bitter poverty in which at times she ate the bread of charity, this remarkable woman, who at fifty years of age was unknown and was literally a homeless wanderer, suddenly began to wield a golden scepter and turned out to be a veritable wizard of finance. She rapidly rose to affluence and died a millionaire, several times over.

As usual with her, she based her money-making scheme on an alleged divine revelation, which she announced in the following terms:

When God impelled me to set a price on Christian Science mind healing, I could think of no financial equivalent for the impartation of a knowledge of that divine power which heals; but I was led to name three hundred dollars as the price for each pupil in one course of lessons at my college; a startling sum for tuition lasting barely three weeks. This amount greatly troubled me. I shrank from asking it, but was finally led by a strange Providence to accept this fee. God has since shown me in multitudinous ways the wisdom of this decision.[1]

It is really pathetic to observe the shrinking modesty with which she recoiled from the idea of fixing a price of three hundred dollars for twelve lessons running through only three weeks, and the extreme difficulty with which she brought herself to consent to it, though she was acting under a divine compulsion and was led by a strange Providence to do it; yet she confesses, somewhat inconsistently, that she could not think of any price that would be a financial equivalent for the knowledge she imparted of divine healing. Yet after all this hesitation as though it went hard with her conscience to charge such "a startling sum" for only twelve lessons, she presently reduced the number of lessons from twelve to seven without reducing the price of the course, thereby increasing the price from the "startling sum" of twenty-five to the still more "startling sum" of forty-three dollars a lesson. In ex-

[1] *Retrospection and Introspection.*

planation of this she published the following notice in the
Christian Science Journal for December, 1888:

Having reached a place in teaching where my students in Christian
Science are taught more during seven lessons in the primary class
than they were formerly in twelve, and taught all that is profitable
at one time, hereafter the primary class will include seven lessons
only.   As this number of lessons is of more value than twice this
number in times past, no change is made in the price of tuition, three
hundred dollars.   Mary Baker Eddy.

When she began teaching, however, she had a different
scale of prices as set forth in the following contract:

We, the undersigned, do hereby agree, in consideration of instructions and manuscripts received from Mrs. Mary B. Glover, to
pay her $100 in advance, and ten per cent annually on the income
that we receive from practicing or teaching the same.   We also do
hereby agree to pay said Mary B. Glover $1000 in case we do not
practice or teach the science she has taught us.[1]

Under this contract she not only got her fee for teaching
her "science," but also reaped a royalty from the fees of
her students.   She was thus sowing seed from which she
could reap a perpetual harvest, and her fine financial
hand was in evidence in this arrangement.   She also
bound her students to pay her a large sum whether they
did or did not practice or teach her science.   Whatever
was done or not done she had everything to gain and
nothing to lose.

Mrs. Eddy's "Metaphysical College," which was in
no proper sense a "college" at all but was really a bogus
institution of the rankest quackery, was a strictly family
affair, for its whole "faculty" consisted of Mrs. Eddy,

[1] Peabody, *Masquerade*, p. 123.

her third husband, Asa Gilbert Eddy, and her adopted
son, J. Foster Eddy, so that its entire proceeds practically
flowed into her coffers. Mrs. Eddy says that "during
seven years some four thousand students were taught by
me in this college." Four thousand students at three
hundred dollars apiece would yield one million two hundred
thousand dollars! One would think that a family of three
with an annual income of one hundred and seventy thousand dollars could lay by something for a rainy day, and
Mrs. Eddy did. She took some charity students so that
some reduction would need to be made, but there never
was very much charity in her transactions. It went
hard with a student that did not pay the tuition, for a
lawsuit was frequently brought to compel payment,
which suits she lost in every instance, the judge in one
case deciding that she had not rendered any useful service
for the fee.[1]

Mrs. Eddy struck a still richer vein of ore in her book
"Science and Health," of which, after the earlier editions,
she herself was the publisher. This book was sold for
three dollars in the cheapest binding and on up to six
dollars for more expensive bindings. Mr. Peabody thinks
the book could be manufactured in those days in large
quantities for fifty cents a copy, yielding a five hundred
per cent profit on the cheapest edition; and Mark Twain,
who was himself a publisher with an unfortunate experience in the business says: "I am obliged to doubt that
the three-dollar 'Science and Health' costs Mrs. Eddy
above fifteen cents, or that the six-dollar copy costs her

[1] Mr. F. W. Peabody, of the Boston bar, says that he has examined
the court record in two of these cases. See his *Masquerade*, pp. 123,
124.

above eighty cents. I feel quite sure that the average profit to her on these books, above cost of manufacture, is all of seven hundred per cent." Our respect for Mrs. Eddy's financial ability is rising. She made money where Mark Twain lost it!

How many copies did she sell? The book, we have seen, passed through nearly five hundred editions before the publisher stopped numbering them. We are not told how many copies were published in each edition, but the total must have mounted up into hundreds of thousands. Where did Mrs. Eddy find a market for such an enormous output of a religious book? In her students and in the membership of her church, every one of whom was expected and induced by notices and commands whose meaning could not be evaded to purchase a copy of this "textbook" of the faith that was of equal rank and authority with the Bible. In the Christian Science Journal for March, 1897, appeared this remarkable notice:

Christian Scientists in the United States and Canada are hereby enjoined not to teach a student of Christian Science for one year, commencing on March 14, 1897. "Miscellaneous Writings" is calculated to prepare the minds of all true thinkers to understand the Christian Science textbook more correctly than a student can. The Bible, "Science and Health with Key to the Scripture," and my other published works, are the only proper instructors for this hour. It shall be the duty of all Christian Scientists to circulate and to sell as many of these books as they can. If a member of The First Church of Christ, Scientist, shall fail to obey this injunction, it will render him liable to lose his membership in this church. Mary Baker G. Eddy.

Can the like of that notice be found in all the religious literature of the world, Christian and pagan? This prophet actually stopped the teaching of her faith for one year in order to reap a larger profit from the increased forced sale of her books during this period! She now included her "other published works" along with her textbook in this order and required every member of her church to circulate and sell as many of these books as possible, the penalty of failing to do this being excommunication from the church! What other prophet or priest ever did such a thing as this?

But we have not reached the end of this business, and the worst is yet to come. There was a reason why so many editions of "Science and Health" should issue from the press. We have seen how the book was always undergoing change, being in a fluid condition. These changes were often trivial, but Christian Scientists were always given to understand that they should have the latest edition! Does the reader not see what this meant? It meant that every new edition put all the previous editions out of date, and loyal Christian Scientists had to get the latest edition of this bible to have the latest inspired word on the subject of their salvation. A bible that constantly needs revising, even though it be inspired, at least has the advantage of always being able to command a large market among the faithful for each new revision.

An astonishing instance of how this scheme was worked occurred when this notice appeared in February, 1908:

Take Notice: I request Christian Scientists universally to read the paragraph beginning at line thirty of page 442 in the edition of "Science and Health," which will be issued, February 29. I consider the information there given to be of great importance at this stage of the workings of animal magnetism, and it will greatly aid the students in their individual experiences. Mary Baker G. Eddy.

Mr. Peabody tells us that at the time this appeared

Senator Chandler happened to be with him in Boston, as they were engaged together as counsel in the litigation then pending in connection with Mrs. Eddy's competency to manage her affairs. The senator was anxious to see this edition as he "was particularly interested in keeping tabs on Mrs. Eddy's mental attitude toward so-called 'animal magnetism.'" Mr. Peabody went out and obtained a copy of the new edition and on opening it at the page and line found the "information" that was of such "great importance" and "would greatly aid the students." "It was just two lines," says Mr. Peabody, "inserted in a blank space at the end of a chapter and necessitated the change of no other plate of a single page in the book." This is what they saw: "Christian Scientists, be a law to yourselves, that mental malpractice can harm you neither when asleep nor when awake." Whereupon Senator Chandler exclaimed: "What a swindle! Do you suppose anyone can be of so little intelligence, who buys that book in consequence of Mrs. Eddy's notice and reads this paragraph, that he does not feel, as we feel, that he has been swindled?" And this is Mr. Peabody's comment: "Only this and nothing more. It is senseless, and yet it cost many thousands of Christian Scientists from three to six dollars apiece to find out, if they could find anything out, that the 'revelator' had sold them 'a gold brick.' And even since the edition of February, 1908, another edition, with only one line added, has been foisted upon the faithful."[1]

In the words of Colonel Sellers, with such a book, "There's millions in it!"

In addition to these main streams of revenue derived

[1] *Masquerade*, pp. 136–138.

from her college and her book, Mrs. Eddy drained off the funds of her followers in various subsidiary tributary streams that helped to swell her flood of gold. She appeared to be always busy in finding means of making money and was fertile in cunning schemes and devices to this end. She took to publishing in the Journal lists of her Christmas presents, giving the names and addresses of the donors, thus flattering their pride to find themselves the recipients of such distinguished mention and honor and suggesting to others that they should do likewise and shine with the same glory. These lists grew with the years in length and variety of gifts, and the "List of Individual Offerings" in the Journal for 1889 mentions thirty-seven articles, consisting of gold-embroidered, hand-painted, eider-down pillows, pictures, perfumery, books, a barometer, and so on, concluding with "two fat Kentucky turkeys," and "hosts of bouquets and Christmas cards."

She grew bold enough in time to solicit such gifts, and four days before Christmas in 1889 there appeared in the Christian Science Sentinel this "Card":

Beloved: I ask this favor of all Christian Scientists. Do not give me on, before, or after the forthcoming holidays, aught material except three tea jackets. All may contribute to these. One learns to value material things only as one needs them, and the costliest things are those that one needs least. Among my present needs material are these three jackets. Two of darkish heavy silk, the shade appropriate to white hair. The third of heavy satin, lighter shades but sufficiently sombre. Nos. 1 and 2 to be common-sense jackets, for Mother to work in, and not overtrimmed by any means. No. 3 for best, such as she can afford for her drawing room. Mary Baker Eddy.

As this request for three tea jackets with particular directions as to material and color and style appeared on

December 21, Mr. Peabody maintains that she very well knew that practically all presents intended for her were already mailed, and this was a shrewd device for getting the tea jackets extra. Apparently it was not the literal tea jackets she wanted, but the money to buy them, as she stated that "All may contribute to these." If "all" really did this, she must have received no mean sum of money by this device.[1] Of course it is amusing to find Mrs. Eddy saying that "One learns to value material things only as one needs them," but how could she say this when her whole philosophy was that material things had no value and were all delusions of "mortal mind" and the very imps of her devil, "malicious animal magnetism"? The truth is that she had a very real and keen sense of the value of such material things as she wanted, especially money. Matter in the form of gold was one demon of "mortal mind" that she never tried to exorcise. She never claimed that money was a "nonentity" that was to be "denied" as a "delusion": that would have ruined her business.

Perhaps the climax of these catchpenny devices or side lines of her trade was the famous "Christian Science Spoon" or "Mother Spoon" that she foisted upon her followers. This was an ordinary silver spoon with Mrs. Eddy's likeness embossed upon it, together with a picture of Pleasant View, Mrs. Eddy's signature, and the motto, "Not Matter but Mind Satisfies." It was sold to the faithful for $5.00, which would net her a profit of several hundred per cent. It was introduced to them

---

[1] For Mr. Peabody's full account of this very peculiar request, see his *Masquerade*, pp. 140-143.

with this announcement and command, which appeared in the Journal for February, 1890:

Christian Science Spoons.—On each of these most beautiful spoons is a motto in bas-relief that every person on earth needs to hold in thought. Mother requests that Christian Scientists shall not ask to be informed what this motto is, but each Scientist shall [here the request passes to a command] purchase at least one spoon, and those who can afford it, one dozen spoons, that their families may read this motto at every meal and their guests be made partakers of its simple truth. Mary Baker G. Eddy.

The above-named spoons are sold by the Christian Science Souvenir Company, Concord, N. H., and will soon be on sale at the Christian Science reading rooms throughout the country.

Again we wonder at the mercenary spirit and effrontery of this thing. Christian Scientists must not let their curiosity get the better of them so far as to ask what this remarkable motto is and thereby get the information free of charge and deprive "Mother" of her rightful profit, but each one "shall" buy his own spoon, and not one only, but, if he "can afford it," at least a dozen, so that the whole family and their guests may read each one for himself this precious bit of inspired wisdom, which apparently exhales its divine virtue only when it is read from the silver spoon itself. If "every person on earth" had hastened to buy this article it would have had a market immensely beyond that of the magic book and there would literally have been "millions in it." Did Christian Scientists swallow this spoon? They did! And yet they affect surprise and are offended when we wonder at their gullibility.

There were still smaller catchpenny devices. "Christian Science emblems," Miss Milmine tells us, "and Mrs. Eddy's 'favorite flower' were made into cuff-buttons, rings, brooches, watches, and pendants, varying in price from

$325 to $2.50." Mrs. Eddy's picture was also exploited, and a copyrighted photograph was introduced and recommended to her followers in a notice which appeared in the Journal for May, 1899, and which read:

> It is with pleasure I certify that after months of incessant toil and at great expense Mr. Henry P. Moore, and Mr. J. C. Derby of Concord, N. H., have brought out a likeness of me far superior to the one they offered for sale last November. The portrait they have now perfected I cordially endorse. Also I declare their sole right to the making and exclusive sale of the duplicates of said portrait. I simply ask that those who love me purchase this portrait. Mary Baker Eddy.

"This portrait," says Miss Milmine, "is known as the 'authorized' photograph of Mrs. Eddy. It was sold for years as a genuine photograph of Mrs Eddy, but it is admitted now at Christian Science salesrooms that this picture is a composite." Even her photograph was faked.

How did Mrs. Eddy spend her large income? Nobody outside of her inner circle seems to know. She contributed to few if any charities, and she gave very little to her own church or propaganda. She always got others to furnish the money to publish her book in its early editions and to build her church, and in general she made her enterprises pay their own way and then yield her a large profit. She was not known as being generous and was generally regarded as being parsimonious and close-fisted. She knew how to drive sharp bargains to get money, and then she knew how to keep it. She gave her son, George W. Eddy, considerable help at different times, and when litigation was brought in her last days she settled on him a modest competence. Shrewd in getting and miserly in spending, she hoarded her money and died leaving a large fortune estimated at over two millions of dollars, which now appears to be a bone of contention and a disrupting power in her church. A lawsuit was a fitting part of her legacy, perpetuating in her death what pursued her, or rather what she pursued, in her life.

Two millions of dollars derived from teaching a religion and selling a religious book and various personal mementos! No small achievement that for a woman who at fifty years of age was unknown outside of a narrow circle in which she was an unwelcome object of charity and who was burdened with infirmities and was a nervous wreck. Along with her other peculiar powers this remarkable woman had a streak of financial genius. She could turn her esoteric stock in trade into gold with a magic that might well excite the envy of many a Wall Street magnate or great business promoter. But, somehow, making money and founding a religion do not seem to go well together. There is an incongruity here that jars upon our sense of the fitness of things. All the great founders of religion were poor men, and the One who was above all had not where to lay his head. Mrs. Eddy will not be remembered for the money she made, much less for the way she made it, if she is remembered at all.

The mercenary spirit still clings to Christian Science. The spirit of its founder did not pass from her church when she went out of the world, for it is bred in its bone and pulses in its blood. It is the only religion we know that is deliberately a system of making money. It has its thousands of practitioners in its churches whose business it is to heal people for pay; they are really business agents of this cult, financially interested in promoting it, and in a large degree it is this money-making spirit and side of Christian Science that keeps it afloat and alive; its "science" would soon sink it. We do not mean to imply that these practitioners are conscious quacks who are simply playing on the credulity of people and are in the business merely for the money that is in it. We doubt not that Christian Science believers and practitioners are sincere and conscientious as a class. But none the less they have no proper medical knowledge and skill, and when they venture outside of certain nervous ailments and offer general treatment to the sick, they are dangerous quacks and a menace to any community. And they know how to charge, too, according to general belief and experience. The author gained personal insight into their methods in an instance in which one of them fastened herself on a family of means and bled them of a large sum of money, which they paid to get rid of her. Wealthy patients pay dearly for their treatment. It is not to be believed that a system of "science and health" that is based on such ignorance and animated by such a mercenary spirit can last.

CHAPTER X

THE APPEAL OF CHRISTIAN SCIENCE

There are reasons for the rise and rapid spread of Christian Science. No movement is grounded in pure irrationality, and every religion can give some show of reason for its faith. We shall briefly indicate some of the reasons that have given and still give Christian Science its impetus and prestige.

1. THE APPEAL OF HEALTH

Health is the primary basis of human activity and happiness, and all the world is in search of it. Disease in myriad forms sows the very air with its seeds and impairs the vitality and strength of such multitudes and so burdens them with weakness and suffering that the quest for some means of relief and cure is eager and intense and often pathetic and distressing. The victims of ill health and disease, especially those that have tried many means and systems of cure only to be repeatedly and bitterly disappointed, grow desperate and are willing to try any remedy that promises relief, however it may be branded in official medical circles as a quack nostrum. Disease in general and particularly functional disorders and depressing nervous ailments are the congenial soil in which all forms of mind cures and all kinds of quackery find rich nourishment and grow rank.

Christian Science promises this cure in a quick and easy

way, and hence its great attraction to those in ill health and its special affinity for those of a nervous temperament. That it does afford genuine relief and even permanent cure in many such cases has been fully admitted in this study; and its work is so far good and is the principal attraction and reason why so many have accepted it and are profuse in its praise.

As was to be expected and could have been predicted, it flourishes most prolifically in regions where nervous disorders prevail as the consequence of climate and as the concomitants of social conditions of wealth and luxury and the high tension of city life. This has been pointed out and strikingly illustrated by Woodbridge Riley, Professor of Philosophy in Vassar College, in his work on "American Thought from Puritanism to Pragmatism." The author here quotes one or two paragraphs as follows:

For an explanation [of the spread of Christian Science] we must have recourse to the comparison of statistics of the sect with conditions in various parts of the country. The statistics are to be found in the last federal census; the conditions are suggested by an interesting, but as yet unpublished map designating the absolute number of Christian Scientists in the land. A first glance at the map shows this threefold distribution of the sect: the East, the Middle West, the Far West. By States this means Massachusetts and New York; Illinois and Missouri; Colorado and California. This confirms the official statement that the influence is strong over comparatively limited areas in the United States. In this threefold distribution the pathological factor is primarily in evidence, for the centers of influence are large cities, with their concomitant nervous disorders, and the health resorts of the mountains and the coast, where it is natural that groups of invalids and semi-invalids should welcome any new therapeutic agency. . . Christian Science has spread largely along the fortieth degree of latitude—the richest pay streak of our civilization. From their personal appearance and from the showiness of their churches, the followers of the "scientific mental therapeutics" are manifestly prosperous. Yet with this very physical prosperity there goes a spiritual change. As in the case of those primitive Christian Scientists, the followers of Plotinus who centered in the rich cities of Alexandria and Rome, so these modern Neo-Platonists tend to revolt against overprosperity. With a plethora of wealth they incline to asceticism, and long for a breath of the upper air of mysticism. In a word, too much of the material has brought a desire for the immaterial.[1]

This distribution of Christian Science is borne out by the fact that while the Christian churches have only forty per cent of their membership in cities of 25,000 and over, the Christian Science churches have over eighty-two per cent of their membership in such cities and are only exceeded by the Jews who have eighty-eight per cent in cities. Another fact bearing on the same point is that while the average female membership in all denominations is fifty-seven per cent, in Christian Science churches it rises to over seventy-two per cent, the highest of all the churches.

The list of churches published in the Christian Science Journal for December, 1919, also shows that these churches are congested along the fortieth degree of latitude. The churches in Massachusetts fill two and one-half columns, in Illinois four, and in California nearly six columns, being more numerous in the latter State, especially in the southern part of it, than in any other on account of the attraction of its climate to invalids and retired people of wealth. But when we pass north and south of this line these churches thin out. Minnesota has one column, Kentucky has one half and Louisiana only one sixth of a column. Christian Science has also made little headway in Canada, the whole country having less than two columns.

This church feeds on ill health, which of course is not to its discredit. The promise of relief is its chief allure-

[1] Pages 44, 45.

ment, and in so far as it fulfills the hopes it creates it is to be commended. But it has been shown that its results fall far short of its promises, and that it puts forth claims that are false and offers remedies that are dangerous and sometimes disastrous. It publishes and exploits its real or imaginary successes but hides its failures, and its victims do not care to make public their experience and retire into silence.

2. THE APPEAL OF COMFORT

A second appeal of Christian Science is its promise of comfort. People that live in conditions of primitive civilization where life is a battle with nature and hardship, danger and daring, are far less sensitive to discomfort and pain than those that are cradled and nursed in the multiplying artificial conveniences and luxuries of our upholstered modern world. Savages seem to be almost insensible to pain, whereas highly cultured, daintily coddled souls may be impatient of the slightest irritation and annoyance. Most of us bear pain badly.

Christian Science is characterized by this unwillingness to suffer pain. Mrs. Eddy could not stand any discomfort and generally had to have any number of people waiting on her. Her father nursed her in his arms after she was grown; a special cradle was made for her and her second husband rocked her as though she were a baby, taking the cradle along with her at their marriage; the people that took her into their homes in her wander years had to pamper her, and in her later years her faithful ones had to protect her from every annoyance, flatter her inordinate vanity, minister to her fastidious temperament and tastes and gratify her every whim. This spirit in no small degree passed into Christian Science and in some measure characterizes it to this day. Its constant aim and effort is to avoid and "deny" any discomfort and to swathe the soul, the "body" having been "denied," in the softness of undisturbed serenity. It has an aversion to all the ills of life, disease and poverty and sacrifice, because these things are unpleasant. There is no heroism in its ideas and aims, little of the soldier spirit of accepting the trials and hardships of life in the pursuit of high ideals, no adventuring upon the sea of duty though it be swept by storms, no noble enthusiasm that triumphs over perils and pains and glories in them as Paul did; there is no cross to its crown, none of the sublime heroism of Jesus, "who for the joy that was set before him endured the cross, despising shame."

Christian Science may promise and does give a kind of comfort, but it is an ignoble kind. It finds its own comfort by forgetting the discomfort of others. It is largely oblivious of the sufferings of the world because it does not believe in the reality of any suffering and thinks that such delusion is a personal fault. It has no social gospel and no form of social service. It is terribly significant and a damning indictment of Christian Science that it has no hospitals and general philanthropies because it does not believe in them. It seems monstrous that in our modern world with its ever-increasing note of altruism a set of people should wrap themselves in comfort and nurse their own souls in ease and deaden their ears and hush their very houses of worship to all the cries of poverty[1] and social distress in the world. Having denied

---

[1] "Poverty is a belief of material lack or material limitation." T. W. Wilby, *What Is Christian Science?* p. 163.

the reality of the material world, it has retired into an unreal and self-contained world of its own. Its comfort is self-centered and selfish.

Frank Podmore, a not unsympathathetic student of Christian Science, throws a searchlight into the heart of this aspect of the system in the following quotation:

The religion of Christian Science oils the wheels of the domestic machinery, smooths out business troubles, releases fear, promotes happiness. But it is entirely egoistic in expression. . . For Christian Scientists there is no recognized service of their fellows, beyond the force of their example. . . There are no charities or institutions of any kind for social service in connection with Christian Science churches. . . Poverty and sin, like sickness, are illusions, errors of "mortal mind," and cannot be alleviated by material methods. If a man is sick, he does not need drugs; if poor, he has no need of money; if suffering, of material help or even sympathy. For the cure in all cases must be sought within. The New Religion, then, is without the enthusiasm of Humanity. It is, in fact, without enthusiasm of any kind. We shall look in vain here for spiritual rapture, for ecstatic contemplation of the divine. There is no place here for any of the passions which are associated with Christianity, nor, indeed, for any exalted emotion. There can be no remorse where there is no sin; compassion, when the suffering is unreal, can only be mischievous; friendship, as we shall see later, is a snare, and the love of man and woman a hindrance to true spirituality. There is no mystery about this final revelation, and there is no room, therefore, for wonder and awe. Here are no "long-drawn aisles and fretted vaults"; the Scientist's outlook on the spiritual world is as plain and bare as the walls of his temple, shining white under the abundant radiance of the electric lamps.[1]

Christian Science in its ethics is a form of hedonism. Having "denied" the body, it nevertheless gives much of its time and thought to this same fictitious body, soothing it into comfort and keeping it in a pleasant condition. After all their talk against it, the followers of this cult appear to be more concerned with the flesh than with the spirit. It is a shallow gospel that goes little deeper than

[1] *Mesmerism and Christian Science*, p. 282.

the very body they affect to disown. Christian Scientists make much of their cheerfulness, exploiting it as though they had got rid of all worry and were cheerful above other people, but we know from personal experience that their cheerfulness is sometimes affected, kept up as an outer appearance in spite of their inner state, proclaiming themselves to be perfectly well and comfortable when they are obviously in pain and are ill and weak to the point of exhaustion. So their comfort is sometimes artificial and false, and at its best it is often a smug self-complacency which we would think would satiate and nauseate a healthy virile soul. Such was the reaction of the man who, when asked why he had left Christian Science, declared that he "got tired of being so monotonously happy."

This shallow hedonistic philosophy will not stand the test of logic and of experience. This world is not a playground and life is not a picnic. Comfort is not the conscience of the soul. Happiness is not the chief end of man. While pleasure is a motive that enters widely into our aims and activities, yet it is not the supreme ideal and pursuit that fundamentally governs our lives. Duty is a star that holds the human soul to its course when pleasure falls as a meteor out of the sky. In fact, when we do seek comfort as our immediate aim we are likely to miss it and meet with disappointment. No people are so apt to be discontented and miserable as those who make the pursuit of pleasure the chief business of life. The way to get pleasure is to forget it. Pleasure is the music that floats off the harp of life when it is kept in tune and properly played, and it is our business to attend to the harp and let the music come of itself; and its music will not all be pure harmony and sweet melody, it will not always soothe us with pleasant songs, for the harp of life sometimes yields minor chords and is swept with storms of agony.

God is not simply nursing us in comfort in this world. He is not merely rocking babies, but making men. The world is made of sterner stuff and life is confronted with greater and graver issues than health and comfort. Health is not holiness. Plato and Socrates, Isaiah and Paul, Luther and Lincoln never thought of comfort, and the Son of God was made perfect through suffering and came to the very culmination and climax of his glory on the cross.

3. THE APPEAL OF IDEALISM

Christian Science, as we have seen, is a form of idealism. It is an ignorant and spurious form, as it declares that matter is a baseless delusion which is to be rooted out of the mind, whereas philosophical idealism does not deny the reality of matter but affirms its true nature and existence as a form and manifestation of mind. Mrs. Eddy appears to have fallen into this mistake as to the nature of matter according to idealistic philosophy through pure misunderstanding or ignorance of the subject. And her position on this point was a needless defiance of common sense, for her system would have worked better without this notion, and in fact it was this initial absurdity that involved her in most of her contradictions and hopeless confusions. A straight-out system of idealism or of pantheism can be consistently carried through, but her system, that was based on the nonreality of matter and yet had to deal with matter at every point, was vitiated by an inner self-contradiction and absurdity that was bound to wreck it.

But few of the followers of Mrs. Eddy know, any more than she did, what philosophical idealism is and that her conception and system of philosophy is ignorant and absurd. Yet idealism, however false it may be in form, makes a strong and fascinating appeal to the human mind. It seems to discard the flesh and appeal to the spirit, and this strikes a responsive chord in the soul and wakes up its noblest music. It is true that Christian Science is inconsistent in that it affects to deny and despise the flesh and yet in practice it is keen enough in its appreciation and pursuit of the comforts and satisfactions of the body and of all material things, especially money. But the human mind has an immense capacity for inconsistency, whatever its philosophical or religious creed, though it is evident that Christian Scientists have much more than their proper share of this aptitude. But with all its inconsistencies and impossibilities, Christian Science strikes the high note of idealism, and this appeals to this age, if only in reaction to its materialism. This is one of its attractions and virtues and must be set down to its credit, though it must also be corrected.

Professor Riley has also noticed this attraction of Christian Science. On this point he says:

Christian Science as immaterialism has had, as a prepared soil the previous American idealism. If a mental isothermal line could be drawn for such a phenomenon, it would begin in Massachusetts, stretch to that historic projection of New England—the Western Reserve—and continue on with the latter's prolongation into Illinois. This, it would likewise be noted, was the path of Puritanism; westward the course of Calvinism took its way, and on this same path, seeking his audiences among those of New England stock,

Emerson brought to the winners of the West the message that "the spiritual principle should be suffered to demonstrate itself to the end."[1]

We have already dug into the subsoil of Christian Science, and have found that the system still carries with it some of the varied and strange forms of idealism out of which it grew.

4. THE APPEAL OF LIBERAL REVOLT

Christian Science has in no small degree profited by revolt against conventionalized religion toward liberal thinking. Orthodox religion is ever in danger of crystallizing into rigid lifeless forms, or of going to seed and drying up into empty husks that have little nourishment and repel some minds so that they revolt from it. We have noted the fact that nearly all Christian Scientists have come out of the membership or out of the training of the orthodox churches, and in some degree they have been carried away by this centrifugal tendency. They simply lost interest in the old churches and were ready to be caught by some wind of doctrine that promised a fresh breeze and breath of air. Mere novelty has in it an attraction and charm for superficial people that have no deep convictions and fixed principles.

Again to quote Professor Riley:

The new gospel of mental medicine is also a system of philosophy. "Hopelessly original," as Mrs. Eddy calls it, the system appeals to those who are inclined to novelties. Tired of the dry doctrines of the churches, to most beginners in speculation, unacquainted with the history of the schools, Christian Science has all the air of discovery. Now such persons, who have, at least, the merit of thinking

[1] *American Thought from Puritanism to Pragmatism*, p. 46.

for themselves, are found chiefly in cities, and the acknowledged preponderance of urban over rural adherents is explained by a third factor, that of freethinking or a liberal attitude toward the unconventional. In the little town it is notoriously difficult to break from the dogma of the local churches; it does not approve of changes in ecclesiastical caste. Freethinking is therefore a potent factor in the spread of Christian Science. The map of distribution by States discloses this. Connecticut and New Jersey, with conservative colleges like Yale and Princeton, are far below the average of their liberal neighbors. It is not so in Massachusetts, that hotbed of heresies; not in Illinois, with its mixture of foreign faiths; nor in Colorado, early home of woman suffrage; nor lastly in California, pervaded with esoteric Buddhism and the doctrine of Maya— of the world of sense as shadow of illusion.[1]

Though Christian Science is a pretentious and fallacious system of philosophy that has no standing or respect in the schools, yet this very aspect of it has been an attraction for a certain type of unschooled and superficial minds. The vague mystic ideas, the strange doctrines, the claim and appearance of being a new "revelation," the peculiar catchwords and phrases of its jargon, and especially the great swelling, sonorous polysyllables, even such uncouth words as "allness" and "somethingness," and the rolling, reverberating sentences have a kind of hypnotic effect, fascinating and attracting minds not given to careful attention and reflective thought, as bright electric lights attract swarms of summer flies and moths. It is a fashionable thing in some quarters to be philosophical and up-to-date in "new thought" and use affected speech, and the high-flown language and esoteric parlance of this cult have supplied some people with "a long-felt want." This is the kind of thing that is liked by those that like this kind of thing.

[1] *American Thought*, p. 45.

5. THE APPEAL OF RELIGION

The strongest attraction of Christian Science, next to that of health, is that of religion. Man is incorrigibly religious and his soul will ever crave satisfaction for this deep need and cry; and if it cannot find, or if it turns away from, the true bread it will feed on husks. Christian Science is a religion, and this fact has given it entrance into many lives. Its very name is artfully contrived to make a popular appeal. The word "Christian" is intended to declare that it is a form of Christianity, and it makes a great show of honoring Christ and the Bible. Many if not most Christian Scientists and the public in general suppose that it is only another form of the Christian religion as one denomination differs from another in some unessential if not unimportant variation. Why, then, are not its followers Christians, and why not join the Christian Science church as well as any other church? The fact that it is a pantheistic religion that cuts up true faith and worship by the roots, that it flatly contradicts Christ and Scripture and boldly brands the Bible when it differs from itself as a "lie,"[1] that it perverts all Scriptural and Christian words to utterly different meanings and uses, that it subverts the whole Christian system, is either unknown or unrealized by Christian Scientists, or else, if they do understand this, they accept the system in all its anti-Christian teaching and spirit.

The name "science" is another attractive word, for what can be more trustworthy and honorable and authoritative in this scientific age than "science"? The fact that the word "science" in this system, like the word

[1] "It must be a lie": *Science and Health* in its comment on Gen 2:7.

"Christian," is used in a peculiar sense and is only one of the characteristic terms of Christian Science jargon, a sense that is utterly contradictory to and subversive of the whole system of true science, is again either unknown to Christain Scientists or else they accept it in its absurdity.

Mrs. Eddy used these two words, "Christian" and "science," as floats to buoy up her system, or as wings to enable it to fly, or as a bait to conceal the true nature of her mixture of pantheism and spurious idealism and false science so as to lure and catch unsuspecting followers, and in this she was exceedingly clever and succeeded beyond her utmost dreams. Yet in spite of all this falsity and absurdity Christian Science does appeal to the religious nature of the soul and affords it some satisfaction. We do not deny that, as in some degree it does restore people to health, so in some measure it does satisfy the religious yearning of the heart. God can get some divine light to a sincere soul even through the dense dark medium of an idol, and can get considerable light through the twilight of pagan faiths into humble souls. We do not and dare not restrict his grace and exclude it from any form or profession of worship. We wish to Christian Scientists all the blessing they can receive from their faith. But we must judge it by the standard of truth and Scripture, and so judged we cannot but believe that at many points the light that is in it is darkness.

The strongest appeal in the religious theory of Christian Science is its doctrine of the "allness" of God, which, excluding its pantheistic implications, in a measure corresponds with the philosophical and Christian doctrine of the immanence of God.   The orthodox view of God has sometimes made the impression of a distant absentee deity, remote from human affairs and especially from our personal needs, as he sits on some far-off throne and rules over the great transcendent laws and activities of the universe.   Such a God is too inaccessible for us to feel his presence, and the very thought of such a vague and shadowy being may give us a chill and leave us cold.   Mrs. Eddy teaches the "allness" of God, the one and only Being that includes us all and in whom we live; and his very presence excludes evil and fills us with good. This brings God near and makes him warm, wraps us around with his Spirit and makes him all in all in our thoughts and lives.   There is a great truth and immense help and attraction in this view of God, and, next to the appeal of health, it is the chief value and asset of Christian Science.

This is simply the Scriptural and Christian doctrine that in God "we live, and move, and have our being," which we shall emphasize later.   Unfortunately, however, Christian Science as usual perverts this truth into pantheism that fuses man with God, obliterating all real distinction between them, and effaces the personality of God, degrading him to "Principle," and then God, in any religious sense and value, is gone, and both God and man are merged and lost in the vast dark abyss of impersonal fate.   In the world of religion there is no harder stone and no more poisonous serpent than this view.

Christian Science thus has a fivefold appeal and attraction of health, comfort, idealism, novelty, and religion, and these are the grounds of its popularity and success. We have admitted the element of truth in each of these, but also shown how this system has perverted them into dangerous error, though it has sugar-coated them so as to conceal their poison and deceive the ill-informed and unwary.

6. THE FUTURE OF CHRISTIAN SCIENCE

Prophesying is perilous. Mark Twain tried his hand at the business on Christian Science, and he fared badly. Though he belabored Mrs. Eddy and all her works so savagely and sarcastically, yet her cult had a kind of fascination for him and he returned to it again and again in writing the articles that make up his book. He was under a spell or obsession as to Christian Science and thought it was destined to become one of the great religions of the world. Writing in 1899 he prophesied as follows:

> It is a reasonably safe guess that in America in 1920 there will be ten million Christian Scientists, and three millions in Great Britian; that these figures will be trebled in 1930; that in America in 1920 the Christian Scientists will be a political force, in 1930 politically formidable, and in 1940 the governing power of the Republic—to remain that, permanently. And I think it a reasonable guess that the Trust (which is already in our day pretty brusque in its ways) will then be the most insolent and unscrupulous and tyrannical politico-religious master that has dominated a people since the palmy days of the Inquisition.[1]

This prophecy, that seemed extremely extravagant and even open to ridicule when it was made, has utterly failed. Instead of there being thirteen millions of Christian Scientists in this year of 1920, there is probably not the one-hundredth part of this number, and, as we have seen, the flood is apparently at or near its high-water mark

[1] *Christian Science*, p. 72.

and may be on the point of subsiding. What Mark Twain says about the Trust being autocratic is true enough, as we have also seen, but no one has any fear of its dominating the government and mastering the world. Such autocracy contains within itself the seeds of revolt and of its own dissolution, and this process appears to be now going on.

A significant fact in the history of Christian Science is that the system early began to break up into divisive groups and sects and has already been prolific in an astonishing number of them. It is so lacking in the coherency and binding unity of rationality and attracts to itself so many peculiar people of aberrant minds and emotional temperaments and erratic individualities, it contains so many seeds of internal disharmony and dissolution, that it is sure to develop its own dissent and disruption. The terrible tyranny of Mrs. Eddy served to hold it together against all rebellion in her lifetime and still acts as a suppressive and unifying influence, but it could not wholly prevent revolt and secession in her day and is likely to grow less effective in the future as her personality recedes and others come forward.

Mr. Horatio W. Dresser, in his recent "History of the New Thought Movement," 1919, gives an account of many of these divisive movements. Speaking of "Science and Health," he writes as follows:

If we are to see any purpose at all in the publication of that book, we may venture to say that it had value in arousing people out of their materialism. The results of the past forty years apparently justify this statement, for to those of us who have known former Christian Scientists as they came one by one out of their radical into more reasonable views it has been plain that something like "Science and Health" was needed to set matters in motion. The first reaction was against the "revelator" and the claims made in behalf of a supposed "revelation." The second was against the theory contained in "Science and Health," which had served for the time to provoke thought. Just as the earlier readers of Mrs. Eddy's book took fundamental exception to it, so increasing numbers have departed from her organization to set up for themselves, meanwhile keeping such ideas as had proved of value. In due time the last Christian Scientist will probably take leave in the same way. In retrospect people will then wonder why such a reaction did not occur long before.[1]

The author has already given an account of the schisms of 1881 and of 1888, and of the secession of Mrs. Woodbury and of Mrs. Stetson.[2] Mrs. Stetson, after her expulsion from the Christian Science church by Mrs. Eddy as an increasingly dangerous rival, set up an establishment in her own home in New York, where she is still carrying on a system of mental healing.

Out of Christian Science has now come the very thing that Mrs. Eddy feared and took every precaution and desperate means to prevent, namely, division and rival sects. It was to stop the very possibility of this that she made her textbook "the Pastor over The Mother Church" "on this planet," without the possibility of change until the end of time, and would not allow her readers to say a word of their own in the church service, or any officer, lecturer, or member to write or speak on the subject of Christian Science except as such statements were submitted to and approved by her own board in Boston. She also tried, as we have seen, very rigidly to control and restrict the books she permitted her followers to read. Nevertheless, in spite of all such precautions and re-.strictions, out of the bosom of Christian Science have

[1] Pages 127, 128.
[2] Chapter VIII, Section 2.

issued sect after sect that are now practically rival denominations.

Among these new forms and organizations of mental healing are bodies that call themselves "Reformed Christian Science," which was founded in 1912, "Divine Science," and "Science of Being." But their number and names are legion, and space would not permit even a catalogue of their names. These separated bodies generally revolt against the absurdities and crudities of Mrs. Eddy, especially her claim to divine inspiration and revelation, her theory of the nonreality of matter, her pantheism, and her other ignorant and nonsensical notions. Mr. Dresser quotes Mr. F. L. Rawson, of London, "whose teaching is almost identical with Christian Science without the claims ordinarily made in behalf of Mrs. Eddy," as saying:

To-day there are many millions of mental workers, containing some fifty or sixty schools. Only four or five of these work on the basis that Jesus did, namely, by turning in thought to God. The remainder work in the same way as the sorcerers and witches of the past and the black magic workers and hypnotists to-day, namely, with the human mind. This means that they use one or other of the five different forms of hypnotism, all of which are more or less harmful, not only to the patient, but to the practitioner.[1]

Many of these movements have been led by individuals who became possessed of and obsessed with some peculiar idea or strange notion and founded a society or started a magazine to propagate it; and many of these mind healers went off into "theosophy," "Babism," and all the wild and weird dreams of Hindu pantheism and Oriental "thought." Of course many of these strange cults were

[1] *History*, p. 265.

short-lived and were dead almost before they were born, strangled by their own absurdity, but they help to swell the number of these variations and splinters of Christian Science. These movements and societies have sprung up most thickly along the track that Christian Science followed, the fortieth degree of latitude, "the richest pay streak of our civilization," running from Massachusetts through Illinois and Colorado to California, through the regions of wealth and luxury and leisure, of cities and high-tension living, of nervous affections and health resorts, and they have been most prolific in "California the natural home of New Thought." An astonishing number of ephemeral magazines were born to live their little lives in propagation of these new ideas, bearing such titles as The Metaphysical Magazine, Practical Ideals, Mind, Unity, The Revealer, The Healer, The Truth Seeker, Eternal Progress, Power, Harmony, and Immortality. "Of the sixty or more miscellaneous publications," says Mr. Dresser, "standing for various phases of the movement only a very few remain. Meanwhile, some of the leading publications, such as Unity, Nautilus, and Master Mind, have grown in circulation and have taken the place of dozens of magazines which once existed."[1]

All these movements have sprung up in some degree as rivals of Christian Science and have grown at its expense. They have occupied the same soil and fed upon the same sustenance and drawn nourishment and strength away from it. Christian Science is being checked and devitalized if not devoured by its own children. Protestantism against it has broken out in its own bosom in

[1] *History*, pp. 315, 316.

many forms and reforms, and revolt may yet prove its ruin. Disintegration is at work.

Besides all this opposition springing up within itself, Christian Science is encountering increasing criticism from without. At first and for many years it attracted little attention and was practically let alone as only another harmless vagary by a visionary dreamer that would soon pass away if left to itself. Serious people did not take it seriously. But when it did not wither and die but grew vigorously and multiplied prolifically and spread widely, observers and students of it began to "sit up and take notice." Metaphysicians and psychologists, ministers and physicians and lawyers, professors and newspaper reporters and magazine writers set about the work of investigating it and writing articles and books in which they exposed its real origin and doctrines and practices. These revelations were startling to the general public and were surprising if not disillusionizing news even to many Christian Scientists. This literature against the system has accumulated and is still growing. It is based on facts that are the result of patient and honest and thorough investigation, conducted in a purely scientific spirit, and it is backed up with documents, photographs, facsimiles, affidavits, and the testimony of many witnesses who had personal knowledge of the matter.

It is difficult to think that Christian Science can permanently withstand all this light and logic. Truth gets the better of error in the long run. Irrationality in time chokes and strangles itself. The more error and absurdity which any theory tries to carry, the more certainly will it break down and go to pieces. Christian Science is surely so burdened with absurdities that it cannot per-

manently stand up. It may last a long time, but its
doom will overtake it. It cannot fool even all Christian
Scientists all the time. Even now the light of truth and
common sense is slowly penetrating it.[1]

Mrs. Eddy took every precaution to guard her followers
from this opposition both from within and from without.
She tried to inoculate them so thoroughly with her own
ideas and to protect them so rigidly from external contagion that they would be immune from all danger of in-
fection. No such censorship as she established and enforced was ever enacted and maintained by any despotism
political or ecclesiastical. But such prohibition cannot be
made effectual in this day of the press. Books and other
literature are multiplying all the while, and are everywhere
sowing the seeds of destruction to this system. All
science and psychology, as well as true religion and sound
morals, are against it. This knowledge is ever spreading
silently and multitudinously as snowflakes fall out of the
sky. It is sown in the very air. No one can arrest
the spread of this knowledge any more than he can stop
the wind or saber the sunlight to pieces. Some of this
light cannot be prevented from penetrating the minds of
Mrs. Eddy's followers and even from filtering through
the windows of Christian Science churches. The marble
walls of The Mother Church itself may not be wholly
opaque! Heresy has broken out time and again in the
very bosom of this church, and it may do so again in a
more destructive form. Christian Scientists still have

[1] In a personal letter to the author from Horatio W. Dresser, he
states that as a result of the Boston lawsuit he finds some of the
leaders of Christian Science inquiring into the facts of the origin
and history and teaching of the system in a way that is significant.

eyes and ears in spite of their denial of them as mere mortal delusions, and they would have to shut them and stop them to escape this pervasive and insinuating knowledge. They cannot keep it from their children and make sure of the next generation; in fact, the next generation is pretty sure to revolt against the whole system. Every Christian Science church has its lapsed members, many have turned back from it who have seen the light and let their common sense rule them once more. Many who once turned from Christ to Christian Science have discovered how false it is to his teaching and spirit and that it has no right to his name.

How long this system will last, no one knows, but the author feels confident that in time, it may be a long time, it will wither away. It cannot live in the world of our modern science and philosophy. It is at war not only with the Christian Church but equally with the common school and college and university. If it is right, then all our scientific knowledge is wrong; but if our orthodox science is going to stay, then Christian Science must go. These two are not agreed but are diametrically and hopelessly opposed to each other, and they cannot walk together or live in the same house or breathe the same air.

Horatio W. Dresser, who has known Christian Science intimately from its early history and knows its present status as few other students know it, says of Mrs. Eddy that "increasing numbers have departed from her organization" and that "in due time the last Christian Scientist will probably take leave in the same way. In retrospect people will then wonder why such reaction did not occur long before."

7. SOME RECENT MIND-HEALING MOVEMENTS

Among the many mind-healing movements that have split off from Christian Science or have sprung up in its wake two are worthy of special mention. These are not forms of or secessions from Christian Science in origin, but they are of affiliated nature.

(1) The first of these is the movement known as "New Thought." The name lends itself to ironic criticism if not ridicule as being neither "new" nor "thought," and the infelicity of the title has been felt and acknowledged by some of the leaders of this school, but it is a survival out of a number of competitors such as "Higher Thought" and "Advanced Thought."

The movement dates back to Quimby and thus sprung from a common source with Christian Science, though it has none of the philosophic vagaries and absurdities of Mrs. Eddy's cult. Rev. W. F. Evans taught some of its ideas, and other leaders of the school were at times more or less closely associated with Christian Science, but the movement in time swung clear of the latter system and has no relations with it. The first writer to use the capitalized phrase "New Thought" was Dr. W. F. Holcombe in 1889. In 1895 Mr. C. B. Patterson published a volume entitled "What Is the New Thought?" Henry Wood has been a prolific author on the subject, his "Symphony of Life" appearing in 1901, and Ralph Waldo Trine has been another voluminous writer, his well-known "In Tune with the Infinite" appearing in 1898.

The most prominent leader and teacher, however, of New Thought is Horatio W. Dresser, Ph. D., who is the author of many books on the subject and whose recent

"History of the New Thought Movement" is the fullest and most authoritative account of this school. This volume shows how widespread is this movement, what are its leading ideas, how various are its manifestations, and how abundant is its literature. The fundamental idea of New Thought is the primary reality and supremacy of the inner spiritual life as dominant over the outer life of the body and the world. As to mind healing the system emphasizes the power of the mind over the body and uses suggestion, autosuggestion, and affirmation as the means of intensifying the recuperative energies of the body and eradicating disease. It has no part nor lot with Christian Science in denying the reality of matter and of sin and suffering and is in sympathy with Christianity.

The author asked Dr. Dresser to give a brief account of the teaching of this movement and he has contributed to this volume the following statement:

WHAT THE NEW THOUGHT STANDS FOR

The New Thought is a practical philosophy of the inner life in relation to health, happiness, social welfare, and success. Man as a spiritual being is living an essentially spiritual life, for the sake of the soul. His life proceeds from within outward, and makes for harmony, health, freedom, efficiency, service. He needs to realize the spiritual truth of his being, that he may rise above all ills and all obstacles into fullness of power. Every resource he could ask for is at hand, in the omnipresent divine wisdom. Every individual can learn to draw upon divine resources. The special methods of the New Thought grow out of this central spiritual principle. Much stress is put upon inner or spiritual concentration and inner control, because each of us needs to become still to learn how to be affirmative, optimistic. Suggestion or affirmation is employed to banish ills and errors and establish spiritual truth in their place. Silent or mental treatment is employed to overcome disease and secure freedom and success. The New Thought then is not a substitute for Christianity, but an inspired return to the original teaching and practice of the gospels. It is not opposed to the churches, but aims to make religion immediately serviceable and practical. It is not hostile to science but wishes to spiritualize all facts and laws. It encourages each man to begin wherever he is, however conditioned, whatever he may find to occupy his hands; and to learn the great spiritual lessons taught by this present experience.

It will be noted that Dr. Dresser affirms the New Thought is not a substitute for Christianity but a return to the gospels, and other writers of this school are quoted to the same effect in his "History." "The clear province of the New Thought school of writers and teachers is not the abrogation of any Christian principles, but rather to give a better interpretation to those principles, consonant with truth, righteousness and health." Yet New Thought is affiliated with "Liberal Christianity" and has small affinity or sympathy with orthodox doctrines. It denies or at least greatly minimizes original sin and affirms the the natural divinity of man and aims at arousing and raising his inner resources to their highest power. It is not a doctrine and system of divine redemption but of human self-realization.

The New Thought movement finds expression in several magazines as well as in a large literature, and it has become organized in many local associations, usually called New Thought "centers" or "churches," in the National New Thought Alliance and in the International New Thought Congress. It flourishes chiefly in the "richest pay streak of our civilization" that follows the fortieth degree of latitude from Massachusetts to California.

(2) The Emmanuel Church Movement was inaugurated in 1906 in Emmanuel Episcopal Church in Boston by its rector, Dr. Elwood Worcester, and several associates, especially Dr. Samuel McComb and Isador H.

Coriat, M. D.[1]   The object of the movement was and is to meet Christian Science on its own ground and restore to the Christian Church the healing ministry which Christianity practiced in the first three Christian centuries. The movement, so far from disowning or disparaging the place of medicine and the physician in the treatment of disease, employs these agencies and does not at all attempt to treat all disease independently of them or by moral means alone; but it also emphasizes the part the mind plays in the healing of the body and utilizes them in its church clinics

In answer to a request for a brief statement of his theory and practice Dr. Worcester sent the following:

We have gone so far in our denial of the soul as a factor of health and disease that our treatment of the sick has become almost entirely material from which we try to exclude religion altogether. If we look no further than the success of the treatment and the recovery of the patient, this is a great mistake.   William James said: "I regard as one of the most certain facts of medicine that prayer is beneficial to the sick."   The two parts of human nature cannot be separated so rudely without great harm to both patient and physician. In every form of disease the moral condition of the patient counts for much, as is proved by the fact that defeated armies always suffer more from wounds and illness than victorious armies, while in almost all forms of psychical and nervous disturbance, physical treatment, apart from ensuing wholesome conditions of life, counts for little and psychical and spiritual treatment alone can be counted on for results.   As Emmanuel has done more than any other Church in Christendom to follow the example of the early Church in a manner consistent with the science and culture of our times, I feel privileged to speak freely on this subject.

[1] These three men were the joint authors of their well-known book entitled *Religion and Medicine: The Moral Control of Nervous Disorders,* 1908, which is still one of the most important contributions to this subject.   The same authors and two other associates have since brought out jointly or singly the following books which belong to the literature of this school: *Abnormal Psychology, What Is Psychoanalysis? The Christian Religion as a Healing Power, The Living Word, The Re-making of a Man,* and *Religious Aspects of Scientific Healing.*

Our work has been going on steadily for nearly fourteen years. During this time a great procession of people have passed through our church, coming from all Christian bodies, including a good many Roman Catholics and also a good many Jews. We have done this work at the cost of a good deal of time and effort without any charge, though we have expected persons of means to contribute to the work in order that we might be free to extend it to the poor, and to provide them with methods of treatment which are frequently costly, such as the care of specialists, sojourns in hospitals, sanatoria, etc., the payment of oculists, dentists, etc. In short our work is based on common sense. For many years we maintained a department for the treatment of victims of alcohol and morphine and other habit-forming drugs, but since prohibition has become a fact our services are much less frequently called on for this type of case. Our work has grown slowly and is represented in several other cities by good and worthy men. We have confined our work to the field of the neuroses and psychoses as this is the field in which all forms of psychotherapy are to be regarded as independent remedial agencies, but we have frequently coöperated with physicians and surgeons in bringing relief to their patients in facilitating their recovery, helping them to an improved moral and spiritual condition.

No exception can be taken to this work from either a medical or a religious point of view, and it sets a worthy example for more service of this kind in all our churches. It should be remembered, however, that our churches are doing this work in a large way through hospitals and other public and private remedial agencies that are so generally supported by the churches and that are predominately Christian institutions and are virtually extensions of the Christian Church. Religion and medicine, that once were united in one person and institution, are now divided and distributed among specialists, and yet both the minister and the physician remain Christian and are doing the work of Christianity. Dr. Worcester himself recognizes and emphasizes this fact in one of his sermons as follows:

It cannot be said that Christians in modern times have neglected the care of the sick. In this country and in every progressive country throughout Christendom splendid free hospitals have been erected, well supplied with devoted nurses and furnished with every equipment for the diagnosis and treatment of disease. Young physicians frequent these hospitals as part of their medical education. Great and famous physicians and surgeons serve in them, without compensation and with a most unselfish expenditure of time and effort.

There were no such institutions for the treatment of disease in ancient times or in the early Christian centuries, and we may venture to assert that Christianity through these and other institutions as well as through its direct ministry of helpfulness and cheer is doing immensely more for the sick and the poor in our day than it did or could do in its early history. Yet there is a call that the churches should give more attention and service to this field of human need, and Emmanuel Church has made an important contribution to this problem.[1]

[1] For a "Review of the Emmanuel Movement," giving "Points in Favor of the Emmanuel Movement," and "Points Against the Emmanuel Movement," see E. E. Weaver, *Mind and Health*, pp. 291–310.

CHAPTER XI

OLD TRUTHS NEWLY EMPHASIZED

We should always learn from the opposition. It may be protesting against some error in our position which we should correct, or emphasizing some aspect of truth which we have obscured or lost. As there is always a soul of good in things evil, so is there always some truth in error which gives it its vitality and growth and which we should see and seize and use. A movement, however wrong it may seem or be, always has some ground of justification, otherwise it could not move or even stand up. Rebellions are usually reactions against wrong which they are trying to set right. Reforms are restorations. Reformations are re-formations. We sometimes must go backward in order to go forward. When we have lost old truths we should recover them and make them new. We should not be in the least ashamed or reluctant to recognize and accept any truth in the possession of an opponent which we do not have, but should be quick and glad to adopt and proclaim it.

Christian Science must have large elements of truth or it would never have attained its present standing and wide acceptance, and we have been conceding this fact all the way through this study. There are "lost truths" in our Christianity which we need to recover and restore to their full force and fruitfulness. The old truths we are about to emphasize have not been wholly lost, but they have in some degree fallen into the background and are not receiving their due emphasis, and Christian Science has seized and claimed them as its peculiar principles and then capitalized them as its popular and powerful assets. But they really belong to orthodox Christianity and always have belonged to it in their true form and force, though at times they have been obscured in the consciousness of orthodox Christians. They are set forth in the Bible all the way through it, and we should cultivate and exemplify them in their fullest degree and finest fruitage.

What are some of these old truths that should be newly emphasized?

1. THE SUPREMACY OF THE SPIRITUAL

Materialism is one of the greatest dangers of our life to-day. We do not refer to philosophical materialism, such as the crass doctrines of Büchner and Haeckel, for these are now so generally discredited in the world of thought that there is scarcely any so poor as to do them reverence. But practice may linger long after the theory of it is gone, and the practical materialism of the bodily life still persists and waxes lusty. The undue emphasis and value put upon business and bread, wages and profits, wealth and leisure and luxury, fashion and pleasure, position and power, whet up our bodily instincts and appetites to their keenest edge and make them fierce and aggressive. Probably more thought and effort are now given to the upkeep and comfort of the body than ever before. Life with many is a mad craving and search for pleasure, a constant itching for a new thrill. Multitudes would turn life into a picnic and moving-picture show with no higher thought than sensuous excitement. The soul is thus being drowned in a sea of sensations and the spirit sunk in the flesh.

The materialistic life has been greatly intensified by our modern science and marvelous machines which have had the effect of enormously extending and multiplying and refining our physical powers. The human body has outgrown the human soul, and from one point of view this is what is the matter with the world to-day. We are now armed with contrivances and powers by which we stride across continents and seas, take to the air on wings, prowl around, like terrible sharks, under the ocean, flash our thoughts and the very tones of our voice along telegraphic and telephonic wires and shoot them on wireless waves through the ether around the globe. Our great guns and high explosives have extended the reach of our arms to sixty or seventy miles and multiplied the punch of the human fist a million times. Our poisonous gases enable us to emit a deadly breath over wide areas that blasts every living thing. The human body has thus become, so to speak, a huge armored steel tank that goes lumbering along spitting fire and a leaden hail of death and trampling everything under its juggernaut wheels, with a little soul rattling around in it. Our science, like Frankenstein, has created a frightful monster which is now getting beyond our control and is crushing us in its steel arms. Steam and electricity, oil and gas, physics and chemistry are now our nimble servants and are making us masters of the earth and sea and sky.

This overdeveloped human body also has an enormous appetite for wealth and pleasure and power. It is insatiable in its greed and is consuming everything in its way.

It is whipping up our life into a hot pursuit and passion for wealth, sowing our industrial order with competition and injustice and strife, corrupting our politics, turning our social life into a mad whirl of pleasure and undermining our morals. It has just devastated the world like a fearful monster breathing out fire and slaughter in a great war. It still threatens to upset the world and wreck our very civilization as it strides over ancient landmarks of law and order, right and duty, and crushes all things under its iron hoofs.

Science and industry have also multiplied the comforts and luxuries of life so that they have wrapped the body in a swathe of softness which breeds effeminacy in the soul. Our fathers labored to conquer their hard conditions of life and bequeathed to us easy conditions that are now conquering us. They struggled in the bitter battle with scarcity which yet disciplined them in plain living and high thinking, but now we must struggle with the corrupting materialism of abundance which debilitates our nerves, relaxes our vigor and virtue, multiplies our temptations, and weakens our wills. They wrestled against flesh and blood, but we must wrestle with spiritual hosts of wickedness and with vast doubts of which they never dreamed.

This development of the human body was inevitable and has in it as great power for good as for evil, but the development of the soul has not kept pace with it and has fallen under its power. Our character and conscience are not equal to the control of our iron muscles and steel nerves throbbing with electricity. The material is mastering and smothering the spiritual, and we must now reverse this relation and put spirit on top, conscience in control. All these material forces and powerful machines are splendid agencies of good when they are subordinated to the spirit.

The cure for and safeguard against this dangerous materialism is the recovery and emphasis of the spiritual. The soul is the primary and supreme reality and value of life, of which the body is only the shell and servant. The body is a good slave when kept in subjection, but a terrible master when it gains the ascendancy. Matter in some degree, controls the mind, but in an indefinitely greater degree mind masters matter. Biology is more and more coming to the conclusion that mind is the architectonic principle that builds the organism of the body. The brain does not secrete mind, but mind carves the brain. We have seen how at times the mind may be kindled into such intensity that it will burn right through the body and melt and mold it to its purpose. The philosophy of idealism asserts this supremacy of the spiritual, and we should translate this true idealism into life and conduct.

The call of the age and of the hour is for a revaluation of our goods, a replacing of the emphasis of life. A truth that we need to have stamped on all our standards and burnt into our consciousness and conscience is, "A man's life consisteth not in the abundance of the things which he possesseth." We need to transfer the standard of value and the emphasis of life from the outer to the inner, from outer wealth to inner worth, from outer position to inner disposition, from the flesh to the spirit. Peace and power have their true throne and scepter in the soul and not in the world. The soul should have large and rich inner resources that are its real treasure and satisfaction, joy and happiness, so that it will carry its own comfort around with it and be independent of external circumstances and vicissitudes. It should have within itself a well of water springing up in a pure stream of life that has its source deeper than the world and is careless of its changing weather. The soul should be kindled into such a glow of thought and aspiration that it will shine through the flesh and transform and transfigure it. We should be so saturated with the spirit that it will purify and refine our vision, and then we shall see the whole world steeped in its splendor. "It is the transcendental or mystical sense, the sense of the Infinite, Idealism, call it what you will, that gives to life its glory and dignity. It gives an added sense of beauty to the world in which we live; it tends to deepen our spiritual experience; it makes us an instrument of good to our fellow men; above all it gives us peace for which the whole world is seeking."[1]

By all the means of grace and education and by all the resolute strivings of the will we should arouse and inspire ourselves to "walk not after the flesh, but after the Spirit." Thus shall we recover the idealism which Christian Science to some extent has capitalized and restore it to its real place and interpret it in its true meaning and develop it into its full power and fruitage.

2. THE GOSPEL OF HEALTH

"Know ye not that your body is a temple of the Holy Spirit?" Then the proper care of "our brother the body," as Saint Francis called it, is a part of our Christianity. The body is the physical basis of our life, even of our

[1] Oscar Kuhns, *The Sense of the Infinite*, p. 261.

highest and finest spiritual life. "A man cannot be a saint," it has been said, "a poet, or a lover unless he has recently had something to eat." Soul and body are closely interwoven into a vital unity and mutually and profoundly affect each other. Religion therefore has always been deeply interested in the health of the body, and, in fact, religion and medicine orginally were united in one science and art. A surprisingly large part of the ministry of Jesus had to do with the healing or the feeding of the body, twenty-six out of his thirty-three miracles being of this nature. "Gifts of healings" were possessed by the early Christians, and the exercise of this power was a prominent feature in the Christian life of the Apostolic Church.

At times theories and practices have prevailed that viewed the body as a hindrance to religion—not as "the brother" but as the "ass" of the soul—to be subjected to all manner of ascetic deprivations and even abuse. But we have swung back to saner views and are rather in danger of going to the opposite extreme. "Health" and "wholeness" and "holiness" are only three variant spellings of the same word, and this fact indicates that these three things have close common roots and relations. "A sane mind in a sound body" is a true ideal. Sickness has some connection with sin, either directly by reason of personal violation of the laws of health, or indirectly through heredity or contagion, or bad sanitary and social conditions and racial history. Pains are penalties, and often this fact stares and stabs us in the face, though at other times the connection may be hidden under one or several generations; even every bitter tear drop has in it some sediment or tincture of sin. And yet also "pain is friendly," as Henry Wood said, meaning that it is a friendly warning or a means to greater good. Even the deadly microbe is a divine messenger for us to resist with the protective armor of vigorous health or to master and thereby rise to higher dominion, for "He hath made every thing beautiful in its time." We are challenged to meet all the germs and forms of disease, not by "denying" them, but by recognizing their reality and penetrating into their condition and cause and overcoming them by the divinely appointed means.   It is therefore a religious and Christian duty to get rid of illness and have that wholeness of body that is health and contributes to the holiness of the soul.

In fulfilling this duty there are appropriate and necessary means to be used.   Primary and fundamental among these is obedience to the laws of health: the proper use of food and exercise, work and play, rest and recreation, sleep and fresh air and sunshine. These means also include medical science and art, for medicine is just as natural and necessary for disease as food is for health.   In fact, medicine is a special kind of food which meets certain abnormal needs of the body as ordinary food meets its normal needs.   Quinine and calomel are as truly products of nature and good gifts of God and as certainly have their uses for the body as wheat and rice and strawberries. The body in health is like a watch in good order: it then needs only regular winding or renewal of its energy, which corresponds with normal food for and care of the body.   But when the watch has a broken spring or is otherwise out of order it requires the watchmaker, who corresponds with the physician and surgeon. The physician, then, is as divinely appointed to minister to the body in sickness as is the clergyman to minister to the soul in its sin. The two offices, which were once united in the same person, are now separated and each assigned to a specialist, but they both have a divine mission and we are to use the services of both in the restoration of the body and the soul from sickness and sin.

The duty of health includes as a vital means the influence of the mind on thh body. Mind healing, as has all along been admitted and seen, is a powerful curative agent. We should therefore have faith in the physician and in the means he uses for our recovery from disease; and we should especially strive to arouse and exercise a hopeful spirit and masterful will that will react on the body and help to drive out disease and generate health. The practice of cheerfulness and hope stimulates the curative and healthful forces of the body and raises the level and increases the volume of its vitality. "A cheerful heart is a good medicine" (Prov. 17:22).

The gospel of health, in common with the gospel of holiness, includes prayer and faith in God. God is sovereign in the material as in the spiritual world and can answer prayer for recovery from disease and restoration to health as certainly as he can answer any other prayer. We do not say that he will do this by a miracle, but he can do it by the use of means, including the physician's skill and medicines, and by his immediate control of the laws of nature without violating them. If man can in some degree control and cure disease, cannot God do the same in an infinitely more effective and perfect way? We do not need to understand just how God answers prayer in the case of disease, but this kind of prayer puts no undue or special strain on our faith, and we should unhesitatingly exercise it in childlike confidence. It does not follow, of course, that God will answer every such prayer by restoring the sick, for he may have wisely and kindly appointed otherwise. But we have a religious and rational right to appeal to him in sickness, and then leave the result with him.[1]

We cannot here go into the question of how and how far the Church can undertake faith healing methods. We sympathize with the Emmanuel Movement of Dr. Worcester, but think such methods should be carefully guarded. It is not well for the minister to undertake work that lies beyond his field and special training, and he should know better than to intrude into the sphere of skilled medical art. Yet the Church can and should emphasize the duty of being well and can help to enforce the use of the means to this end and especially of right living and of the holiness that is so vitally connected with health. Churches are also now employing physicians and nurses as part of their ministry, especially among the poor.

It is the special office of the Church to enjoin and practice faith and prayer in connection with disease and to raise all life into harmony with God. Religion is sanitation of the body as well as sanctification of the soul,

---

[1] The Report of the English "Clerical and Medical Committee on Spiritual Healing" made in April, 1914, the committee consisting of ten eminent clergymen and ten eminent medical authorities, says that they "desire to express their belief in the efficacy of prayer," and that "they consider that spiritual ministration should be recognized equally with medical ministration as carrying God's blessing to the sick," and they add, "Too often it has been forgotten that health, bodily and mental, is capable of being influenced for good by spiritual means." P. 15.

and by fulfilling its duty more efficiently in this field the
Christian Church will render another form of service
which rightly belongs to it, but which Christian Science
has sought to appropriate as though it were its own
peculiar possession. "And the God of peace himself
sanctify you wholly; and may your spirit and soul and
body be preserved entire, without blame at the coming of
our Lord Jesus Christ" (I Thess. 5:23).

3. THE DUTY OF CHEERFULNESS

To be saved is not to be sad. Some doctrines and practices of religion have given the impression that it is.
Asceticism reduced the body to the lowest terms in order
to raise the soul to the highest power. And there is some
truth in this theory. The body should always be kept
in subordination to the soul, and it may be well at times
to subject it to special discipline. Puritanism seemed to
think that there was something divine in discomfort.
Pleasure in all its forms and degrees was thought to be
dangerous, and the only way to be safe was to be miserable.
A heatless church in winter was supposed to be a means
of grace. The Sabbath especially was made a day
of restriction and harshness. Worldly activities and
thoughts were banned, and the day was given over to
religious exercises. To laugh or play was held to be a
desecration of the sacred day, and sometimes the impression was given that even to smile was a sin. Religion is rightly associated with reverence, but simply to
look solemn is not to be sanctified. A long-faced visage
is no proof of piety. John Foster long ago exposed this
species of sanctimonious cant in his celebrated essay

"On Some Causes by which Evangelical Religion had been rendered unacceptable to Men of Cultivated Taste."

When we open the Bible we do not find this ascetic, somber, depressing religion, but the religion of cheerfulness. "Serve the Lord with gladness" is a voice that rings through the Old Testament, and the New Testament is equally a book of joy. Joy was the first note in the angel's song at Bethlehem, and the very word "gospel" means "good news." Of Jesus himself it is said that he was "anointed . . . with the oil of gladness above thy fellows," that is, he was the gladdest man and most jubilant optimist that ever lived. Paul, writing farewell words to the Philippians and summing up and emphasizing his most important message, says: "Finally, my brethren, rejoice in the Lord." Then a little later he says: "Rejoice in the Lord always: again I will say, Rejoice," thus iterating and reiterating this injunction and giving it a threefold repetition and emphasis. Joy is the very message and music of salvation. If we believe in God we shall have abiding confidence and hope and cheer in all conditions and in the darkest hour. God is not a God of gloom, but of sunshine and blue sky, flower blossom and bird song. If we catch the light of his face it will make our faces shine. A truly sanctified soul is the sweetest soul, full of peace and happiness.

Cheerfulness can be cultivated. At this point the power of the mind over the body is again manifested, and the mastery of the will over the states of the soul and over its circumstances asserts itself. By simply looking sad we can feel sad and make others feel sad and can even make ourselves cry and shed copious tears. But by willing to be cheerful and putting on a pleasant smile, the heart can be quickened, gloom can be dissipated, and lively spirits will diffuse themselves through the whole soul and body. The practice of cheerfulness will in time beget a cheerful disposition and wreathe the face in smiles. Character carves the countenance. Our very face has been molded by all our thinking and feeling and "is the result," says Victor Hugo, "of a multitude of mysterious excavations." The face of Moses shone when he came down from communion with God on Sinai, and Jesus was transfigured on the mount when his divine glory was unloosed and permitted to stream through his flesh and steep it in splendor. In a weaker degree we may be molded and stamped by our habitual thoughts and moods until the inner peace and hope and cheer transfigure and shine through the face.

A sour, grumbling, morbid, miserable Christian is a self-contradiction. Piety has no affinity with pessimism. The way to get rid of such an evil spirit is to forget it. It can be banished by an act of will and by being busy in doing good. Work crowds out worry. Let us learn to see the bright side of things and cherish a cheerful spirit. Much of this morbid depression is due to a self-contained, selfish life. When we shut ourselves up within our own hearts we grow stagnant like a foul pool; but when we send our life outward in streams upon other lives like a fountain we keep pure and sweet. Let us sink the roots and springs of our life deep into God and live in his fellowship, and his blessedness will become our gladness. "Why art thou cast down, O my soul? And why art thou disquieted within me? Hope thou in God; for I shall yet praise him, Who is the health of my countenance and my God" (Ps. 42:11).

Christian Scientists make a point of "denying" worry and being cheerful. Many have doubts whether they succeed in acquiring this grace better than other people, and personal experience with them has not removed these misgivings. But they have no monopoly of this grace or special means of acquiring it, and the deepest secret and source of peace and cheerfulness is not in "denying" any of the realities of the world, but is faith in God in Christ. As we enter more fully into fellowship with him, his Spirit flows into us and fills us with his peace, and then we have a rational reason for and an unfailing spring of blessedness. "And let the peace of Christ rule in your hearts, to the which also ye were called in one body ; and be ye thankful" (Col. 3:15).

4. THE PRACTICE OF THE PRESENCE OF GOD

There is a certain fascination about pantheism, and its charm appears to be due to the fact that it brings God near to us. A distant or absent God is fatal to human interest in him and to real religion as it puts him beyond our pale and reduces him to a cold proposition. But pantheism brings him near and immerses us in his immediate presence and warm life. The fatality of pantheism, however, is that it brings God too near and merges man and God in one common impersonal abyss and fate, and this last state is worse than the first.

The truth and attraction of pantheism are found in Christian theism in their full force and value without any such fatal defect or excess. The Bible brings God very near to us and yet not too near. It declares that God is not far from any one of us but is nigh us, even in our heart, so that we do not need to ascend into heaven or descend into hell or fly to the uttermost part of the earth to find him. Jehovah God created man in his own image and breathed into him his own divine breath. God is spirit and man is spirit, and thus they are of the same fundamental nature and have deep common faculties and affinities which are the ground of their fellowship and of all religion. The divine immanence and the whole system of idealism is expressed in Paul's profound saying, "In him we live, and move, and have our being." The Scriptures are pervaded with the doctrine of the divine immanence which makes the creation a visible manifestation of his presence.

"God is here" was a saying of Henry Wood, and it is a truly Christian saying. The practice of the presence of God means that we cherish and realize a sense of his presence in all things. The conception of nature as an enormous mass of matter and mighty machine interposes an opaque obstruction between God and us, but the Hebrew conception of nature as the immediate presence and will of God brings him near. Then the "stormy wind" is his "will," and the heavens a dome of many-colored glass through which his glory streams. "Earth's crammed with heaven, and every common bush afire with God." From this point of view we see the world saturated with God and we breathe his breath. The laws of nature are the laws of God's own life which we share as it pours through us. We then feel in nature a presence that disturbs us with a joy and have a sense

Of something far more deeply interfused,
Whose dwelling is the light of setting suns,
And the round ocean and the living air
And the blue sky, and in the mind of man.

Not only Wordsworth, the poet of nature, but all the great poets and prophets and mystics have had this sense of the Infinite that immerses the human spirit in God, puts a "new splendor on the grass," brings heaven near, and "makes all the earth enchanted ground."

Providence is the presence of the immanent God in all things working out the divine plan and purpose. Prayer makes his presence more vital and vivid as it brings us into conscious personal communion with him and admits us into the secret place of the Most High, where we are still before him and are calmed into peace and receive suggestions of his will and come forth strong and brave to do and dare in his service.

This divine immanence or mutual indwelling comes to its most intimate and finest expression in the relation of Christ and Christians. Christ gave the very formula of such mutual immanence in his prayer, "As thou, Father, art in me, and I in thee, that they also may be in us." "Abide in me, and I in you." Paul elaborated the doctrine that Christ is in Christians, and Christians in Christ. "It is no longer I that live, but Christ liveth in me." More and more we learn to do all things as in his presence and for his sake, so that whether we eat or drink, buy or sell, pray or play, we do all for the glory of God. While not always conscious of his presence, yet we grow into a disposition and habit of mind and heart that enable us to do his will as by an act of conscious obedience and fellowship. This divine immanence is the truth which Christian Science has exploited under the crude idea and name of the "allness of God," but which is of the very substance and heart of Christian faith.

In proportion as we realize this divine immanence shall

we see the world ablaze with God and be able to live in the light of his face. We shall then know that all things are the expression of his wisdom and will and are working together for our good. Our life will merge in his life in fellowship and obedience, love and joy. The flesh will melt into the spirit, and we shall live in the spirit. The world will dissolve into the splendor of God, and in his light we shall see light. As Dante expresses it, we shall live "where God immediate rules."

The supremacy of the spiritual, the gospel of health, the duty of cheerfulness, and the practice of the presence of God are four principles that Christian Science has emphasized and in a degree capitalized and popularized, and in so doing it has rendered the world and the Christian Church a good service, in spite of the absurd philosophy and perverted Scripture which it has associated with them. It is these truths and not its errors that have given the system its vitality and growth. The Christian Church has not lost but it has in a measure obscured these truths so that they have not stood out as conspicuously and as helpfully in its teaching and practice as they should. Not a few people in our churches have more or less consciously felt this lack and have gone to where they thought they could find these satisfactions and where in a measure they have found them. This is why thousands have left our Christian churches and why on many an avenue their costly and generally well-filled Christian Science edifices stare us in the face. Those churches must be meeting some need which we have failed to satisfy. We should profit by our failure and set about restoring these truths to their full force and fruitfulness. It is useless for us to berate or ridicule or even expose the fallacy and falsity of Christian Science unless we can ourselves do the work that it is doing.   There is little hope of winning back the followers of this faith by mere logic, however convincing to us it may be, but if we can fully meet the needs that they are satisfying with their poor bread, then the fallacy and folly of their system will in time cause it to wither.   These truths and satisfactions are inherent in the very substance of Christian faith where they are found in their rationality and purity unmixed with the error of Mrs. Eddy's cult.   We have let Christian Science grow at the expense of the Christian Church because we have not done justice to these truths, and it has been able to give the impression that they are its peculiar possession and power.   They have belonged from the beginning to Christian doctrine and living, and the church must show this and give them their rightful and full place and power in its teaching and life.

The author's task is done.   He has endeavored to tell the truth about Christian Science in a fair and not unkindly spirit, setting down naught in prejudice and affirming nothing that is not written in the records and backed up with trustworthy evidence.   He would not rob anyone of any genuine comfort that may be derived from this faith, but the truth should be told though it may evoke indignant criticism or give temporary pain. And the truth in time will prevail and bring forth the peaceable fruits of righteousness.   He has laid bare the nature of this system and uncovered its foundations, and its origin and history and doctrines and doings do not commend it.   As a form of religion it is not worthy of

acceptation, and we do not believe it can last. We turn
from it with relief to escape from its unreality and absurdity to Him who is the Way, and the Truth, and the
Life. These little human schemes of salvation that have
swarmed along the path of the Christian centuries all
have their brief day, but he is the same yesterday, to-day,
and forever. Heaven and earth shall pass away, but his
words shall not pass away, and not one jot or tittle of his
truth shall fail.

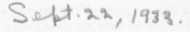

Sept. 22, 1933.

INDEX

of idealism, 266ff; its appeal of liberal revolt, 270ff; its religious a p p e a l, 270ff; the future of, 273ff; divisions and rival sects in, 275ff; growing opposition to, 278ff; its war against Scripture, science and common sense, 280; elements of truth in, 287ff.

Scripture, Mrs. Eddy's use of, 106, 107, 124, 137ff, 171ff, 216ff.

Senses, The, Christian Science view of, 145, 146, 155, 172.

Shakerism, affinity of Christian Science with, 17, 18.

Sin, Mrs. Eddy's doctrine of, 104, 134, 153, 155ff, 158, 169ff.

Smith, Rev. Charles M., 54.

Smith, Joseph, founder of Mormonism, 19.

Soul, and body, relations of, 223ff, 239ff, 298.

Spirit, Holy, Mrs. Eddy's doctrine of, 107, 126, 169.

Spiritualism, 20; Mrs. Eddy's belief in and practice of, 30, 31; her doctrine of, 110, 111.

Spofford, Daniel H., student of Mrs. Eddy, 38, 39; condemned by Mrs. Eddy, 44, 45, 46; 114, 175, 176, 195.

Stanley, Charles, student of Mrs. Eddy, 158, 159.

Stetson, Mrs. Augusta E., 154; her rival church in New York and expulsion from The Mother Church, 183ff; 191, 192, 195; quoted, 208; her own system of healing, 275.

Sturge, Miss M. Carta, quoted, 148.

Suggestion, Hypnotic, 227.

Surgery, Christian Scientists not to attempt it, 131.

Testament, Expositor's Greek, quoted, 232.

Tilton, Mrs. Abby, sister of Mrs. Eddy, 35, 36.

Toplady, Augustus, 212.

Townsend, Luther T., his challenge to Mrs. Eddy, 238, 239.

Transcendentalism, in New England, 15–17.

Trine, Ralph Waldo, "New Thought" writer, 281.

Truth in Christian Science, 259ff, 287ff; summary of, 303.

Tuke, Dr. D. H., 226.

Twain, Mark, his book on Christian Science, 12; his critical e x a m i n a t i o n of "Science and Health", 84ff; on Mrs. Eddy's use of the name "Mother Mary," 100ff; his characterization of the M a n u a l of. The Mother Church, 190, 191, 192, 193; on Mrs. Eddy's profits, 249, 250; on the future of Christian Science, 273ff.

Unitarianism, 15.

Voltaire, quoted, 172.

Walcott, Mrs. Julia, 33.

Warfield, Dr. B. B., 230, 231; on counterfeit miracles, 233.

Watts, Isaac, 212.

Weaver, E. E., on the Emmanuel Church Movement, 286.

Webster, Captain, 33.

Wentworth, Charles O., 70.

Wentworth, Horace, 34; his affidavit as to Mrs. Eddy, 69-70.

Wentworth Mrs. Sally, 34, 69, 81.

Wesley, Charles, 212.

Wheeler, Mrs. James, 33.

White, Andrew D., quoted, 46.

Whittier, 212.

Wiggin, Rev. James Henry, his testimony as to Mrs. Eddy's dependence on Quimby, 75, 76; Mrs. Eddy's literary re-